The Calendar of the Soul

The Calendar of the Soul

An Inner Journey through the Year

Karl König

Edited by Richard Steel

Floris Books

Karl König Archive Publication, Vols 6 & 7
Subject: The Inner Path
Series editor: Richard Steel

Karl König's collected works are issued by
the Karl König Archive

Translated by Simon Blaxland de Lange

First published as two separate volumes:
Vol. 6 *An Inner Journey through the Year: Soul Images and the Calendar of the Soul* by Floris Books in 2010. First published in German as *Bilder des inneren Jahres* by Verlag Freies Geistesleben in 2009
Vol. 7 *The Calendar of the Soul: A Commentary* by Floris Books in 2010
First published in German as *Anleitungen zum Seelenkalender* by Verlag Freies Geistesleben in 2009. Includes essays published as *Rudolf Steiner's Calendar of the Soul: A Commentary* in 1977 by Rudolf Steiner Press, London

This combined edition published in 2025

www.florisbooks.co.uk Authorised EU Representative: EasyAccess System Europe, Mustamae tee SO, 10621 Tallinn, Estonia
gpsr.requests@easproject.com

British Library CIP Data available
ISBN 978-178250-975-2
Printed and bound in Great Britain
by TJ Books, Padstow, Cornwall

Floris Books aims to make environmentally friendly choices, including choosing sustainable inks, when printing our books.

FSC
www.fsc.org
MIX
Paper | Supporting responsible forestry
FSC® C013056

Contents

An Inner Journey through the Year

Editor's Remarks

Originally, this book was published as two separate volumes, *An Inner Journey through the Year,* and *The Calendar of the Soul.* The former contained drawings made by Karl König in 1940, while the essays and lectures, which he gave to his closest friends, as well as the drawing for the 'Metamorphosis of the Cross' contained in the latter, were all developed later. *The Calendar of the Soul* is placed first in this collection as it is more general.

In the first part of this book we have made available to the reader documents of various kinds from the Karl König Archive on a common theme: addresses, drawings, manuscripts, essays, texts and excerpts from notebooks and diaries.

The texts of the four addresses given in English consist of unrevised notes. Everything else was originally written by Karl König in German. The manuscript for the 'Guide to the Use of the Soul Calendar' was intended for publication, but was never completed. The essays appeared in *Mitteilungen der Anthroposophischen Gesellschaft in Deutschland* (Journal of the Anthroposophical Society in Germany) between 1963 and 1966 and were then first published in book form in Stuttgart in 1970. His notebooks and diaries were not, of course, intended for publication; on the other hand, König expressly — even in his last will — regarded them as part of his literary estate.

The drawings of the 'medallions' from p. 193 are facsimiles of the 13 pages as König created them. The originals are 25.5 x 31.5 cm and have been reduced to fit the pages of the book. Hitherto only copies of these 'Metamorphoses of the Cross' have been published, due to the assumption that the originals had faded. However, recent research established that, contrary to earlier assumptions, the originals had not faded (as can clearly be seen from the legibility of the ink in which the verses were written), but are virtually in their original state. The paper has yellowed and shows signs of use; but the only change in the colour of the drawings is through friction, the drawings having been just piled on top of each other in an envelope for so long, and is not so considerable that the artistic effect cannot be fully experienced today.

Both in König's handwriting and also to some extent in the text, some of the German wording in the *Calendar of the Soul* verses differs from the present (2006) edition. These divergences have not been corrected here; to some extent they reproduce the edition of 1923. Steiner's manuscripts also show many differences which have been noted in the new edition. In one place we presume that König intentionally replaced a word. The context in question is verse 26: the Michaelmas mood. As there are similar alterations in many other documents in the Archive, we may assume that at Michaelmas he did not want to write the word *Feuermacht* (fiery strength): when he was writing this in 1948 the distortion of language through propaganda was for him still too close. Thus when he was writing out the 'Metamorphoses of the Cross,' König substituted the word *Feuerkraft;* whereas in the 'Guide' — written in 1955 — the word *Feuermacht* was again used in the appropriate place.

In the second part, previously published as *An Inner Journey through the Year,* for each weekly verse of the Soul Calendar, one of König's pictures describes an experience of the inner situation of any particular step on the meditative path through the year. A substantial part of this volume is given over to the 52 drawings which were made in 1940 on ordinary paper and with coloured pencils. The pictures differ in size and have been slightly reduced in the reproductions.

The originals of the 52 drawings have now been framed both for their protection and for exhibition purposes. They are currently kept in the Karl König Archive in Aberdeen, Scotland, and were formerly in the private possession of König's widow, Tilla. After their 'rediscovery' at the end of the 1960s they were shown for the first time to a small circle of people. It is owing to the graphic artist and painter Günther Lehr that these pictures could subsequently be made known to a wider public.

Some acknowledgements should still be added here, because some friends have worked industriously in the background on behalf of this volume. Special mention should be made of Elisabeth Schaefer, who was always prepared to draw up textual data files, and Prof. Reinhold Fäth, who helped to reconstruct the drawings associated with the addresses and was, in addition, invaluable for his artistic advice regarding the original drawings (and also their frames). A considerable debt of gratitude is owed to Christof-Andreas Lindenberg, who not only agreed to write about his experiences as a colleague of König, but also for his essay which emanates from his having lived for so long with König's pictures, and helping us to find our own path to them. He devoted many years to Archive work and can today still help out a newcomer to the job. Together with a small group of faithful friends he spent many hours examining, organizing and listing the vast number of papers left by Karl König in his rooms in Camphill House, Scotland. He currently leads the Dorion School of Music Therapy in the Camphill School at Beaver Run, Pennsylvania.

The Quartets

Before we go on the journey through the year, it may be helpful to show how the groups of four weekly verses are connected. These groups are the subject of König's drawings and guiding thoughts.

In using these verses it soon becomes clear that two are always strongly linked through their language and content. For instance, the first verse at Easter is connected to the last of the year, verse 52. Indeed, it is like a total reverse to the Easter mood:

1. When from the realms of space
The sun to man's beholding speaks

52. When up from depths of soul
The spirit turns toward world's existence

In the same way all the verses have their 'counterparts' which can be found easily by content, but also by following the numbers: verse 1 corresponds to 52, 2 to 51, 3 to 50, and so on, right around the circle of the year to verse 26, at Michaelmas, which corresponds to verse 27. This correspondence is a reflection.

On closer observation another correspondence becomes apparent showing another level of correlation between the verses. Each verse corresponds to the one of the opposite time of year, 26 weeks ahead (or behind). Rudolf Steiner added a letter to each verse to show this opposite correspondence. Thus verse 1 corresponds to its opposite, verse 27, and verse 52 to 26.

Taking both the reflected verse and each opposite we now have a group of four related verses: 1, 52, 27 and 26; Easter and the week before Easter on the one hand and Michaelmas with the week after Michaelmas on the other.

Following this we find that verses 2 and 51 correspond to 25 and 28, then the next quartet being 3 and 50 corresponding to 24 and 29.

The Translation

There are a number of different translations into English of the Calendar of the Soul. For this volume we have chosen to consistently use A.C. Harwood's translation as being contemporary with the time that these studies were written. Their sometimes unusual words are close to the original German, and on the whole help bring out many of König's ideas. Harwood's translation was also used in the original English publication of König's Guide to the Calendar of the Soul.

Introduction

Richard Steel

Once he was released from the internment camp on the Isle of Man, Karl König could return to the recently acquired property of Camphill Estate, where he was able to continue his work of pioneering a therapeutic community. The time was October 1940. With a verse of dedication he had given his wife, Tilla, the 52 coloured drawings, indicative of the distinctive path that he followed in his work with the *Anthroposophical Calendar of the Soul* during the solitude of his 'double exile.'[1] The Soul Calendar was to occupy him for the rest of his life, though now from a quite different perspective. Having recorded impressions of his imaginative soul experiences in artistic form, he now turned his attention over the coming years more to the temporal aspects.

The historical and biographical background to König's work with the Soul Calendar is worthy of attention purely on its own merits; but I have a particular interest in introducing it now because the currently prevailing conditions of our new millennium are such that it is directly relevant. The increasing dominance of technology over our lives, the resultant loss in this electronic age of the temporal dimension as a realm for social relationships and as a sphere of influence of hierarchic beings, together with the apparent waning of our capacity to master our soul-life through exercises and self-development, present a considerable challenge to each of us who — in full awareness of what our age demands — feel ourselves to be free beings.

It is now nearly a hundred years (or 3 x 33$^{1}/_{3}$ years) since Rudolf Steiner made his great disclosures about the development that would be necessary for the future (that is, now!) to prepare human consciousness and forms of society for a new connection with the being of Christ. The Soul Calendar derived from the same period.[2] In view of this situation, and out of a mindfulness of the rhythms of history, we offer this book — which König himself had hoped to publish — to those wishing to use the Soul Calendar as a practical tool.

The time element

Studying his notebooks and diaries, we can learn much about König's endeavours to come closer to the riddle of time, which had already occupied him deeply during his youth. These studies led him to consider how evolutionary aspects find expression in the dimension of space, with the theme of metamorphosis coming into the forefront of his attention. Thus as a 22-year-old he was led from zoology to medicine and then, with the question of developmental processes in the human form, to the new science of embryology. This opened up the pathway to Goethean science and to his meeting anthroposophists interested in Goethe's work — above all Eugen Kolisko — and finally to the work of Rudolf Steiner and his medical assistant Ita Wegman.[3] König's discovery of the seed of eternity within the human soul, which was of such a reality for him at that time, surfaces on a new level during his work in those initial years of Camphill in Scotland. The elements of time, music and the form of the Soul Calendar merge together with the questions of *inner* development, with the inner growth of the human soul, while also finding their place within the greater cosmic setting which ultimately constitutes both the path and the goal of all evolution. The composition and structure of the Soul Calendar is revealed to be of not merely human origin but to derive from the source of creation that created the human form itself.

In 1942 König gave lectures about the Soul Calendar and the importance of the element of time for one's own inner development to those working in Camphill. From his notes we know how he wrestled to understand this time-structure. To begin with he made a diagram of a lemniscate, as he had also done in previous years. This was to show the relationship of the verses to each other and their characteristics in the four seasons. This time he found the drawing was inadequate. We can follow his quest and experience how his deep and earnest strivings not only point the way to an understanding of the inner structure of the Soul Calendar but also conjure forth further pictorial impressions:

> Some time ago I gave a lecture for the friends in Heathcot in which I tried to describe the inner path, the inner thrust of the Soul Calendar.
>
> It had always been a question for me how one could discern the cycle of the year within the Soul Calendar and in what way the 'archetypal plant' of the year could be found there.
>
> For some years I have increasingly had in my mind the image of the lemniscate, but this was not sufficient. It was not good enough because, for instance, the two verses
>
> 'I feel ... spell-bound' [verse 15, July] and
> 'I feel the spell dissevered' [verse 38, Christmas]
>
> would not correspond to one another properly in their respective positions. They were in turn too far from and too close to the crossing-point of the lemniscate.
>
> So I kept searching and then a linear image formed that seemed to correspond more to the course of the year; for the year is a unity of time that must therefore return to itself but nevertheless also progress, a self-contained structure which has the potential to continue ...

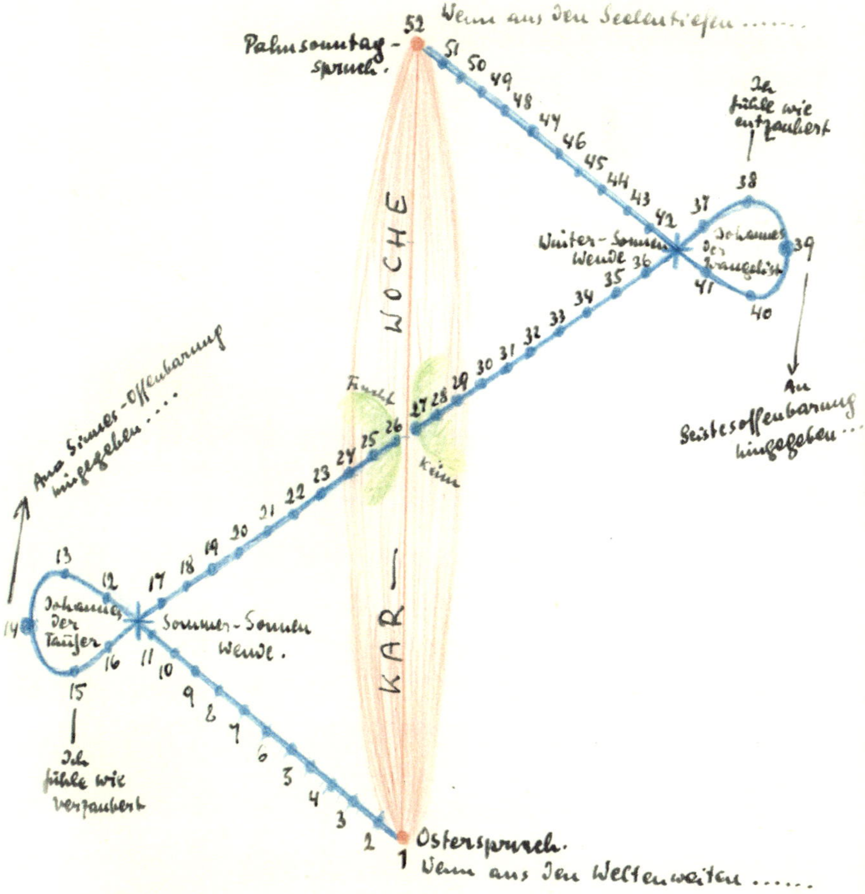

So löst sich der Seelen-Kalender in dieser Linie auf & gibt die Form des Jahres-Laufes wieder.

Space is singular in character, whereas time is manifold. Thus time and especially the 'year' does not merely have a simple form but, while following a general direction, must nevertheless have loops in its ongoing course. We do not, after all, go in a straight line from one Easter to another. We go this way and that, turn around and look back, have experiences that coincide with those that we have already had; then we set off again in another direction. Then we stop to consider and wait, and sometimes it may need a jump if we are to find the path that leads us on.

Bearing all this in mind as I continued searching, the following form suddenly presented itself: (see drawing page 16).

This line is the same one that corresponds to the course of the sun. The planets take the same course, striving upwards. It is the main line of time! Now the verses fall into place. The two outermost ones respectively begin with the words:

> 'Surrendered to the spirit's revelation' (verse 39) and
> 'Surrendered to the senses' revelation' (verse 14).

At the crossing-points are, respectively, the winter and summer solstices; and much more could be said.

In contemplating this line, however, a further image arises which can be depicted as follows (see page 18).

König's search for the meaning of the Soul Calendar in a line, reflecting the form of the yearly cycle

Im roten Mantel, das blaue Unterkleid
tragend, dem Sommer hingegeben:
DEMETER.

Im blauen Mantel, das rote Unterkleid
tragend, dem Winter anvertraut:
PERSEPHONE.

So lebt die Seele in der Welt!
So lebt die Welt in der Seele!

12. Juli 1942

In the red cloak, wearing the blue slip and devoted to summer: DEMETER.
In the blue cloak, wearing the red slip and entrusted to winter: PERSEPHONE.
So lives the soul in the world!
So lives the world in the soul!
12 July 1942

The lectures that have been collected in this volume show how König followed up this temporal aspect of the Soul Calendar, finding ever more clues for applying the verses to the path of inner schooling. Again and again he spoke with his friends and colleagues about his discoveries, and encouraged them to pursue a similar path. In his diaries we have a testimony to his endeavours in this respect over many years, dwelling as he did sometimes just over the meaning of a single word. Much of this work flowed over time into lectures and later into the essays included in this collection. The lecture notes, transcripts and preparation notes that have been preserved allow us to follow a trail of discovery, to identify with the deep questions with which he was living, to share in his tentative beginnings to answers and in his joy when — as in the above quotation — something reveals itself to him on this journey: 'Bearing all this in mind as I continued searching, the following form suddenly presented itself.' And the image of a movement reveals itself to him in such a way that he seems to experience the movements of the planets themselves. After a few years of living with this impression he was able to formulate it in an address during Advent 1947 (see page 47):

> The Soul Calendar can indeed be seen as a path of initiation that leads into the planetary sphere and thence to the sphere where the etheric Christ lives.

König's intensive work with the verses in the internment camp — not only with his young Camphill colleagues who were interned there but also with fellow German-speaking anthroposophists such as Willi Sucher and Ernst Lehrs — led to certain experiences which he did not immediately recognize from his study of Steiner's lectures, but of which he was later able to make sense with their help. Among the experiences of this time was the impulse which over the coming years led to the inauguration of the Bible Evening, later to be embodied as one of the 'three pillars' in the social organism of the Camphill Community.

In his notes for that Advent address we find the following

words (in English) that König seems not to have used on that evening (they do not appear in the transcript, though it must also be said that in those days note-taking was done less professionally than it is now):

> The calendar of the soul is written out of the region of the Geister der Umlaufzeiten [Spirits of the Cycles or Rotation of Time, or in König's phrase — below — Spirits of the Time Courses].
>
> In the aetheric sphere of the earth — elementary beings.
>
> In the astral sphere — Spirits of the Time Courses — They direct the elementary beings to bring about the seasons.

Thus in König's view the Soul Calendar could grant access to the realm where the seasons themselves are created, even perhaps to the process of time's creation. In this respect we may recall one of the few instances where Rudolf Steiner himself made reference to the Calendar of the Soul, this being two weeks after the first edition had been published at Easter 1912:

> Before we turn to the object of our considerations today, I should like to refer you once more to the anthroposophical Calendar which has now appeared, where I have tried to restore a living impulse to the use of such a calendar by tracing the nature of time, and the forces subsisting in temporal relationships, back to their origin, thus enabling them to be recognized in occult imaginations ...
>
> You will find meditative verses for each week of the year. You should take these meditations quite particularly into your hearts, for they contain something that can spring to life in the soul and truly corresponds to a living relationship of soul forces to the forces of the macrocosm. What we can call the progression of time

> is directed and guided by spiritual beings who, in their mutual relationships, in their living, spiritual connections with one another, actually bring time about — they make time, one could say.[4]

The musical element

König's strong connection to music enabled him not merely to gain an overview of the structure of the Soul Calendar but especially to perceive correlations between individual verses, deriving as these do ultimately from relationships between spiritual beings themselves; soon he began to be able to hear and describe the character of the respective voices that sound through the verses and their interconnections. Is music not a medium that leads us to the interweaving relationships between the spiritual beings of creation? It was this inherent quality in music that led König to research its therapeutic effects and possibilities. He also worked with people who were interested and talented in this area — for example with the singer Valborg Werbeck-Svärdström, the musician and curative teacher Edmund Pracht, and — in Camphill circles — with the doctor Hans-Heinrich Engel, Christof-Andreas Lindenberg and Susanne Lissau (later Müller-Wiedemann).

These elements of the structure and musicality of the Soul Calendar as an expression of creative forces in the spirit world inspired König during the post-war years to work on a comprehensive study to help find 'what can come to life in the human soul' through the verses, as Rudolf Steiner put it. From his addresses at various festivals we can discern the path that König was taking in this study, which he began to write in 1952 as a 'Guide for the Use of the Soul Calendar.' (It is perhaps of interest that the original hand-written Guide turned up after being passed on through the family from his wife to their daughter and then granddaughter, who presented it to the Archive on the day that the German edition of this volume was published in September 2009. Some diagrams are included in this English

edition for the first time, along with the dedication that he wrote on presenting the meticulously written book to his wife, Tilla.)

Metamorphoses of the cross

König discerned how the opposite verse and the complementary verses (those an equal number of verses before or after Easter and Michaelmas) described a kind of cross, that changes through the course of the year. In 1948 he drew 13 'medallions' to demonstrate this, showing for each set of four verses the special character or mood of relationship. Around these metamorphoses of the cross are the four corresponding verses in his handwriting including the respective musical voice. These pictures are published for the first time in this volume.

The Guide

After his artistic experiences of metamorphosis through drawing and musical moods, in 1952 König began to make a first draft of his Guide, which he finished in September. He gave it the simple title, *Rudolf Steiner's Calendar of the Soul,* and the manuscript was given to Trude Amann as a birthday present in April 1953: she was a member of the founding group of Camphill and had been close to him since the time in Vienna. This version was quite short and ended with an interesting afterword, which has been included here (page 188).

In 1957 König went on a first trip to South Africa, where again he discerned the importance of the Soul Calendar. He was struck by the question of the Archangels of the seasons and their relationship in the different hemispheres. He sensed a new dimension to his own work with the verses, and could see how significant the practical application of this particular approach could be. The address on this theme that he gave in Scotland immediately on his return inaugurated a new phase of this work, which was concluded in 1955. At that time only a small number

of personal copies had been made for a few friends, including some who then moved from the original Scottish focus of the Camphill movement to make a start with the work in South Africa.

The question has often been raised why this work — of such importance to König — remained a fragment, because there are descriptions only of 27 of the 52 verses. There was, however, an intention to publish much more than just the essays of the 1960s. In 1962 he was in touch with the publishing house Freies Geistesleben in Stuttgart, who were to publish the completed book 'soon.' In a letter to Dr Lauer dated February 9, 1962 König wrote:

> I believe that it would be of great help to many people not only to be able to see the structure of the Soul Calendar clearly in front of them but also to have some guidance as regards the right mood for meditating the individual verses.

A fragment?

König often spoke about thirteen groups of four and had drawn thirteen metamorphoses of the cross; and in the Guide he went round the thirteen groups more than twice by writing about 29 of the verses, each in their connection to three others. Of course, the experience of each group of four is different when looked at from the perspective of each season represented there, each of the four taking turns to put its own voice forward. But the Guide can only indicate a direction for the inner work of the individual and not describe *everything*. The more detailed writing of 1955 never had a conclusion or afterword, and so in a way did remain a fragment. Perhaps the afterword of 1952 could no longer be adapted and the deep question of the heart as an organ of encounter between man and macrocosm could no longer be developed due to König's workload. Or perhaps it was because

his underlying heart problems became particularly evident from 1954 onwards.

Questions remain, but the Guide offers such a thorough introduction to this particular way of experiencing the Soul Calendar that it seems unwarranted to refer to it as a fragment, even though König was unable to finish the book that he had in mind.

The essays

In 1966, the last year of his life, König completed his essays which approach the structure of the Soul Calendar in a completely different fashion. The relationships to one another of spiritual beings living in and creating the cycles of time are explored out of the essence of the word itself. He had spoken about this in many of his lectures in the 1960s, especially in Berlin (a city that he so loved to visit), where in November 1963 and again in May 1965 he had been asked to speak about the language of the Soul Calendar. It was important to him that aspects of the various verses should be demonstrated in eurythmy. Unfortunately only his notes are available in the Archive. However, it would appear that — apart from one matter that we are about to consider — the content of the lectures was identical to that of the published essays.

Enigmatically in 1965 König prepared two further essays which were never finished. These were not intended to go into the planned book, nor were they mentioned in his diary, where he always reported on his research. The themes were thoroughly compatible with the other six essays and had the potential of being just as interesting and important. They were about 'Becoming and Resurrection' and 'Light and Darkness.' Facsimiles of these notes are in the Appendix of the German edition.

König's approach to the Soul Calendar in the essay form is quite different. The essays were of course intended for a wider

public, but their starting point was the word. On the one hand we notice that König was presenting thoughts that, according to the available evidence, had been ripening over several decades. But there was now also a quite particular biographical maturity to which Hans-Heinrich Engel, his personal physician during his severe cardiac arrests, drew attention.[5] Another factor is that König had moved from Scotland to begin a new encounter with Central Europe during this last phase of his life. This move was in response to a call to his heart, to his deep sense of responsibility towards the being of anthroposophy, and to his conscience towards history.[6]

The essays, published in *Mitteilungen aus der Anthroposophischen Arbeit in Deutschland* (Journal for Anthroposophy in Germany) between 1963 and 1966, were intended to become a book. At this time, amidst his many other tasks of those last few years — the founding of the school community in Föhrenbühl and of the first German village community at Lehenhof, journeys to Dornach for meetings with the Executive Council of the Anthroposophical Society, giving medical courses and other lectures — he continued to wrestle with the riddles of the Soul Calendar. Thus we read in his diary on July 12, 1965:

> Later I can finish writing the work on 'sense of self.' That is another step towards understanding the Soul Calendar; this is the fourth essay in this series. For the Christmas issue this should be followed by some words about the 'heaven's own fruit of hope.' Perhaps a little book will emerge from all this after all. I hope I will be able to manage that.

This 'little book' could only be published posthumously, as the essay was finished for Christmas. And on January 20, two months before his death, we find this entry in his diary:

> Yet again I am astonished at the architecture of the words of these verses, whose every fibre is imbued with what

> Rudolf Steiner intended. It is as though the cosmic word itself comes to expression in them. During the course of the day I have come a good way further and have arrived at new and truly wonderful results that fill me with awe.

This essay for Christmas is something like a final legacy. König rounded it off by likening the Christmas verses to the Foundation Stone Meditation, which Rudolf Steiner had laid into the human heart.[7] Karl König's last words in this connection were as follows:

> The heart and Christmas are one. For Christmas is the revelation of the heart of the world and the heart is the hidden Christmas of the developing human soul.

Karl König's Work with the Calendar of the Soul in Camphill

Christof-Andreas Lindenberg

Karl König's work with the Soul Calendar has a quite particular place in the history of the Camphill movement. The little group of refugees had hardly begun their curative-educational community-building task in Scotland when, at the outbreak of the Second World War, all the male members of the community were interned on the Isle of Man as 'enemy aliens.' There they met with other Central European anthroposophical friends, and in this state of captivity an active intellectual life based on mutual exchange of ideas arose. König took advantage of this extraordinary opportunity by drawing the pictures for the Soul Calendar that he could discern inwardly as imaginations on small pieces of paper with coloured pencils that he had brought with him. The simple, unpretentious style of the drawings proved to be helpful to those who already knew the verses to gain a deeper access to them.[1]

If we peruse this sequence of pictures through the year, in the weekly rhythm of the verses, we become aware that many of these pictures have arisen from a deeper soul level than would be the case if they were merely illustrations. Many of the pictures are so rich in meaning that Peter Roth — one of König's closest colleagues and also in the camp — spoke of an 'occult

imagination.' This prelude to the work with the Soul Calendar took place at first privately and intimately, but then through the lectures, essays and other indications that he gave subsequently it extended to a growing community, and ultimately through publications became generally available. As I took part in this development of the Soul Calendar work, I should like to present a brief survey of it.

In 1942 the date of Easter fell on the original day of the Resurrection, April 5. This occurs only three times or sometimes four times in a century. In the twentieth century the relevant years were 1931, 1942 and 1953. The next time will be 2015. In that special spring of 1942 König gave the newly emergent Camphill Community a first lecture about the Soul Calendar. From his own brief notes we know that he spoke about the cycle of the year and the Soul Calendar in connection with the Goetheanum building. From the ground-plan of the building it is easy to imagine a lemniscate representing the course of the year together with the great in- and out-breathing of two circular forms of unequal size. Unfortunately none of the notes made by those who listened to this lecture are extant.

Five and a half years later, on October 13, 1947 in Bristol and to mark Advent Sunday in Camphill, he took the theme of the Soul Calendar further. He quoted a remark of Rudolf Steiner's about the Spirits of the Cycles of Time, who with the help of the elemental beings bring about the changing of the seasons out of the astral sheath of the earth (see page 20). König concluded from this that the Soul Calendar had been derived by Rudolf Steiner from this spirit-region.

There is a time-structure in the year that comes to expression in the Calendar. Thus we see that verse 1 is connected with verse 52; the second with the penultimate verse; the third with the third from last, and so on; then the Michaelmas verse 26 is related to verse 27. We enter into a dynamic flow and, from a structural point of view, rectangles arise as connecting lines in the great circle of the year. Thus one can discern the way that

the verses relate to one another as groups of four. According to König each group bears a name, for one can see the connection of the thirteen groups of verses with the twelve apostles and with Christ. In this respect König had something new and significant to say deriving from his own experience: that for an event in one's life at the time of verse 30 one can seek the impulse for it, or in a certain sense its cause, at the time of verse 23. An event in week 25 similarly has a consequence in week 28. In this way one might also trace the relationships in the 'opposite' time of the year, if one has first recognized the rectangle of the four verses in the circle (see the illustration on p. 49). With this a first major step in understanding has been taken. Awareness of time processes is of great importance not only for the individual but also for a community. And in conclusion König refers to the possibility of reaching through the experience of time, through the Spirits of the Cycles of Time, to the planetary spirits.

The next step concerns the sequence of pictures published in this volume 'Metamorphoses of the Cross.' The artist in Karl König was again at work in 1948, a year after the lecture referred to above. Out of the previous work with the groups of four verses there now arose a sort of cross which he discovered in the concentric circles that he had drawn when depicting the 13 groups of four verses (see illustration on page 78). A cross is formed from verses 1 to13 (from the centre to the periphery); from verses 14 to 26 at right angles to it but in the opposite direction (towards the centre); from verses 27 to 39 on the same line, but again reaching out to the thirteenth circle; and finally back into the centre at right angles to the previous line with verses 40 to 52. Thus the cross consists of a vertical Easter dimension, from Easter to St John's and from New Year to Easter (Palm Sunday), and a horizontal Michaelmas dimension, crossing the centre. The lines with arrows describe a hidden lemniscate around the cross. A time cross now appears before us in thirteen lunar orbits with a lemniscate in quarter segments. Each circle in turn becomes a group of four verses which belong together

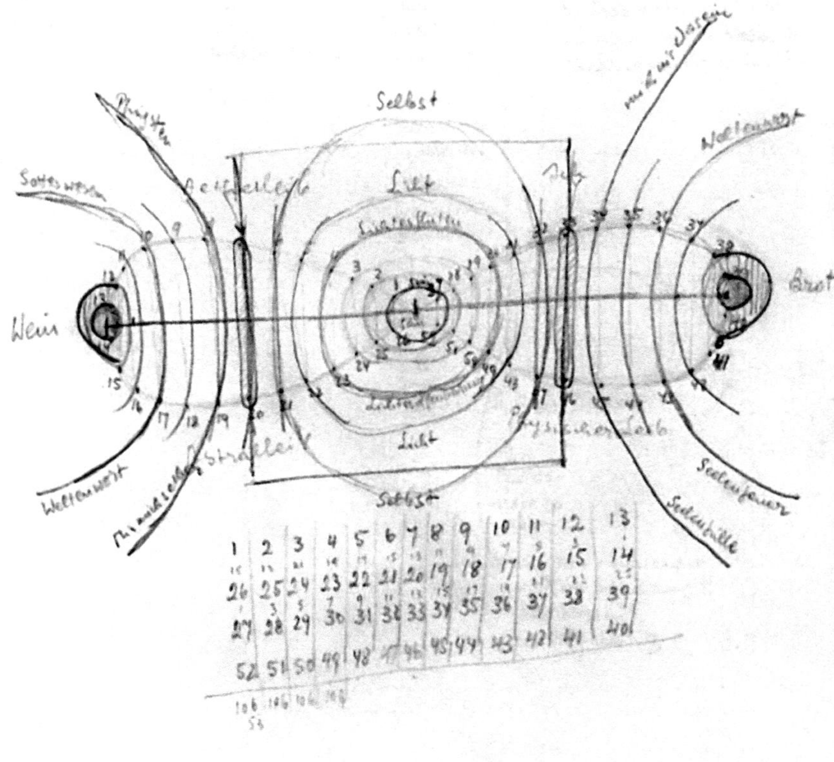

The Calendar of the Soul and the Goetheanum.
Sketch from spring 1942.

and manifests its own identity, individuality deserving its own name — for example the names of the twelve Apostles and Jesus. König then freely metamorphosed this cross form that changes from week to week in the cycle of the year into the 13 cross medallions, which correspond to the character of the verses in question.

König wrote the verses belonging to these (with a few spelling mistakes!) around the 'roundels.' We see two sides of Karl König: in his writing a person imbued with will and in his drawing the artist of feeling. This is also how he was experienced by us in life and in his leadership of the Community: a personality of both heart and will.

In the introduction to the Guide his intention comes to expression in a succinct way. The date of the drawing is March 1948 and it was probably shown to his colleagues, for several sketches relating to the Soul Calendar were now made for study purposes and might have served as preparation for evenings of conversation or similar events. If we try to imagine the intimate nature of a study session with Karl König, it would have been thoroughly possible at that time to see the 52 pictures together with the 13 metamorphoses of the cross (a synopsis that we can easily achieve today through their publication); but unfortunately we younger ones failed to request this on such occasions. The soul's experiencing of the cycle of the year is deepened and enriched by imaginations of this kind.

During his first post-war visit to the Clinical Therapeutic Institute in Arlesheim, Karl König was able to report about this communal work on the Soul Calendar in a lecture on June 17, 1948. In Scotland it was the custom for him to give addresses at Whitsun and St John's Day. As in the meantime a branch of the Anthroposophical Society — the Ita Wegman Group — had been formed, in the following year König took the opportunity to speak about the Soul Calendar at festivals and in the anthroposophical group. Now the subject was the place of the Whitsun festival in the Soul Calendar; and König's view was that, just as

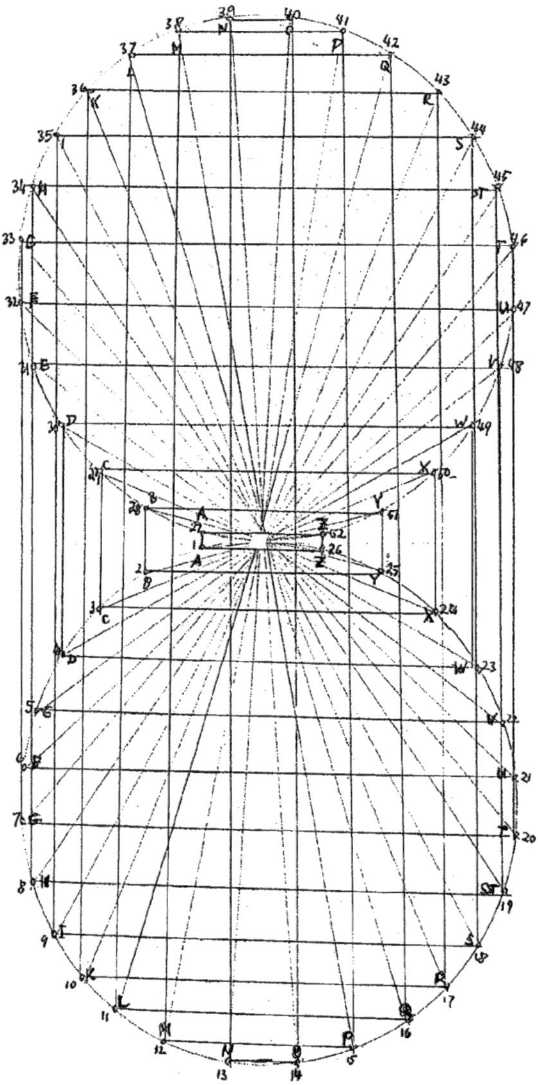

One of König's lemniscate drawings, probably from around 1948 as a study of how the groups of four verses belong together. This drawing was made available to some of his long-standing colleagues together with the Guide in the 1950s.

the thumb is a distinctive fifth digit on the hand, so the Whitsun festival has a role alongside the four 'fingers' of the main festivals. He introduced the new idea that at Whitsun something is conceived that comes to birth roughly at the end of February, interpreting Rudolf Steiner's observations in such a way that in our time the child, the image of the human being, would have to stand in the place of the dove of Whitsun. In his address for St John's Tide which followed shortly afterwards he spoke of the future of John the Baptist as the representative of I-existence and, in connection with the group of four verses 13, 14, 39 and 40 (the two weeks after St John's and the two weeks after Christmas), he developed a fourfold aspect of the self — from a process of self-discovery through the renouncing of all intellectuality (the 'beheading') to a growth towards the communal meal of Christ. The mystery of the 'I am' stands before us; this time in the figure of the Baptist, who gives this cross of verses its name. Just at St John's König frequently arrived at unusual, unique trains of thought.

As well as the addresses for Whitsun and St John's Tide, König's basic work on the Soul Calendar in the 1950s is for the most part contained in this volume. In 1952 he wrote the essay 'Rudolf Steiner's Calendar of the Soul' as a precursor to the Guide. In six chapters the musical element of the four voices was considered — a theme that had previously only been hinted at. It is music to my ears when he speaks of the soul 'singing this a cappella' with the help of the score of the Soul Calendar. 'This song has four voices ...' Should one sing the Soul Calendar? This was not what Karl König meant! Nevertheless I would like to insert a personal experience here.

When I came to Camphill, Scotland, in 1950, I lived in Heathcot Cottage, where the house-father, Rudolf Walliser, stood on the stairs every morning and sang the weekly verse from the Soul Calendar with his clear tenor voice! The melody — which was different every day — rang out in a freely improvised way and was intended to wake us (adults and children) up.

Some passages of the melody held firmly on to one or another vowel; the singing became expansive and for Peter B, one of the children who slept in my room, the warbling became a lullaby! For me it was the impulse some years later to undertake the setting of one of the groups of verses to music. The Whitsun cross was first performed at the Soul Calendar Conference in Föhrenbühl, taking into account the movements of the voices as described by König.[2]

In the mid-1950s, following directly from his morning meditation one day, König decided to express something of the essence of the Soul Calendar, and out of the moment wrote a foreword to the *Guide to the Soul Calendar.* His diary shows the date as being April 17, 1955. He was really ill at this time — since the late autumn of 1954 he had been suffering from heart attacks and had to put much of his work aside, even though entries regarding further work were constantly appearing in his notebook. It was as though he felt called to pass what he had discovered on to the friends associated with Camphill, probably also because of the presentiment of death which he felt throughout 1955. Perhaps because of these circumstances the essay remained a fragment. Margarethe Reuschle put together a selection of König's poems and special writings into the book, *Wanderer ins Morgenrot* (Venturer into the Dawn) for König's sixtieth birthday. She had recognized the decisive quality in this foreword and included it in the book.

In 1957 König travelled for the first time to South Africa, where he experienced the Soul Calendar in the southern hemisphere. During his lecture tour he spoke twice about the enigma of the reversal of the seasons in connection with the Soul Calendar and, after his return, gave a report full of wrestling thoughts about this phenomenon. In the southern hemisphere, should one write the names of the four Archangels only above the seasons and not above the principal festivals that are for us associated with them? The report is included in this volume (page 69). These questions concerned him greatly, and a year later he spoke in Nürnberg and

Krefeld mainly about the north-south theme. König returned to this theme at Advent 1959, at the Sheiling School in the south of England, and indicated how the self stands in opposition to the earth's great breathing rhythm of the globe with its northern and southern aspects. Then he went briefly into the 'cross of the soul's probation' of the Soul Calendar, which we may also call the 'Judas cross' (verses 7, 20, 33 and 46). This is the cross of the testing criteria which stand before the principal festivals, as is particlarly evident before Advent — a time that inherently has a testing character. Advent, according to König, is the beginning of the year for the human soul; and on the four stages of the path to Christmas (35, 36, 37, 38) it is as though the soul becomes a child again, a child who has to go once more through the steps of walking (the second week of Advent), speaking (the third week in Advent) and thinking (the fourth Advent verse), so that at Christmas it can say 'I am' out of itself.[3]

Observations of this nature were made by König on several occasions to the life of Camphill and were for us younger members of the community like the steps of a ladder. If one of us was unable to be there, all this was passed on, or someone would make notes for us. (I still have a lot of notes of this kind from my friend Michael Lauppe, as I was in Glencraig, Ireland for some of this time and he wrote it down for me in Scotland. We took these mutual services for granted.) In this way — and also with the help of older Camphill friends — we were able to participate in the developmental steps of those years.

How should one look at 'opposite' verses? König's various drawings — the lemniscate and loops, the rectangles in the lemniscate form, the cross medallions — were steps that were able to help us on our way. Then he drew attention to the central significance of the crossings of the threshold in the Soul Calendar: sleeping in summer, wakefulness in winter; to the various births within us; and finally to the four-part nature of the 13 Soul Calendar crosses, which of course had an indispensible quality to a musician. He described to us how the tenor voice

sings from Easter to after St John's Tide; the bass-baritone voice sounds from beyond this summer threshold to Michaelmas; the soprano has to do with the power of thought for verses 27 to 39 leading to the dark time of the year; finally the alto, who after the winter threshold leads from the Holy Nights to the time before Easter. I was able to speak with Karl König about this singing aspect of the Soul Calendar. There were many questions! The weekly verse of the Soul Calendar appeared as a eurythmic prelude to festival lectures. I experienced the first Camphill eurythmist, Irmgard Lazarus, in solo performances; later Susi Lissau (Müller-Wiedemann) in a eurythmy group augmented by lay-eurythmists — a colourful splendour of movement in a very small space.

We shall take a further step on our pursuit of developments with the Soul Calendar. In January 1960, after some Camphill meetings with friends from all over the world, there were many conversations in house communities about the inner path which, through Brigitte Köber's question, led to Karl König's lectures in February that year on that theme. Regarding the use of the Soul Calendar there was a lack of clarity. So König gave a brief guide to the timing of the verses.[4] For most Camphill colleagues the way they worked with the verses was always resolved privately; Sunday always signified beginning with a new verse, and depending on the date of Easter, one had to compress or extend (rather like an accordion) the verses after Candlemas and before Lent, likewise between Whitsun (8) and St John's Tide (12). König's little list was welcomed by everyone. (I had, for example, hitherto paid no attention to the difference between a threshold that had to be crossed in a state of sleep or dream and the waking consciousness of winter.)

König thoroughly approved of the Soul Calendar being read together in house communities or in pairs, but he did not like meditations or other esoteric material being drawn into everyday life. It often occured that, at a meeting about a child, the weekly verse corresponding to the child's birthday was read at the end of

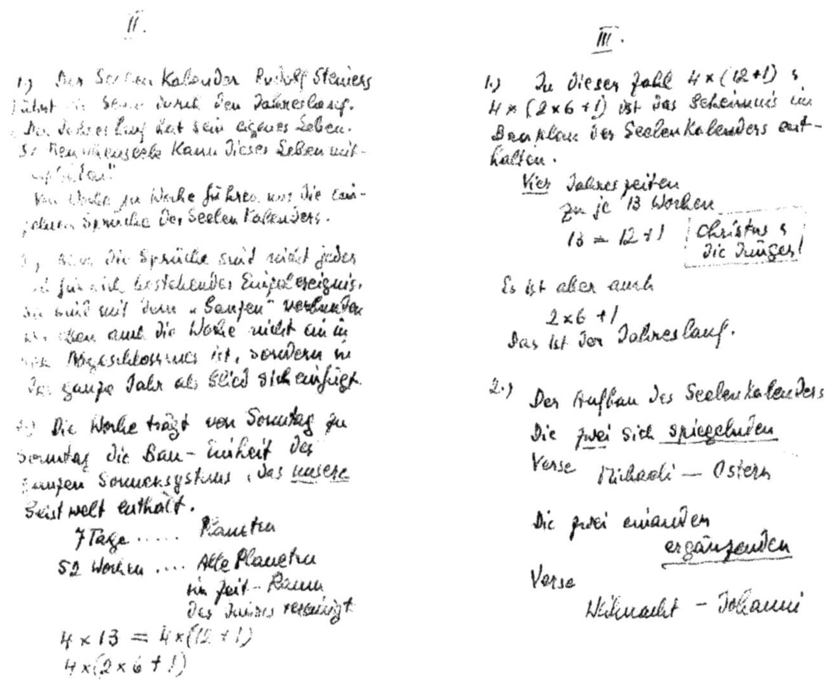

II.

1.) Der Seelen Kalender Rudolf Steiners führt die Seele durch den Jahreslauf.
„Der Jahreslauf hat sein eigenes Leben. Die Menschenseele kann dieses Leben mitempfinden."
Von Woche zu Woche führen uns die einzelnen Sprüche des Seelen Kalenders.

2.) Aber die Sprüche sind nicht jeder ein für sich bestehendes Einzelereignis, sie sind mit dem „Ganzen" verbunden, wie eben auch die Woche nicht ein in sich Abgeschlossenes ist, sondern in das ganze Jahr als Glied sich einfügt.

3.) Die Woche trägt von Sonntag zu Sonntag die Bau-Einheit des ganzen Sonnensystems, das unsere Geistwelt enthält.
7 Tage ..... Planeten
52 Wochen .... Alle Planeten im Zeit-Raum des Jahres vereinigt
4 × 13 = 4 × (12 + 1)
4 × (2 × 6 + 1)

III.

1.) In dieser Zahl 4 × (12 + 1) & 4 × (2 × 6 + 1) ist das Geheimnis im Bauplan des Seelen Kalenders enthalten.
Vier Jahreszeiten
zu je 13 Wochen
13 = 12 + 1 Christus & die Jünger
Es ist aber auch
2 × 6 + 1
Das ist der Jahreslauf.

2.) Der Aufbau des Seelen Kalenders
Die zwei sich spiegelnden Verse Michaeli — Ostern
Die zwei einander ergänzenden Verse Weihnacht — Johanni

II

1. Rudolf Steiner's Soul Calendar leads the soul through the course of the year. 'The year has a life of its own, and the human soul can share in that life.' The individual verses of the Soul Calendar lead us from week to week.

2. But the verses are not separate events that exist only for themselves. They are connected with the 'flow,' just as a week is not an entity in itself but is an integral part of the whole year.

3.From Sunday to Saturday the week encompasses the unified structure of the whole solar system which constitutes our world of spirit.

7 days ... planets

52 weeks ... all planets united in the period of the year

4 x 13 = 4 x (12 + 1)

4 x (2 x 6 + 1)

III

1. In this number 4 x (12 + 1) and 4 x (2 x 6 + 1) the mystery residing in the structural plan of the Soul Calendar is contained.

Four seasons

each of 13 weeks

13 = 12 + 1 Christ and the disciples

But it is also

2 x 6 + 1

This is the course of the year.

2. The structure of the Soul Calendar

The two verses that reflect one another

Michaelmas — Easter

The two mutually complementary verses

Christmas — St John's

From the preparatory notes for the lecture given on 3rd November 1963 in Berlin.

the meeting. Note was taken of the date of Easter in the year of the child's birth, for the links between the dates and the verses shifted each year. It was therefore necessary to be sure to take account of the factor of Easter, even though in 1913 Rudolf Steiner had told Johanna Mücke in response to her question that there was little significance in this shift, on the grounds that three verses always maintained the same mood.[5] Nevertheless the five weeks of the possible shift of the date of Easter, from March 22 to April 25, and the subsequent shift of Ascension and Whitsun, are of considerable consequence for the birth of a child.

We shall now look briefly at the 1960s. In the Camphill Schools in Scotland, where König had lived since 1940, there was a great sense of expectation at the beginning of the decade that a central hall would be built. This culminated in the festive opening of Camphill Hall, Murtle Estate, in September 1962. Karl König could give his lectures in a hall — with the spiritual name 'Hall of Memory and Conscience' — and both his listeners as also other lecturers had the sense of a new beginning. The Calendar of the Soul was often mentioned in his series of lectures, particularly in two of his annual addresses for St John's in 1964.

Here König spoke again of the crossing of the threshold encompassed within the Soul Calendar in the course of the year and compared the halves into which the year was divided with the circulation of the blood; red blood towards St John's Tide, blue blood towards Michaelmas and Christmas. The only verses that contain words which have to do with the heart are around Christmas, whereas the great expansion in the verses around St John's Tide takes place as though through a network of capillaries. Just as the abyss opens up where a threshold is crossed, one stands before a trial which under certain circumstances results in mental confusion. For if these thresholds are striven for unconsciously or in an involuntary way, in a 'nebulous fashion,' this can lead to mania and depression, just as in the other, opposite side of the year (the side of the red blood) it

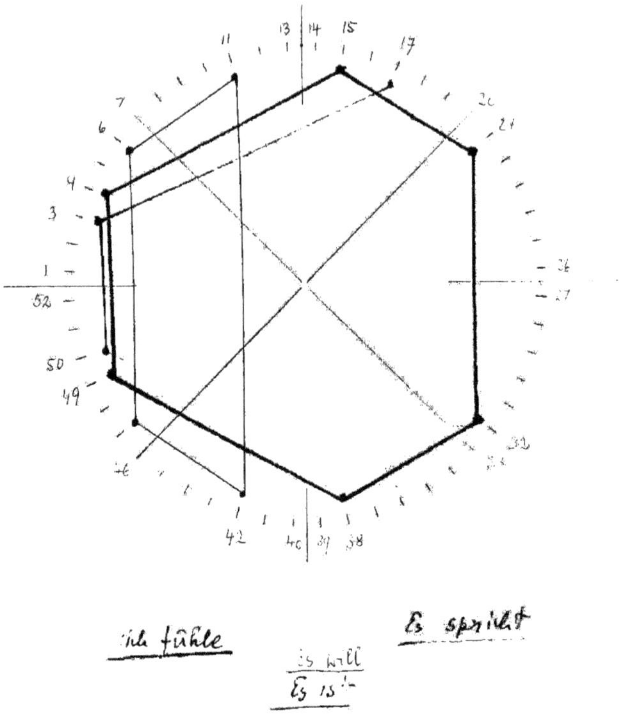

A page from Karl König's studies of the word structure of the Soul Calendar, 1964

can lead to schizophrenic states. König had never spoken in such a deeply distressing way about the Calendar of the Soul.[6]

Half a year previously he had responded to the request — between his regular lectures in Berlin — to speak there about the Calendar of the Soul. He took the opportunity to develop the themes that he was also working with in essay form; they are included in this volume (see pages 207ff). Some of the concisely formulated trains of thought contained in these notes are reproduced here, as they show the unfolding theme again from another side (see page 36).

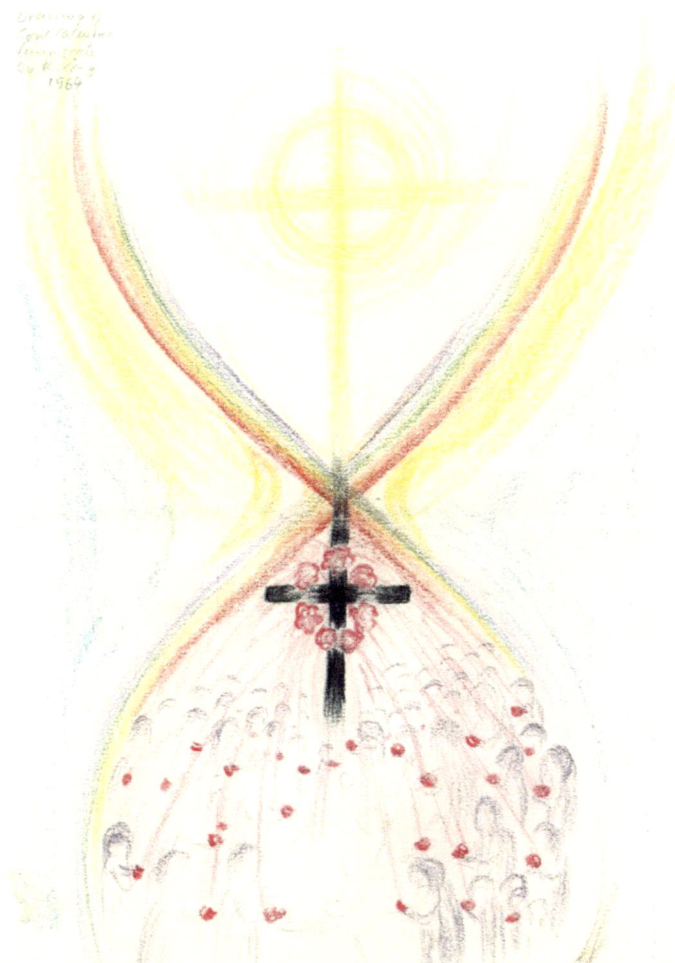

Late Summer
From Karl König's Notes 1964

From the autumn and winter of 1962 he began a new way of studying the Calendar by looking at certain words in the verses. New connections opened up and König would go off on journeys of discovery in a realm which he had already researched so deeply.

In Advent and at Christmas time König held a lecture cycle about the Word in the new hall. The second lecture, on December 26, 1962, was wholly conceived out of the Soul Calendar. The question was, what did Rudolf Steiner mean by the 'cosmic word'? Here is a reflection from König's diary on the day of the lecture:

> In the afternoon I begin preparing for the evening lecture. I know that I must speak about the Soul Calendar verses of Christmas time. But they are complemented by the opposite verses of St John's and gradually there arises the picture of two Christmases: at St John's comes the fertilization of the human soul with the seed of the cosmic Word; at the time of the Holy Nights comes the birth of the cosmic Word out of the human soul into the world. All this is presented quite calmly, so that a beautiful festival may arise.

In the Karl König Archive there are large numbers of folders with loose pages of study material. Karl König had formerly had a book for his studies in addition to his diary; it could also be described as a log-book of the growing insights that he gained, despite consisting of some loose sheets one of which, from 1964, we include here (opposite).

In the course of his studies he would sometimes again include drawings, though this was seldom the case in the last years of his life. The drawing opposite is untitled, but its theme is late summer time, drawn in 1964, and it represents a kind of festive meal such as had become possible through John the Baptist. The upper part of the lemniscate is more in accordance with the winter verses; the Rose Cross in the centre is probably intended

as a contrast to the Celtic Cross in the open segment of the lemniscate at the top of the picture. Some questions have to remain unresolved.

Hitherto König's descriptions of the work with the Calendar of the Soul had been confined to Camphill; but he increasingly received requests from other groups of people, and this led to the essays on the Soul Calendar appearing in the *Mitteilungen der anthroposphischen Gesellschaft* (Journal of the Anthroposophical Society); they also appear in this volume (pages 207ff). Words, concepts and connections from his work with the entirety of the Calendar of the Soul were now in the foreground, and this constituted a considerable broadening of his work on the structure of the verses.

In 1963 he wrote a first essay on the word 'Boding' *(Ahnung),* in late 1964 on the winter and Christmas verses; further studies were then published culminating in the study on 'Forgetting and Losing: Seeking, Finding and Gaining' in the last months of his life, in 1966. Two further essays were to follow but were not written.

These new insights came after his move early in 1964 from Camphill in Scotland to Brachenreuthe on Lake Constance. It was a kind of return from exile — an event in his life that should not be underestimated. In autumn 1963 he gave lectures at the newly opened school community of Föhrenbühl, and thereafter his activities were directed towards Central Europe. He wrote increasingly for German journals, with the result that his work was shared among a wider circle of people.

What had originally started in internment on an island west of Great Britain, and was then developed in the exile of the north that became his new home, finally came to a flowering with the work in Central Europe. This work on the Calendar of the Soul helped imbue a community-building impulse with a feeling for time that relates to our present consciousness, and then the focus on the individual words opened up the inner space of the course of the year. König's contribution on the feeling for time and

space — born out a deep connection to the Spirits of the Cycles of Time through the Soul Calendar — helped to prepare many people for a new vision of Christ.

The following words from Karl König's pen are fitting conclusion.

> The Soul Calendar has its own *specific* place
> within the cycle of the year
> *and*
> within the human soul
> for all denominations
> for all human beings
> for all hierarchies.

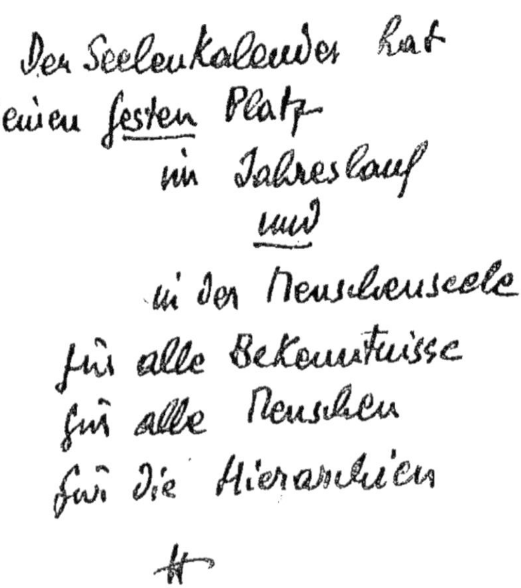

Der Seelenkalender hat
seinen festen Platz
im Jahreslauf
und
in der Menschenseele
für alle Bekenntnisse
für alle Menschen
für die Hierarchien
K

The last page of the preparatory notes for the lecture lecture of November 3, 1963 in Berlin.

Four Addresses on the Calendar of the Soul

Advent Address

Given at Camphill on Advent Sunday, November 30, 1947

It is a few years ago — five and a half, to be precise — that I first spoke about the Calendar of the Soul. It is indeed the case that if one lives for years and years with the mantras which Rudolf Steiner has given, one is led to an ever greater understanding of what lives within the human soul — but also of what lives out in the cosmos. Rudolf Steiner wrote the Calendar of the Soul thirty-three years after 1879, that is, after the year when the Archangel Michael had taken over the leadership of our epoch. It was a Michaelic deed to write the Calendar of the Soul, and it is a Michaelic deed to take this Soul Calendar earnestly into one's own heart and soul and to live with it.

Only by living with it can one gain a certain understanding of the course of the seasons. The more one lives with the Calendar of the Soul, the more the question arises in one's mind: out of what regions, out of what spiritual realms, was this Soul Calendar written? It is not a compilation of simple — or even complicated — poetry, nor is it a collection of symbols and metaphors. It is more than this; and the longer one lives with the question the more one sees that there is something else involved. This Calendar of the Soul is written out of the sphere of the spiritual course of time itself, where dwell those beings whom Rudolf Steiner calls the Spirits of the Cycles of Time.

Rudolf Steiner asks that one first calls to mind the earthly globe and the physical substance of the earth.[1] If one penetrates the further regions of earthly existence one enters the sphere of

life, the etheric body of the earth, where the gnomes, undines and all the elemental beings live. But our earthly globe does not only have an etheric body, and if one penetrates a step further into the astral body of our earth one meets in this astral realm the Spirits of the Cycles of Time. It is they who direct the elemental beings and call upon them to bring about the seasons — spring and autumn, summer and winter. One meets these beings if one wakes up in the spirit-land; that is, wakes up in one's astral body in a region where one is normally asleep. The encounter with the Spirits of the Cycles of Time can only happen if one is awake in sleep. We are all in the region of the Spirits of the Cycles of Time when we are asleep. But where do these Spirits of the Cycles of Time come from? We must say that they are children of the First Hierarchy, of the Seraphim, Cherubim and Thrones; they are sent down to direct the seasons and changes of seasons on the earth. That our earthly globe moves through cosmic space is due to the Spirits of the Cycles of Time. The Calendar of the Soul is derived from an encounter with the Spirits of the Cycles of Time. Those who live with the Calendar of the Soul will soon make the following discovery.

You know that there are always two verses which mirror one another. This process begins with verses 1 and 52, which stand next to one another in the yearly cycle. Then it continues with 2 and 51. So that we have:

1.	When from the world's wide bounds ...
52.	When from the depths of soul ...
and 2.	Into the utmost fields of sense ...
and 51.	Into the inmost life of man ...

and the same pattern continues with verses 3 and 50, 4 and 49 and so on. With every step the two weekly verses so to speak move further apart.

Then we must observe that Rudolf Steiner not only numbered them but gave each one a letter. Few people have taken note of this, but it must have been for a good reason. One must

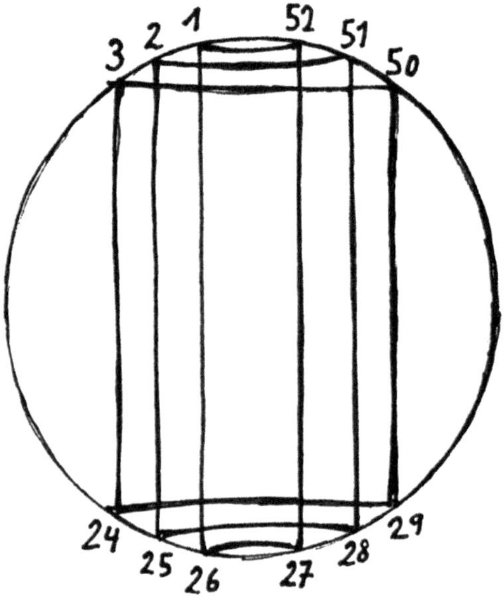

therefore suppose that the two verses that bear the letter 'A' must have some kind of connection with one another. If one marks them on the circle — the two verses that mirror one another and the two 'partners' which have the same letters — a rectangle of one kind or another emerges.*

Then we see that there is a fourfoldness going through the whole Calendar, so that out of the 52 verses there are always four which together form an entity. Four times 13 is 52 - that is to say, the form of the Soul Calendar is made up of 13 entities; and their individual elements lie in different parts of the year.

I should like to say something further which can be helpful for one's own orientation; for the more one grows into a study of this kind, the more one learns to observe that, for instance, what one has done in week 30 has its impulse in week 23. The verses which stand opposite to one another do not only belong together

* The letters have been omitted in this book, as the lettering differs in the German and English as well as in different editions of the Calendar. In any context, König always looks at the oppoiste verse, together with the mirrored ones.

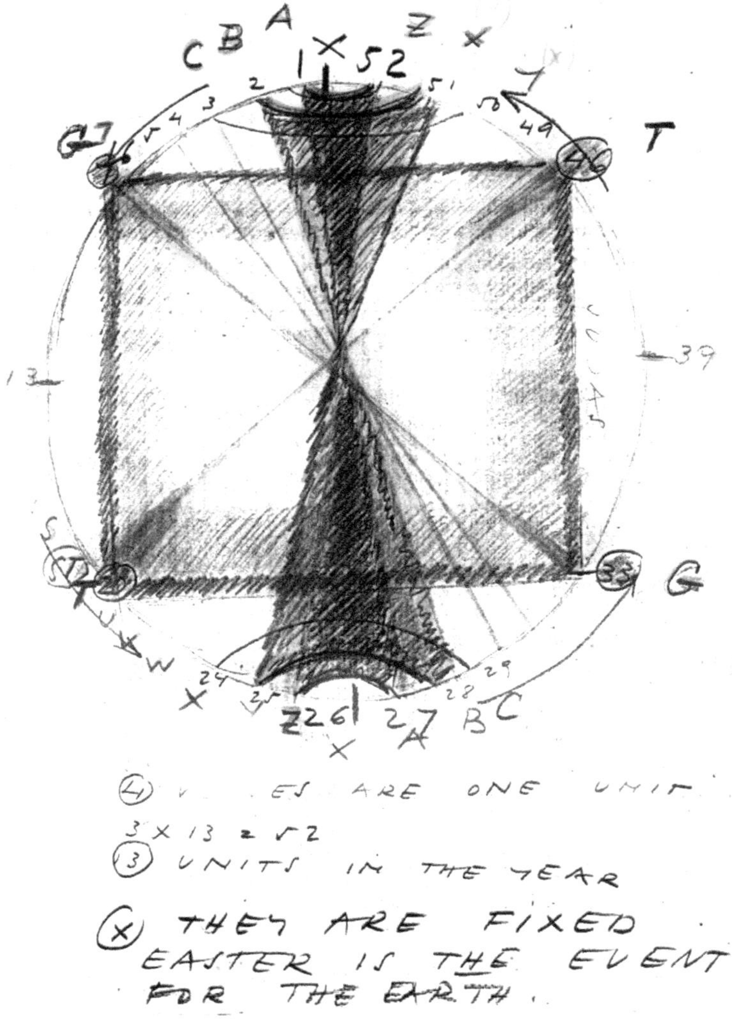
1
52
13
39
46
33
26
27
3 X 13 = 52
UNITS IN THE YEAR
THEY ARE FIXED.
EASTER IS THE EVENT
FOR THE EARTH.

through their content but also belong to the same course of time that the human soul lives in. If something happens in week 25, the effect will manifest in week 28. One learns to experience time not as something linear but that time becomes space, and that this space is penetrated by the most wonderful lines of power. The answer to experiences that one may have in July will be found during Christmas time; but events that happened in June and at the beginning of March or the end of February will be connected with them too. Contemplate the experiences of the past year, and see how the one is determined by the other. There are thirteen essences or beings, each consisting of a time-span of four weeks; together they form the whole etheric or temporal structure of the year. This is what the Calendar of the Soul can give us — that we may learn to live within this structure.

Let us take an example from the middle of the year:

7. If one is not strong enough, one will become part of the earth.
46. The earth tries to overcome one.
20. The centre of the Calendar of the Soul.
33. The razor's edge of the soul.

These four verses represent a kind of balance within the whole course of the year. One should try very consciously to apprehend this fourfold essence which stands exactly in the middle of the seasons.

All the other fourfold essences are built up in the same way. Let us take verses 38, 15, 41 and 12:

38. The spirit-child has woken up in the womb of the soul. At Christmas we are born for the first time and open our eyes.
15. The spirit-child lies asleep in the womb of the world, as an embryo surrounded by etheric forces.
12. We experience the weaving forces of the light and warmth in such a way that we notice: my own self, which

has spiritually become an embryo, can
live in the weaving forces of St John's Tide.

41. In these verses one can easily see how the love of man is the light of the world, and the work of man is the warmth of the world.

All fixed festivals need movement; for we are in the realm of ether, not of outward space, when we live within the Calendar of the Soul. Easter is fixed — it is the first verse. Michaelmas is verse 26. In between one has a certain flexibility. Then there is the leap to the final verse 52 and the related verse 27. The totality is encompassed on the path from Easter to Michaelmas. Thus there are thirteen essences or beings who build up the course of the year; thirteen beings each consisting of four parts. And the more one works and involves oneself with the affinity between any of these four parts, the more clearly will one experience that each of these time-beings has its own face, its own character and even its own name. The examples that I have given you will — if you really live with them — reveal their names; as will the others as well — as will the one that I have called at once the balance and also the razor's edge of the year.

The harmony between the verses for Christmas and St John's may suggest the name of John to you. The other example reveals the name of Judas. The names of the twelve Apostles are inscribed in the thirteen groups of four; while those which belong to Easter and Michaelmas are called Jesus, as the Thirteenth among the Twelve.

If you read what Rudolf Steiner has said about the Spirits of the Cycles of Time, you will see that the path is indicated whereby one can penetrate to the spirit-beings of the planets. Moreover, it is also possible to see that behind the whole Calendar of the Soul there stands the Last Supper.

The Soul Calendar can indeed be regarded as a path of initiation that leads into the planetary sphere and leads to that sphere where the etheric Christ lives.

Whitsun Address

Given at Camphill on June 2, 1949

In the circle of all the other festivals, the festival of Whitsun is more or less the youngest. But what lies behind the festivals — the real festivals, that is, and I am not merely speaking of the Christian festivals — reaches far back into the very earliest times.

Whitsun sprang up entirely out of the festive customs for the communal life of the Jewish people. Pentecost is the Greek name for the festival and comes from the word for 'fifty.' It has always had a connection with fifty; *Shavuot*, as it is called in Hebrew, was the fiftieth day after the Passover Feast, just as Whitsun comes the same number of days after Easter. But it was not only a yearly festival; it was also a festival with a special significance every 50 years and was celebrated as such. Every fiftieth year among the Jewish people was a year of freedom; this was the Whitsun year, or Jubilee Year.

But there was something else that happened in these Jubilee Years. If someone had bought land, it had to be given back after 50 years. The karma that had accumulated over 7 times 7 years was rescinded. The Whitsun festival was established when the Jews were trying to establish a proper social order.

Now, as you know, Whitsun always falls on the fiftieth day after the festival of the event of Golgotha. All the other festivals — Easter, St John's, Michaelmas, Christmas — are deeply inscribed into the course of the year. These festivals belong to what one would call 'the Creation': the annual renewal of the whole of nature, of the whole of earthly life, is given by those other four festivals. An additional festival — but nevertheless

a true one — was added; first by the Jews, then sealed by the Apostles and, subsequently, by the Christ himself.

It is not a festival that is clearly inscribed into the course of the year as the others are; it differs from the other festivals. One could not say that it lies in the middle of summer, nor that it is in the middle of spring; it is not so bound to the course of the seasons as are the other festivals. Hence I would say that the other festivals are in the realm of creation; they are illumined and irradiated by the being of Christ, but they are still in the womb of the Father God. Whitsun is the only festival that has gone beyond the circle of natural existence. It stands in a similar relationship to the other festivals as does our thumb to the other fingers.

With the arising of this number five, with the appearance of this festival of community among the Jewish people, something new was achieved amongst humankind: a festival that reaches beyond creation, a first individual human achievement. But on the other hand, dear friends, if we again look at the yearly cycle we see that Whitsun does belong to it — it must, after all, be held at a certain time, even though only out of its relationship to Easter and not directly in connection with cosmic rhythms. Whitsun, although beyond nature, is inscribed into the whole realm of the seasonal round.

Some of you may remember how we considered the thread of Ariadne which is given to us in the Calendar of the Soul. You will recall that there are 52 different verses, which belong to the 52 weeks of the year. In their structure and wording, however, they are not formed around the idea that the fifth verse comes after the fourth, and so on; one has to look more closely in order to establish how any one verse is connected with other verses in the totality of 52. There are always four verses which are connected with one another. If you imagine the yearly cycle as a circle, that is, spatially, you will find that any particular four verses that are connected with one another are not at an equal distance from each other. The corresponding experience to Christmas, for example, is St John's. If we can be aware of this

web of time, we can experience something very special. There are 52 weeks in the year, and any four of these form a cross; so that we have 13 such crosses in the cycle of the year. What manifests here is none other than the Twelve and the One. That is how the yearly cycle is formed.

If we now consider Whitsun — although as a festival it is beyond nature, beyond the womb of creation — and study it as part of this yearly cycle, we can ask ourselves which of the other verses belong to it. In what context do we find the Whitsun mood inscribed?

If we now turn to the Calendar of the Soul, we find that the verses 7, 20, 46 and 33 form a cross. A cross manifests itself within the circle of time. The seventh week is that of the Ascension. It is a threatening week, and contains what only Christ could consciously accomplish:

> 7
> My self threatens to break away
> Through strong enticement of the light of worlds.

The only possibility of protecting oneself is:

> Now rise, my boding power,
> Assume in strength your rightful throne,
> Replace in me the might of thinking
> Which in the senses' show
> Is like to lose itself.

Let us now turn to the other three verses which belong to this cross.

> 20
> Now first I feel my being —
> Which, torn from world existence,
> Within itself must quench the self,
> And building on itself alone
> Must kill the self-enclosed self.

33
Now first I feel the world,
Which, reft of my indwelling soul,
Would as a frozen waste
Unfold its feeble life,
Create itself anew in human souls,
That in itself could look for death alone.

46
The world threatens to stupefy
The inborn forces of my soul.
Now rise from spirit-depths
In all your radiance, memory.
Establish my beholding,
Which only through the force of will
Can hold itself erect.

Only in these verses do the words 'death' and 'kill' appear. Here is the threshold; and the human being has to break through here. Nowhere else in the Soul Calendar will one find the word 'death.' Here is the cross, which belongs precisely to springtime, to the week of Ascension. Beyond the cross, beyond the threshold, Whitsun reveals itself:

8
The senses' might grows great
Bonded with the gods' creating;
It thrusts the force of thought
Down to the drowsing of a dream.
When godlike being
Will join in union with my soul,
Then human thinking
Must bow in peace to dream existence.

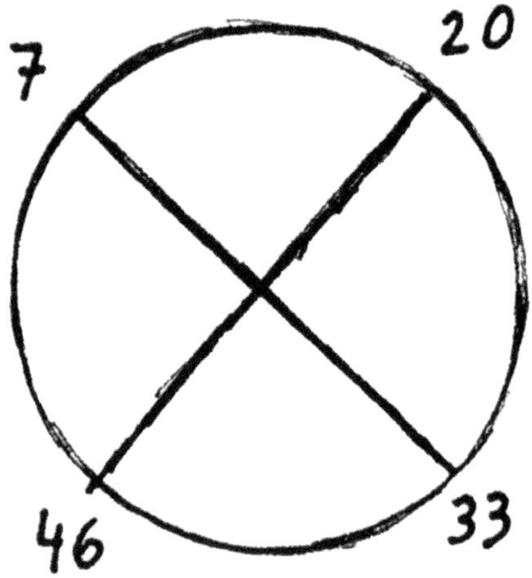

This is the Whitsun experience:

> When godlike being
> Will join in union with my soul

This experience is described as an outer event in the second chapter of the Acts of the Apostles. Those who listened to Peter thought that those who were 'speaking in other tongues' were 'filled with new wine.' But he cited the prophet Joel: 'And your sons and your daughters shall prophesy, and your young men shall see visions and your old men shall dream dreams.' Human thinking had entered a dreamlike state. So it is at Whitsun; our power of thinking is overpowered, and we are as though blinded in our thinking. A kind of veil is drawn around our thoughts, and the experience can arise that a godly being would seek to unite with our soul.

This eighth week is the central experience of the whole year. From this point onwards the human soul wrestles to safeguard the divine seed that has been given to her. What has been implanted in the soul at Whitsun is the cosmic word itself. At

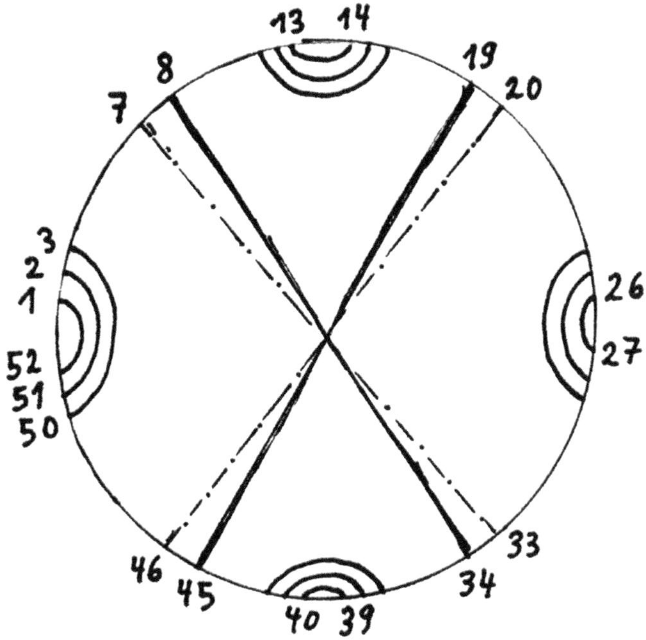

harvest time it is this event to which we look back; the divine seed is preserved throughout the light of summer, until at the time of harvest the soul can say:

> 19
> To wrap the new-conceived germ
> In memory's secret folds
> Be now my striving's master aim:
> Gathering strength to waken
> Force of my own within me,
> Emergent, it shall give myself to me.

The crib of memory can now be woven around the divine seed. This brings me to the point where I can find myself.

In times to come it will be necessary for us to become more and more conscious of this 'web of time'; but the intellect will

not be able to achieve this. To be able to live in any particular week so that we do not only live in one but simultaneously in four will have to become a matter of course. What matters is not that every morning we babble the verse of the week — or not — but that we become as much aware of time as we are now aware of space.

Week 34 is the last week before Advent; the week that leads us into the time of Advent. We have had the experience of Whitsun and harvest time, and now the dawn of Christmas is approaching:

34
To feel through selfhood new uprisen
The treasured dower of old
Stir secretly to life within
Shall, waking, pour into my human deeds
A tide of universal powers,
And so, maturing, grave me in existence.

First the divine seed is surrounded by memory; and now something is secretly stirring to life within. It is coming up to the birth. And yet only in the middle of February is this birth complete. We find this in verse 45:

45
The power of thought stands firm
Bonded with the spirit's birth,
On the dull spurrings of the senses
Raying the fullness of its light.
When plenitude of soul
Will join in union with the life of worlds,
Then must the senses' revelation
Embrace the light of thinking.

Only then has Whitsun come to fulfilment!

First human thinking had to be dimmed down, thrust down to the drowsing of a dream. Now in February, out of the

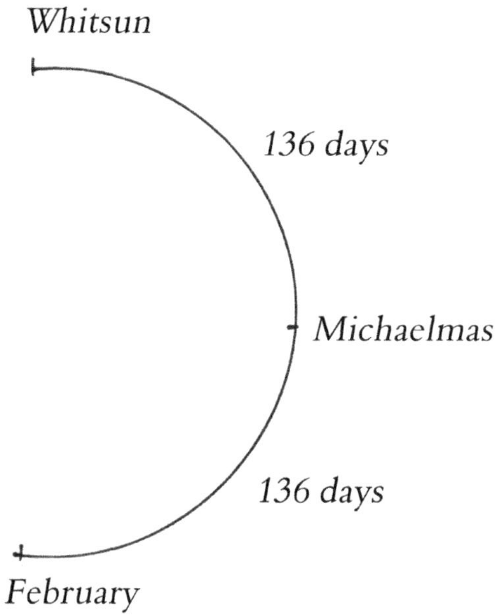

divine seed of Whitsun, does the spirit-birth come about. Here one finds the manifestation of what Rudolf Steiner otherwise expressed in the verses he gave for Whitsun; how behind the sensory world, the world of *maya,* there lives the power of the spirit. If one reads the February verse in the right way, one finds in it the expression of the Whitsun event as it has been fulfilled within the human soul.

The time that Rudolf Steiner chose for his entry into earthly existence was the month of February. From Whitsun until Michaelmas, and from Michaelmas until February is 272 days.

The period of 272 days is the time that the embryo needs for its development in the mother's womb. A child who is conceived at Whitsun would be born roughly in the second half of February. So this is the time that the spirit seed needs to develop within the human soul.

Through this fact we may gain a better understanding of something that Rudolf Steiner has told us, namely, that until now the image of the Holy Spirit has been a white dove.[2] But the more that the new Christianity which is flowing into the world through the being Anthroposophia will develop amongst humankind, the more will the image of the Holy Spirit change. The white dove as an image of the Holy Spirit will be replaced by the image of the human being, as it is expressed in the child. The child will become the true image of the Holy Spirit.

Eve of St John's Day Address

Given on June 23, 1949 at Camphill

On a day like this, which is the eve of one of the greatest festivals in which the human soul is allowed to participate — on such a day, we are justified in looking back to primeval times, asking ourselves what may have happened when we took part at that time in the experiences of midsummer, both by night and by day. How was it for us then? How must it have been when we did not as yet have the possibility of having a clear ego-consciousness; when we did indeed already live on earth but part of our existence was still in the womb of the gods, in the realm of the hierarchies?

Rudolf Steiner has revealed to us how in former times the priests of the mystery centres led those for whom they were responsible through this time of the year.[3] He gives us the following picture: messengers were sent out from the mystery centres to lead their fellow human beings into an experience of midsummer time through music and poetry. These guides of humanity taught a special kind of singing and chanting. On June 24 and 25 not only did the flames leap up into the sky, but also the words and voices of human beings dancing and singing together in their hundreds. Moreover, they were told and also instructed that a response would be given from the spirit realm to their souls as they were borne up into the heights through their voices. They were led into a mood whereby they could send out a question into the heights and know: if we learn our songs, our dances, and perform them within the beauty of nature, in the warmth and light of the soaring earth existence, all this will be sent up into the heavenly realms and an answer will come.

The answer was this: in those who had learnt to listen a window would open, in which their own ego-being, their humanity, their own higher existence, could manifest itself. It was known that only at a particular time of the year — when the sun has reached its highest point — was it possible for us to perceive ourselves. Our own being is otherwise in the womb of the Godhead; but during this time of midsummer we are able to experience or meet ourselves, our own ego. When this meeting between that part of human beings which is earthbound and the part which has remained in heaven had taken place, it meant so much for us that we were able to carry on throughout the whole coming year strengthened and individualized, in the awareness that we had to fulfil our task here on earth, even though our higher self is still in heaven.

If one carries such an mage in one's heart, one learns to know how midsummer was experienced once upon a time — in other words, how we ourselves experienced it. We know, of course, that everything has changed: that what lived as an ego-nature in the womb of the Godhead is now here within our earthly body. No longer do we have part of our being in the heavenly world, but rather have we learnt to say 'I' to ourselves. Nevertheless the time of midsummer is approaching and we must learn to experience it in a new way. To experience midsummer in a manner appropriate for today means essentially that we need to develop a closer relationship with the mystery of our own ego, with what we call our 'I am.' It is very easy for an anthroposophist to say that the human being consists of four members. But the more one tries to get to know, to really get hold of, the nature of our ego, the more one knows that it is veiled, that it is a mystery within our innermost existence. It is as much an earthly as it is a human mystery.

During the time of midsummer we are called by the processes of nature to lose ourselves in light, in warmth and in beauty. And yet this call to surrender oneself already presupposes the question 'What is the I?' It is impossible to answer this question; no earthly language can furnish an explanation. All one can do is

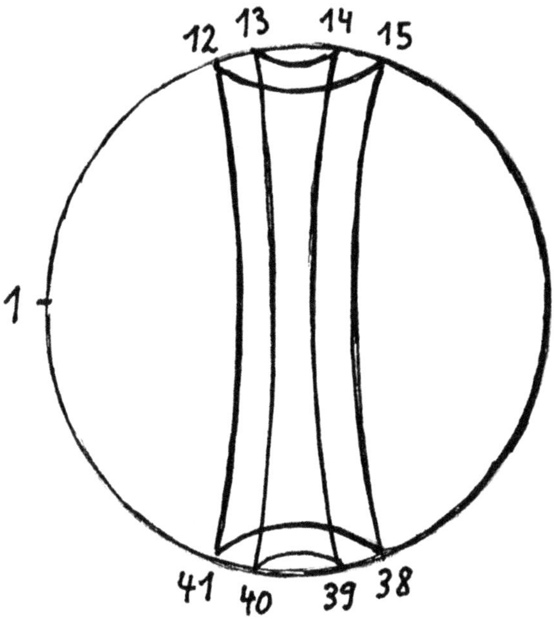

to try to describe it, to try to draw near to such an explanation. There is only one being who can take our hand in this quest, and that is John the Baptist. For he is the guardian of the mystery of human ego-existence. He is the one whom Rudolf Steiner calls 'Adam,' the first-born of humankind, who reappeared as John the Baptist.[4] He is the guardian of the mysteries of warmth and fire, of ego-existence.

At Whitsun I tried to describe some of the verses of the Calendar of the Soul [see the previous address]. Beginning with Easter (verse 1) we rise with the ascending arc of the sun and arrive at midsummer with verses 12, 13, 14 and 15. Verses 13 and 14 belong together, as do 12 and 15. Then we come to the depths of winter with verses 38, 39, 40 and 41. If one familiarizes oneself with the content of these verses, one experiences how they lead one into the heights of nature and into the depths of the spirit. These four form one temporal unit in the year. Verse 13 already reflects what will happen in verses 14, 39 and 40.

We are now in the heights of our experience of nature. Here is reflected our spiritual experience of the depths of winter; and so verses 12, 15, 41 and 38 belong together in a like manner.

In the St John's verse (12 and 15) the human soul is overwhelmed by nature. In verses 41 and 38 midsummer experience becomes an experience of the depths of winter.

This is one of the mysteries of human ego-existence: to lose oneself in order to find oneself again. The one who followed and suffered this path in advance of all human beings — and this is the mark of the ego — was John the Baptist. There were four main aspects of his existence, which have become signs indicating how we may learn how to deal with our selfhood.

Take verse 13 into your heart:

13
Am I then in the heights of sense —
So kindles in my depths of soul
The truth from spirit worlds of fire
The gods themselves proclaim:
'Seek through your boding power
And find in spirit ground
Your spirit brotherhood'

If you let it grow day by day, you will be able to say to yourself: it is John the Baptist who is speaking in my heart, the same voice that called to the people in Judea: *metanoéte*, change the aim of your existence; the spirit realms have indeed come near.

14
Surrendered to the senses' revelations
I lost my being's proper urge,
And felt, in dreaming thoughts bemused,
My selfhood stolen away.
But waking presses on me still
World-thinking in the senses' glow

If you listen clearly to verse 14 you hear the words, 'He must increase, but I must decrease' (John 4:30f). This is the second great event in the life of John the Baptist. John stands by the River Jordan in the knowledge that the one who is greater is coming. You see the window open and there appears the dove. Only John is able to hear the voice of the Father. This lives in the words of verse 14.

The midwinter verse 39 now tells us:

39
Surrendered to the spirit's revelations
I win the light of universal life.
The force of thought grows strong in clarity
To grant me selfhood,
And in me, from the thinker's power
Leaps into wakefulness the sense of self.

I have started working with my own thinking and am bringing my own self to birth. If we really try, even if only outwardly, to approach the mystery surrounding the figure of John the Baptist, we stand — in so far as we are being clear-minded — before the question: Why was it that the one who paved the way for the Christ was not permitted to become his disciple? Why did he have to go into the depths of prison in the castle of Macharus? One can read in the Gospels that in this rock-bound prison he began to doubt. He had to send messengers to ask: 'Are you the one whom we are awaiting?' (Matt.11:2f, Luke 7:18f). In uttermost loneliness, the greatest among earthborn men was sitting in prison, doubting and waiting for an answer. John had to find his 'self' through doubt, tragedy and denial, which led to his being beheaded. This is the third great event in John's life. Through this, he redeemed what he had done when as Adam he had gone through the Fall. The sacrifice was made, the head of John was presented on a silver platter. The third step reached fulfilment.

The fourth step is contained in verse 40:

40
Am I then in the spirit's depths —
So in the roots of soul profound
From out the heart's wide worlds of love
Illusion vain of selfhood fills itself
With powers of fire from the word of worlds.

This experience can be read in the Gospel, in the scene where the Feeding of the Five Thousand is described (John 6:1–15). This is the spirit realm where souls come to Christ in our time. Andrew says to Christ: 'Here is a youth who has five barley-loaves and two fishes.' This youth is none other than the spirit-being of John. He brings all that he has won from earth-existence — in the fivefold world of the senses of our head (taste, smell, sight, hearing and touch) — this he offers up to heaven in the form of five baked barley loaves. The two fish are the sign of the sacrifice of the 'self' that he bears within him. Christ accepts this sacrifice, and with this he feeds the five thousand. This is the fourth metamorphosis of John — of human ego-nature.

I shall now bring these four steps together in the sense of the modern path of experience and practice:

First: We call upon others, as John also did, when we awaken to an experience of our own self.

Second: Then we experience within this self the cosmic thinking, the Logos. We know that we must surrender ourselves if we are to receive the cosmic thinking and make it our own. We must bring our own self to birth out of the intellect.

Third: Only through this will we be able — if we are inherently ready for this — to make the great sacrifice, the beheading of our powers of thought. The challenge here is to surrender our intellect once we have succeeded in gaining the self.

Fourth: If we are then willing to bear the consequences, they will become food in the hands of Christ.

In this way our thoughts can draw near to the mystery of the ego. But behind this there stands another mystery, the mystery of the other ego-being: not of Adam but of Lazarus. There, too, we can find a fourfold path.

Thirteen in number are the spheres which surround our year.

Twelve in number are the weeks of the Apostles. The thirteenth — in the light and the depths — is that of John the Baptist. And in these four weeks of midsummer and wintry depths we stand before his sacrifice, before the mystery of the 'I am' of the human being.

Impressions of South Africa

An address given on July 17, 1957 at Murtle, Camphill Scotland

It has always been a great question how to celebrate the festivals on the other side of the earth and how to work there spiritually with the Calendar of the Soul and in other similar contexts. All that I can offer is merely tentative, and it is given with a great deal of reserve. It should be taken only as a suggestion, as what I can visualize as possibilities for understanding this problem.

The way that our work develops there out of Rudolf Steiner's impulses — in Africa, Australia and South America — will have a decisive role in our understanding of the being of the earth on its other hemisphere and of how we may understand the festivals there. We shall have to abandon all the traditional images of the various festivals which are ingrained in us.

During the last few days the provinces of Transvaal and Natal were so snowed up that traffic came to a standstill — something which has never happened before. And this was at St John's time, the time when the earth reaches its cosmic heights. But there is in a certain sense a true winter in those parts; some mountains in Cape Province have a covering of snow every year, even though it is (from our European perspective) in the height of summer, the crowning-point of the year, when the human soul has given itself up to the light and warmth of the cosmos. On the other side of the earth it is winter; so it is quite justified to ask whether one should not change the festivals there and reverse their order. But it is not right to celebrate Christmas in June and St John's in December; one cannot divide the earth in two parts and all those

who are Christians with it — and as far as the being of the earth is concerned the whole of humanity is Christian.[5] We would even have to celebrate Christmas twice if we went travelling in September!

This impression has been strengthened by my own experience. I was, for example, travelling by car on the Saturday before Palm Sunday through the mountains of Natal. Everything became very quiet; nature was holding its breath, deeply imbued with the mood of this festival. It was imminent; Easter week was approaching, and I had the experience that Easter is Easter, Michaelmas is Michaelmas; the festivals over the whole earth are at the same time. And to confirm this a rainbow — not a full one but a pillar of the most beautiful colours, like a fountain — appeared as the sun was setting. From this moment on, we were convinced: whatever the season is, Easter was Easter. All over the earth it is Easter at the same time. Easter has this special quality of manifesting itself in the very essence of matter, independent of the season. This was confirmed for me as an experience on Easter Sunday, when I held the first Children's Service for the children in Hermanus: even though out in nature it was Michaelmas, it was Easter in autumn. We could see that it was necessary to give up all traditional images — the stable in a snowy landscape, the child in a cradle with Joseph and Mary (as a sign of Christmas), to free oneself from the St John's fire and the burning of torches, and from the budding and sprouting life-forces of nature as a sign of the Easter festival. We have to come to new images, arrive at new experiences. We have to learn how truly to celebrate the festivals on the other side of the globe, how to adapt a festival to the particular circumstances where it is taking place. The deeper needs of the children demand this of us. With Rudolf Steiner's help it will be possible to find a solution; for it is a matter of creating new images that can go in place of the old ones. New ones need to arise; and they must grow in the souls of those who take up such work on the other side of the earth.

However, we already have an experiential guide in this respect

in the Calendar of the Soul. If we really work with the Soul Calendar and follow this meditative path, we will observe that the verse of any particular week is only a quarter of what lives and works during that week. The Calendar of the Soul is written for the whole of the earth, in order that the human soul may be led to an experience of the whole of humankind.

The verses are not only marked with numbers but also with letters, so that there are four verses which belong together. They form a quartet and sing new melodies with the four voices — soprano, alto, tenor and bass. When they sound together, they are singing to one another. If we sing only the song for this week, we will already understand this week's quartet:

> 15
> I feel the spirit's weaving
> Spell-bound within the world's array
> In drowsiness of sense
> It wraps my selfhood in —
> But all to dower that self
> With strength, which cribbed and impotent
> Mine I shall never give itself.

I want to go into the verses for this week. The verse just quoted is the leading verse — it has the dominant voice and gives the theme of the fugue: 'I feel the spirit's weaving spell-bound within the world's array.' Now imagine that we are in South Africa; there it is winter, but here it is summer. We have to unite summer and winter; but we should not take the verse that is precisely opposite, because it has already passed in South Africa. We could imagine a cross; the St John's verse is the Christmas verse in South Africa. One has to count a certain number of weeks back from Michaelmas and then a similar number back from Easter. Imagine the earth in minature — around it turns the wheel of the seasonal forces, revolving continually around the earth. The heavenly equator, the etheric equator (as Rudolf Steiner describes it in his imaginations of the seasons), moves

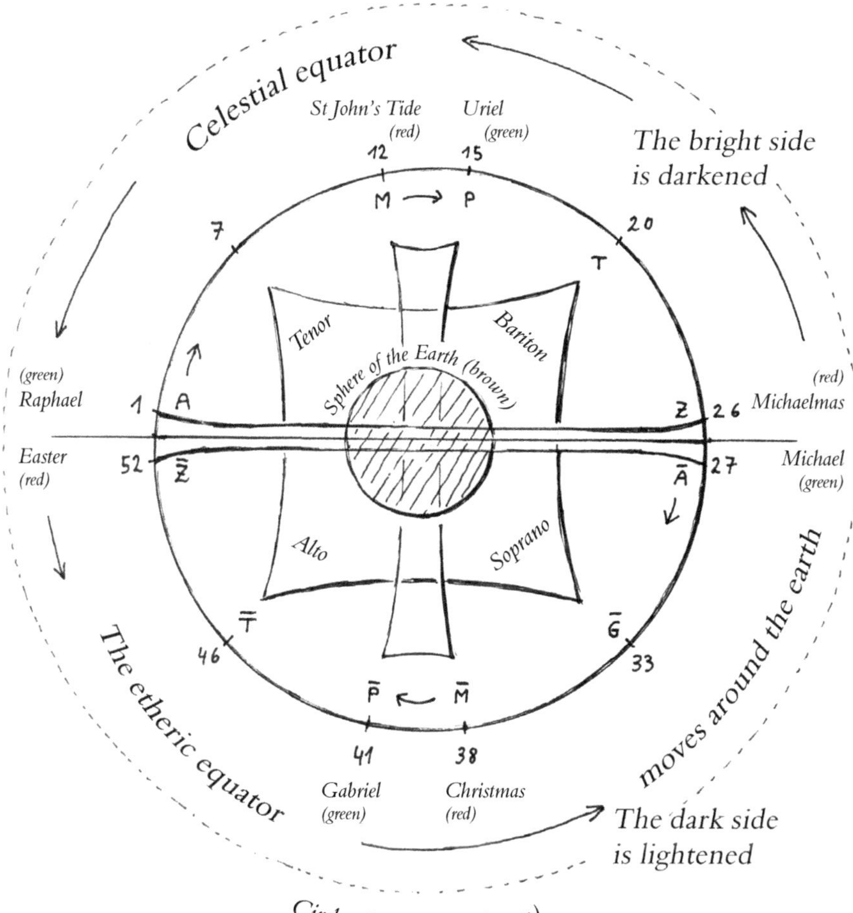
Celestial equator
St John's Tide
(red)
Uriel
(green)
The bright side
is darkened
12
15
M → P
7
20
T
Tenor
Bariton
Sphere of the Earth (brown)
(green)
Raphael
(red)
Michaelmas
1
A
Z
26
Easter
(red)
52
Z̄
Ā
27
Michael
(green)
Alto
Soprano
T̄
46
Ḡ
33
P̄ ← M̄
41
38
Gabriel
(green)
Christmas
(red)
The etheric equator
moves around the earth
The dark side
is lightened
Circle of the festival (green)

around the earth.[6] If you recall how Rudolf Steiner has described the seasons, with the powers, or spirits, guiding and ruling over them, you encounter the names of Uriel, Gabriel, Raphael and Michael. You can ascribe the names of the Archangels to the verses; but you cannot allow yourself to write 'Christmas' but only 'Gabriel,' and not 'Easter' but 'Raphael.' The Christian festivals have inserted themselves into earthly existence. Now the problem is that it is necessary to celebrate Christmas in connection with Uriel, a Michaelic Easter, a Raphaelic Michaelmas. Easter can equally well be in spring and in autumn; Christmas and St John's can have a connection both with Uriel and with Gabriel. It is probably even necessary today to celebrate Christmas with Uriel and Easter with Michael.

At this time of year Gabriel is associated with the southern hemisphere; with us Uriel is ruling over the summer. Down there it is certainly possible to experience something akin to Christmas. But Gabriel is a reality — as is St John's. We must now turn to the question how we may celebrate a Gabrielic St John's festival. Can we connect the work of Gabriel with the deeds of St John? Why should we not in winter imagine St John as the 'voice in the wilderness,' in the empty spaces of the earth? Why should we not conceive of a John amidst the wintry earth, accompanying the Nathan child as an earthly brother? St John is the Adamic being, who from the beginning prepared the earth for the coming of Christ. This, too, is John. Why should John not be considered from the aspect of winter? It would make no sense to light a St John's fire in South Africa. One has to find a different way of expressing it.

Why should we not learn to connect the outward Michaelmas festival with the inner aspect of Raphael? We experience Raphael as a bestower of breathing forces, as a being of healing, as a spirit-being who lives among us human beings, whereas Michael works from out of the spiritual heights. Michaelmas under the wings of Raphael could be a festival where we may become conscious of our responsibility in our devotion to animals;

where we stand as the helpers of our fellow men, as healers of the earth and of nature. In a similar way we can look for true images of midsummer in the African winter, when with us the heat is almost unbearable and the splendour of the light so mighty. What does the south expect at this time? If we imagine a Urielic Christmas we could, for example, think of Christmas as the festival of cosmic thoughts, for Uriel is the bearer of cosmic thoughts. Christmas could then really become a festival of the sun's victory, and we would have to surrender ourselves in a Christmas-like way — but not as our traditions and customs determine!

Christmas can also be experienced in such a way that the earth itself is the child, in the great womb of light of the cosmic being of Christ — and this would be closest to our hearts. As we behold Easter in a Michaelic context, the fruits have ripened; and we may serve the earth as the body of Christ: 'Anyone who eats my bread walks upon the substance of my body.' Michael gives the fruit which has become ripe through the Christ: the feeding of the five thousand is a Michaelic Easter event. If humankind could take steps in this direction to celebrate festivals both in their cosmic and their earthly aspects, healing would come about for the whole of the earth.

May some of these images accompany our friends who are going to South Africa. If we could increasingly manage to think in an imaginative way, it would be more possible for non-European people to come to an experience of Christianity. This, in turn, could help to overcome tremendous difficulties. Although this may be music of the future, you could already be making a start by reading the St John's imagination at Christmas and the Michael imagination at Easter.[7]

A Guide to the Anthroposophical Calendar of the Soul

The mysteries of the yearly cycle lie hidden in the Calendar of the Soul. Once these mysteries gradually become apparent to the human soul that endeavours to discern them, the course of the year manifests itself as a lemniscate rather than a circle. The form of this lemniscate cycle is indicated overleaf. The year runs its course against the background of thirteen concentric circles, and these circles are the thirteen lunar orbits within a year.

On two occasions in the year the lemniscate depicting the course of the year passes through its midpoint; these are during Holy Week and during the week leading up to Michaelmas. At these two festival periods the directions of the earth's course are such that they are at right angles to one another, hence, forming the image of the cross. Its horizontal dimension is formed at Michaelmas, its vertical dimension at Easter. At Easter heaven and earth are united; at Michaelmas cosmic forces are united with the dying of the earth.

At Easter the Word became flesh.
At Michaelmas flesh shall become word.

Thus the cross becomes an archetypal picture of the yearly cycle; and in the following pages an attempt was made to depict the metamorphoses of the cross in the lemniscate course of the year. The form of the cross changes thirteen times, corresponding to the thirteen orbits of the moon. Just as the Christ worked through Jesus and the twelve Apostles, so has the earth's course through the year become a thirteenfold experience of the cross.

Camphill
in
May
1948

Die Geheimnisse des Jahreslaufes sind im "Seelenkalender" verborgen. Werden diese Geheimnisse der Menschenseele, die strebend sich bemüht, allmählich offenbar, dann ergibt sich der Jahreslauf als eine Lemniskate nicht als ein Kreis. Umstehend ist die Figur dieses Lemniskaten-Laufes angedeutet. Das Jahr läuft auf dem Hintergrund von dreizehn in sich feststehenden Kreisen & diese Kreise sind die dreizehn Mondenumläufe innerhalb eines Jahres.

Zweimal im Jahr durchläuft der Jahreslauf als Lemniskate seinen eigenen Mittelpunkt. Das ist während der Osterwoche & während der Woche, die zu Michaeli hinführt. Die Richtungen des Erdenlaufes sind zu diesen zwei Jahreszeiten so, daß sie aufeinander senkrecht stehen & damit die Figur des Kreuzes erbilden. Der wagrechte Balken wird zu Michaeli geformt, der senkrechte Balken zu Ostern.

Zu Ostern wird Himmel & Erde verbunden. Zu Michaeli werden die kosmischen Kräfte dem Erdentod verbunden.

Zu Ostern ist das Wort Fleisch geworden.
Zu Michali soll das Fleisch Wort werden.

So wird das Kreuz zum Urbild des Jahreslaufes & in den folgenden Blättern wurde versucht, die Metamorphosen des Kreuzes im Jahres-Lemniskaten-Lauf darzustellen. Dreizehnmal, den dreizehn Monden-Kreisen entsprechend, wandelt sich die Kreuzgestalt. Wie der Christus durch Jesus & die zwölf Apostel hindurchwirkte, so ist der Jahres-Erdenlauf alljährlich zum dreizehnfachen Kreuz-Erlebnis geworden.

Camphill
im
März
1948

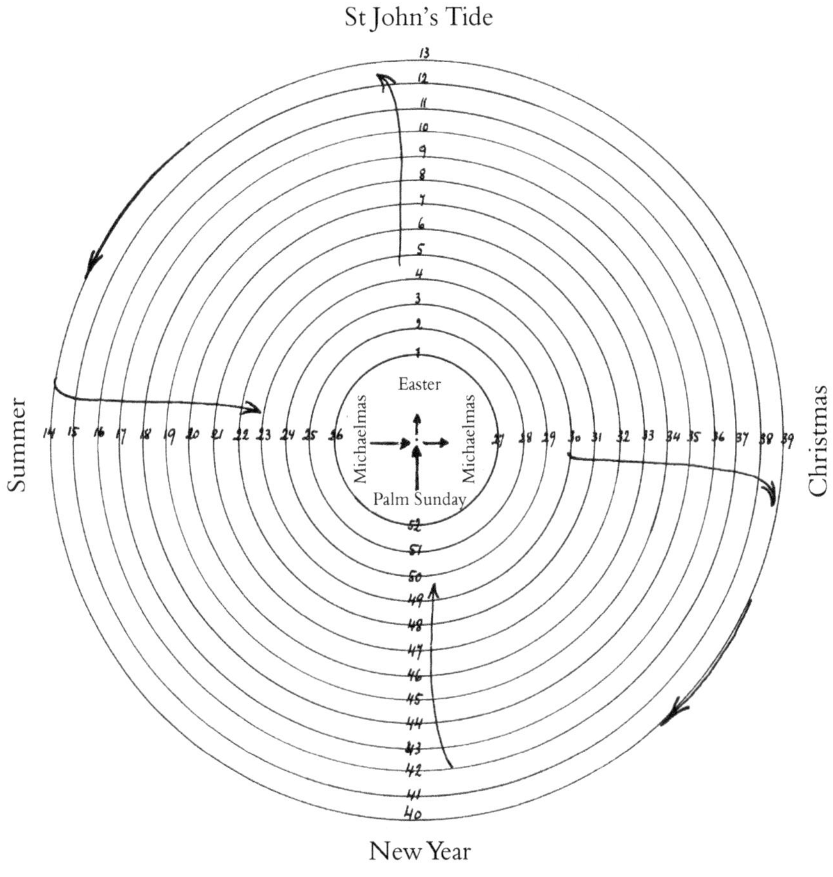

Calendar of the Soul — cross form

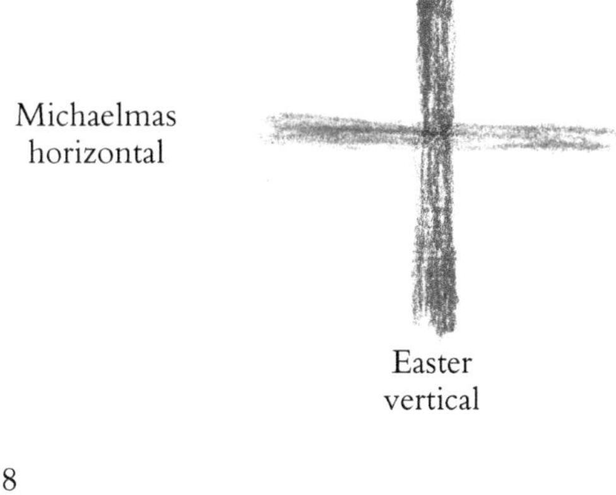

Foreword

Camphill, March 1948

Anyone who understands how to resolve
His relationship to time
Is learning to live in eternity.[1]

'There are two paths.'[2] One is the human soul's gradual awakening to its life and existence within the earthly world in such a form that it acknowledges the necessity of its earthly imprisonment and resigns itself to it in inner contentment, stillness and humility; it begins to integrate itself into this earthly life. To this end the soul cultivates step by step the virtues that it needs and so learns to bear all that is ordained for it, both pain and joy.

What is described in the books of schooling, as for instance Thomas à Kempis's *Imitation of Christ*, is an endeavour to follow this path.

Integrating the soul into the earthly world and its transformation is intimately linked with the acquisition of the Christian virtues. If every effort is made to follow this path, many a soul will be filled with what theology describes as grace. Then parts of the spiritual world will be revealed to the soul in the intrinsic nature of its manifestations. But it can also be the case that Christ himself, the Risen One, appears by grace in human form.

The second path is that of the spirit. The human spirit does not merely seek the integration of its soul into the earthly world, but seeks entry into the world it came from before entering into earthly existence — the world where it dwelt and was active before birth. This second path does not wholly differ from the

first, but it is of another quality. For it demands that the candidate who is ready for it, subjects himself to certain spiritual and soul exercises that are not to everyone's taste.

Anyone can follow the first path who has become self-aware and who at the same time wants to try to do good on the earth. This can happen in all sorts of different ways, provided that the aim of this quest is directed towards a meeting with Jesus Christ.

The second path can also be attempted by anyone, and for a certain part of the way it is almost identical with the first path; but where the hurdles are encountered and trials lie in wait one person can go further whereas another will have to be content with little progress. For where the path of trials is chosen, worlds begin to reveal themselves which the person concerned has known about, but which have become remote and closed to their experience. Now, however, they begin clearly to notice that there are immense differences between knowledge and experience. One can know much about the spiritual world; but to experience and have direct knowledge of it is something entirely different.

Living with the Soul Calendar is an aspect of the first path. Uniting oneself with this jewel of the world-spirit only has an indirect connection to the second path. The Soul Calendar gives the human soul the possibility of attaining by degrees through the yearly cycle the perceptions necessary as a foundation for what Rudolf Steiner calls 'cosmic communion.'

Each single verse of the Soul Calendar contains not only a spiritual content which can be grasped intellectually but a powerful and substantial emotion, a strong feeling that changes from week to week. It is more important to carry this feeling in its ever-changing form through the year, than to connect oneself with the intellectual content of the verses — though this is necessary to achieve that feeling. If this is achieved, both in the course of the year and with the passing of the days, one's awareness is expanded and can gradually become a consciousness that extends over weeks, months and a year; and the result of this is

that the human soul is able to live in harmony with the earthly world and the spirit-world.

Challenges and temptations will not be lessened but will perhaps grow even stronger. However, humility and the power of endurance become greater and the inner swings between suffering and pleasure grows more balanced. The soul thus develops to a stage where it is akin to being a warming fire in a cold room — it fills the cold surroundings with a steady warmth becoming a source of help and comfort.

A soul prepared in this way becomes a constant, warmth-giving fire. It is the same fire that Christ kindled on the shore of Sea of Galilee when he was awaiting those disciples who had gone fishing. Perhaps the Lord then graciously took one of the 153 fishes that the disciples caught and placed it on one or the other of the fires that the willing men kindled within themselves. This is then grace and will shine as a light in the darkness of the earth.

Note
This work remained a fragment: there are descriptions only of 27 of the 52 verses. Noticeably verses 14 and 18 are missing.

Holy Easter Sunday

1 *Easter. April 7–13*
The sun speaks to the sense of man,
And joy from depths of soul
Grows one with light in gazing,
Then thoughts from selfhood's narrow case
Draw outward to far spaces
And mutely bind
Man's being with the spirit's life.

With this verse the soul year, the 'spiritual year,' begins. However much the Easter festival can move within the early part of spring according to the configurations of the spring Full Moon, this verse falls with absolute certainty on Easter Sunday irrespective of the date; its position is therefore fixed. For its position as the verse leading into the spiritual year, depends on its being experienced together with Easter Sunday.

Everything prior to this has as it were disappeared from view. Our gaze reaches not backwards but forwards. For the first time we stand surveying the coming year. All has become future and is in movement! We try to listen to this future, and from it the coming year begins — faintly and barely audibly at first — to sound.

If the right basic feeling for the Soul Calendar is to be acquired, it will always be necessary not merely to experience the individual verse for the week to which it belongs, but also the verses related to it.

Three additional verses belong to each particular one, so that only a quartet of verses can bring a full experience both of feeling and of understanding. The four verses form a true quartet and sound forth in four voices:

As tenor from Easter to St John's.
As baritone from St John's to Michaelmas.
As soprano from Michaelmas to Christmas.
As alto from Christmas to Easter.

Thus the radiant tenor voice rings out and sings:

1. When from the worlds' wide bounds
The sun speaks to the sense of man

But then from the far future there answers a tender alto voice, which softly sings:

52. When from the depths of soul
The spirit turns towards the life of worlds

These two voices interweave, strongly in the tenor, gently in the alto. The soul is overwhelmed by the feeling that Easter has indeed come, Passion has been vanquished, the Resurrection has become a reality, and the sun is manifesting itself from the worlds' wide bounds. The senses experience the light that reveals itself to them as a pair of outspread wings; a mighty breath of light glides forwards, loving, warming, weaving and enlivening. The soul begins to sound forth at the touch of this breath of light, as it resonates, and the soul's bliss of joy comes to birth. Thus from outside, from beyond the soul, the light-breathing miracle of spring approaches us and enkindles joy within us. The world's breath of light reaches right into our heart.

This is different if the words of the alto voice sing in the week for Palm Sunday for then the breath is released not from without but from our inner being, the spirit is turned towards the life of worlds and the beauty welling from the wide bounds of space is received into his heart. But at Easter this stage is now overcome. Easter morning rays forth and the world reveals itself to us.

However, this Easter verse has two distinct points of emphasis: when ... then. When what has been described happens, something else also comes about:

Then thoughts from selfhood's narrow case
Draw outward to far spaces

The approaching light is so powerful that it causes the structure of the human sheaths to tremble, quivering with the approach of newly awakened nature; now thoughts are liberated from the bodily being — selfhood's narrow case — that draw upwards, outwards to meet the dawning light, thus binding human beings in a consciousness of dream and sleep with the spirit's life.

Thus there is something of a twofold nature that we are to experience here: with the approach of the breathing world of light, not only does joy arise within the soul but the body releases the substance of thought which is united with and wedded to the spirit's life. Our answer to nature's summons is twofold: joy is born from the soul, and thoughts from the body.

With this our origin in the spirit comes to fulfilment. The longing that will fill the alto voice at the year's end, which yearns for the beauty of the wide bounds of space and softly mingles with the loud singing of the tenor, is not now present. The tenor radiantly proclaims what is actually taking place: the world of nature and the world of the spirit have turned towards the human soul. The 'when' and 'then' have been consummated. But now a new twofold voice mingles, like a very quiet undertone, with the two other voices. A dark baritone strikes up its song:

26. Nature, thou soul of motherhood,
I bear thee in the essence of my will

and it is joined by a song coming as though from a bright, soaring soprano voice:

27. To dive into my being's depths
Stirs up a yearning in me, boding well

In these two verses the 'when' and 'then' proclaimed in the verse for Easter Sunday comes to fulfilment. The verse for Michaelmas week, beginning with the words 'Nature, thou soul

of motherhood,' speaks of the total union between nature and the human soul. Whereas the message proclaimed in the verse for the first week after Michaelmas, when autumn has truly arrived, refers to the seed which then appears at Easter in the 'then.' Thus the 'when' of Easter leads to Michaelmas, whereas the 'then' is the last part and the completion of what comes about directly after Michaelmas.

These indications will have to be sufficient for now; they can be supplemented by what is said about the corresponding verses for Michaelmas.

The cross-beam of the cross of the year is being referred to here. The tension between Easter and Michaelmas has been established, and so the basic outline of the whole of the coming year has been given. The world opens up in its rejoicing; joy fills the human heart; but there sound forth voices which utter these words of warning:

O man, take heed!

Sunday after Easter

2 April 14–20
Into the utmost fields of sense
The force of thought resigns its separate life.
The worlds of spirit find
Anew their offspring, man,
Whose seed in them,
But his soul's harvest
Must in himself be found.

Here, what in the first verse of the year was expounded, is now taken further. The thoughts that have been drawn from the sheaths of the self into the world expanses, thoughts that carry us with them and awaken wanderlust within us, are now directed wholly to the fields of sense, so strongly that they lose their separate life. This is proclaimed by the tenor. It sounds like a warning and is, nonetheless, a necessity.

Out of the distance of the year's end the soft voice of the alto chimes in and sings:

51 Into the inmost life of man
The senses pour their wealth ...

What now streams outwards as the force of thought will pour back again into the inmost life of man. It is important to consider the comparisons:

utmost [outermost]	inmost
fields of sense	life of man
force of thought	senses' wealth

Then, however, it goes on resounding, and what was described in the first verse as more from without now comes to expression

in its inner essence. The worlds of spirit are giving birth to their son; through the Easter event he has turned again to them, and they receive him as one who during autumn and winter has been in search of the fruits of his self-consciousness.

Intermingled with this there sounds the ever-strengthening voice of the alto, as though explaining and interpreting:

> The spirit of the world beholds
> His mirrored image in the eye of man

Yes, just as the eye is a small but significant 'offspring' of the human body, reflecting in miniature in its structure the entire universe — and also man — so is the human offspring related to the world of spirit. Man is an eye of the spirit-world; and he now turns again to where he originally came from and repeatedly.

Here the comparisons are particularly important, because they are not so obvious as in the first part of the two verses. They are as follows:

worlds of spirit	spirit of the world
human offspring	eye of man
seed	mirrored image
soul's harvest	power
must be found	must create

What in Easter week was still a dim experience ('and mutely bind man's being with the spirit's life') can now become a conscious encounter. The force of thought is still drawn outwards; but because of that man's true being is revealed in its seminal power. This seed is, like any seed, a part of our will that strives upwards in order to meet the spirit-world. At the end of the year the image — the mirrored image — of the spirit of the world will stand over and against this seed.

This seed is my self, the higher self that belongs to the worlds of spirit but which now, in this special week, is of particular emotional significance. For it is through the worlds of spirit finding it that the human offspring finds its true being. That is,

the human offspring has an intuition of it, knows of it in the manner that it can say:

> More radiant than the sun,
> Purer than snow,
> Finer than the ether
> Is the self,
> The spirit in my heart of hearts.
> I am this self.
> This self am I.[3]

In each of us there lives this seed which has an effect on us, even though it abides in the womb of the spiritual powers. This verse would teach one to be mindful of this moment in the year when Easter time quietly makes the transition to the approaching event of the Ascension.

> Recognize the seed! It leads to death.
> Have an intimation of the image! It leads to birth.

When this has been rightly felt and tenor and alto have learnt mutually to keep the balance, the two other voices begin to join in. The baritone starts singing the autumn song:

> 25. My self, now made my very own,
> May shine abroad its inner light
> In dark abysms of space and time.

And then the soprano sounds forth:

> 28. Quickened anew within
> I feel the vastness of my being ...

In these two songs there rings out as though from afar what can come about in autumn, in the weeks before and after Michaelmas. For 'my self, now made my very own' means none other than that self and I are now united in the most perfect harmony and are thereby able to bestow inner light upon dying nature. And from this there arises the experience

of the vastness of my being, which can now decipher life's riddles.

The worlds of spirit find my seed — my manas. They carry it up in all that develops on the sunlit earth in the approaching summer. But I must set off on my way if I am to follow what has gone before me.

Have courage, thou soul-wanderer!

Second Sunday after Easter

3 April 21–27
Speaks to the universe,
Itself forgetting
And mindful of its primal form,
The waxing I of man.
'On you, from cramping fetters
Of isolation breaking,
I ground my own intrinsic being.'

What has prevailed in the first two verses now changes. For the first time (and this will appear again and again in the course of the soul's year) the phrase, '[there] speaks' appears. With this a quite specific nuance of feeling arises which needs to become an inner reality — a will-related element manifests itself. The tension that was present between 'when' and 'then' and was also discernible in the second verse now changes into the active element of '[there] speaks,' and the message in this speaking is communicated.

For now, once worlds of spirit have found their human offspring, this human being confronts the universe as a waking 'I' and tries to become conscious of their situation. As they speak, the ego begins to express what it feels in this encounter. It seeks liberation, freedom from bondage, in order to be able to meet its own higher nature.

We shall arrive at a right understanding of this experience if we call it to mind in the picture: it is spring; nature has awakened. Each day brings to light new miracles of existence. The soul rejoices and longs for the light of the sun. This turning to the world of the sunlight, this state of being flooded by the cosmic power of the sun, engenders in the soul the urge to wander

out into the depths of the country, far from everyday life, away to an experience of the boundlessness of forest and mountains, streams and rivers, clouds and wind — such is the blissful longing of the soul.

> I hear a streamlet rushing
> From out its rocky spring,
> Down to the valley rushing
> So quick and silver-bright.
> (Wilhelm Müller)

Yes, the soul longs to go off into the unknown, the unrecognized, so as to get to know it.

If the light of the moon overwhelms a person in waking consciousness they become sleepwalkers and walk while asleep in the arms of this light. But if the light of the sun has an overpowering effect on someone, the dreamy urge to wander arises in the soul. This verse helps this impulse to rise up into the domain of consciousness and to form from it a longing for a higher state.

> On you, from cramping fetters
> Of isolation breaking

This does not only happen when we become a wanderer or a keen rambler but when we embark upon the inner path of the soul. We find here the same mood in which Christian Rosenkreutz begins his journey on the second day of the *Chymical Wedding:*

> With mirth thou pretty bird rejoice,
> Thy maker's praise enhanced,
> Lift up thy shrill and pleasant voice,
> Thy God is high advanced.
> (Tr. E. Foxcroft)

Once all this has been sufficiently internalized, the voice of the alto again begins to sound out of the far distance and calls:

50. Speaks to the human I
In strong self-revelation,
Enlarging all its being's powers,
The bliss of growth in world existence.

Here we have the opposite: world existence summons the human soul in order to be able to come to manifestation through it. And just as the human I seeks to extricate itself in the time after Easter from its bonds formed from personal isolationism, so in the pre-Easter period does world existence endeavour to free itself from the enchantment which winter has imposed upon it.

In the image of the lemniscate it has the following aspect:

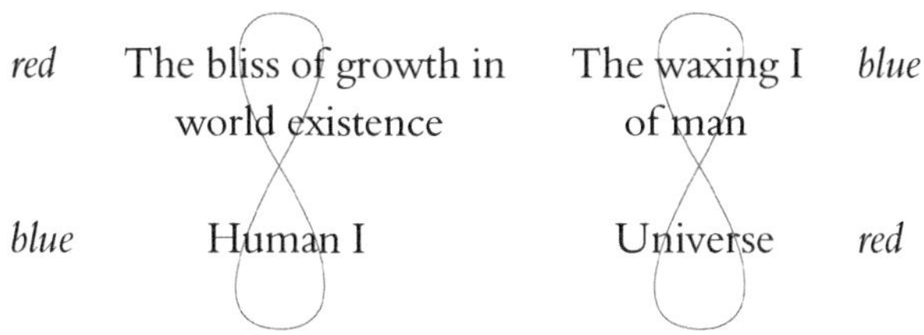

In the time before Easter the universe has taken steps towards being able to meet the human soul. Now, however, the human soul sets out on the path of entrusting itself to the universe.

At this point two voices — those of the baritone and the soprano — begin to sound forth, pointing towards the goal that it is possible for the path of the soul's year — if followed in this way — to reach. It leads to a process of self-discovery within human beings.

The baritone speaks:

24. Unceasingly itself renewing
The soul grows self-aware

and the soprano intones:

29. To light in me the lamp of thinking
And fan with inner force the flame

In both verses that sound forth in early autumn, the words in German *'sich selbst'* (emphasizing the personal aspect of the soul element) appear, together with the resultant consequences.

Thus the soul that at the beginning of this week cheerfully embarks upon the path hears from afar the object of the journey ring out, and at a further distance that promise that the bliss of growth in world existence itself will undertake to the soul to make its own.

Third Sunday after Easter

4 *April 28 – May 4*
'I feel my being's very being,'
So speaks the feeling soul
Which in the sunlit world
Unites itself with floods of light.
It would bestow on thinking
A gift of warmth for clearness,
And into wholeness
Weld man and world together.

The journey continues. It now leads up to the first hill of the spirit, and the soul becomes free and open. It is given over to the world of the dawning light that manifests itself ever more strongly and endeavours to unite itself in the sunlit world with all the streaming floods of light.

It is not the waking ego that now speaks, as in the previous verse, but feeling. The ego — itself forgetting — has pointed, making a gesture towards the universe and has addressed it. But I and world were then still separate from one another. Now one being comes up against another: the floods of light of the inner being unite with the waves of the light that is liberated from the world and union takes place. Just as two lovers at first see only one another but then find themselves, so do world and feeling interpenetrate one another, recognize this and say: Thou art I, I am thou.

From this, warmth of soul — which always arises where a self-sacrifice has been made — is born. It is the

Creative fire of love
That holds sway from man to God.[4]

With this, however, the light of thinking is filled and enveloped by the substance of warmth, and from cold light is engendered a wisdom that bestows blessing and resolves life's riddles. Thus man becomes the consummating element in the world, and the world becomes man's acknowledged father. This is the split that has been overcome in unity.

This basic theme appears as a sort of archetype in every spring song that poets have ever sung. What was separated is united, from the deeper regions to the highest level. Love brings together all that was separated, divided, split, and from this union there again arises the *creative fire of love*, as a renewing and renewed substance.

At the other end of the year, where the first signs of spring are announcing themselves at the beginning of March, what here becomes fulfilment is still hopeful expectation:

> 49. 'I feel your strength of life, O worlds,'
> So the clear voice of thinking cries

It is that clear voice of thinking which as yet lacks substance that is engendered here. But it knows this, and so the wistful alto sings:

> And to the world-day as it nears
> Bending its inward rays of hope.

This should be felt right into the gesture: the inclination similar to the way a young woman inclines her head when she is awaiting the lover. In a similar way the approaching world-day is still awaited; nevertheless the rays of hope turn towards it in expectation of its warming power.

And now, again coming from the autumn time, there sounds the voice of the baritone and the soprano in this reverberating duet. Just as yearning in the pre-Easter time and fulfilment in the time after Easter mutually support one another, the baritone sings as follows:

23. Subdued to autumn's mood
The spurrings of the senses die away,
Veil upon veil, the mist
Dims the still radiant light.

Here the soul is gripped by a mood of farewell. What was united must now be dissolved; the rising mists separate the world from the soul, and the soul must find the path to itself.

The counter-voice, sung by the soprano, now intones:

30. Warmed in the sunshine of the soul
Ripe fruits of thinking thrive,
To sureness of a self aware
All feeling is transformed.

Renunciation has grown out of separation, and in renunciation the soul has grown beyond itself and now has the certainty:

Winter shall wake in me
The summer of the soul.

Thus the mood of expectancy forms part of the joyous experience of the union that comes about between soul and world; and this is again permeated by the feeling of separation and renunciation.

What otherwise takes place constantly in engaging with human destiny is here directed towards the encounter between the human soul and the spirit of the world. But the deeper it is experienced the more strongly it is felt that we find here the archetype of what as a reflection takes place in human destiny. For on earth the seeking and finding, parting and renunciation that happens between us human beings is only a picture of the path that — on a grander scale — we, each of us as a lost son, have to follow back to the Father.

In this week of the soul's year, something comes about for the feelings that will eventually, when the New Jerusalem is built, come about for the entirety of the human soul.

Fourth Sunday after Easter

5 May 5–11
In light, that from the spirit's depths
Plays fruitfully through space
And manifests the gods' creating,
Shows forth the being of the soul
To world existence magnified,
And resurrected
From narrow selfhood's inner power.

Once the union between the human soul and the universe has come about, once the soul has been enabled to bring the 'essence of its being' to experience, something new occurs.

The uniting process began on the hills of the spirit that had to be climbed; but now that sphere of the world where this encounter has taken place reveals itself to the soul. This sphere is the light; that light of which Novalis says:

As life's inmost soul
It is breathed
By the giant world
Of restless stars
Who swim in its blue ocean,
By the sparkling stone,
The peaceful plant,
By the creatures'
Many fashioned
Ever-moving life.
It is breathed by the clouds
Many-hued, by the zephyrs ...
(Tr. Mabel Cotterell)

The soul now finds itself in this light that pervades and

penetrates the universe. It weaves in the rays of this light; it shines in the colours of this light; it creates and finds its form in the forces of this light and it begins to sense the power of this light.

> As a king
> It summons each power
> Of terrestrial nature
> To numberless changes,
> And alone doth its presence
> Reveal the full splendour
> Of earth.

What Novalis describes in this first *Hymn to the Night* is also experienced by the human soul which has awoken in the light. A transport of delight takes hold of it in this experience of having escaped from selfhood's inner power and being able to participate in the activity of the gods which from out of the periphery pervades the whole of space and time. Thus the rejoicing tenor rings forth, expanding our soul and extending to the bounds of the horizon.

But from the realm of the year's end the admonishing tones of the alto are heard, reminding the soul that, in addition to the light from spirit's depths in which it now weaves, there is another experience of light — the light from heights of worlds:

> 48. In light, that wills from heights of worlds
> To stream again into my soul

This is a different light, not one that brings things about, such as the light from spirit's depths, but one with a blessing quality — a light in which world thinking solves the riddles of the soul and engenders love in human hearts.

Just as we have both fire and warmth — the former being creative and formative and the latter warming and nurturing — so, too, does light come from spirit's depths and from heights of worlds. Only by experiencing both do we become inwardly free.

We experience the power of creation, but we can also get to know and love what has been created.

Once this has been experienced, two different voices ring out which similarly have something to say about the experience of light.

The baritone's voice resounds:

22. Light from the worlds' wide bounds
Unfolds in me its life of power,
Changing to light of soul,
Illumining my spirit's depths

And the soprano sings:

31. Light from the spirit's depths
Strives outward like a sun,
It turns to life's own strength of will
And shines into the senses' gloom

Now we begin to sense that there is a mighty cycle of light pervading the universe and the soul, and that the human soul, each individual human soul, is also a heart and works in the world as such a light-filled heart. Just as the blood within us is of a different quality depending on whether it streams from or to the heart, nevertheless it is still blood, though in different forms, so too does the human soul experience light in four different ways.

Novalis gives expression to this in the first of his *Hymns*, when he beholds light as a breathing being and says:

It is breathed by the clouds
Many-hued, by the zephyrs,
And, above all,
By the glorious strangers,
With the thoughtful eyes,
The swinging gait
And the sounding lips...

These strangers are the bearers of the human soul, which is a light-filled heart and unceasingly communicates with the creative and the blessing light of the universe.

The experience of the light-filled heart first penetrates into light's spiritual depths; it is given to us here in this verse for spring. From here the experience changes and becomes the 'light from the worlds' wide bounds' (verse 22), which then becomes the light of soul and now thrusts its way within us into the spirit's depths and rises up out of them again (31). And then this uplifting process leads it to become the light from heights of worlds that streams again towards the soul (48). This streaming of light from the soul into the world and from the world to the soul is the sphere that is brought to manifestation in this verse for the fifth week.

Fifth Sunday after Easter

6 May 12–18 (the week of Ascension)
There has arisen from its separateness
My self — to find that self
As worlds made manifest
In powers of time and space.
The great world shows me everywhere
As the gods' primal image
My imprint's truthfulness.

From experiencing oneself in the sphere of creative light something new has now arisen. The self is not only 'resurrected from narrow selfhood's inner power' but finds itself, after this uplifting process, spread out over the wide world. The self has become a revelation of all worlds, it lives in the cycles of time and the widths of space. This is a state which belongs to the most intimate experience of an incipient spirit-pupilship.

O man, experience thyself!
They speak their promise inwardly
only in gentle tones, reaching my spirit's ear.
They carry in them hope
that they can lead man's spirit in its growth
from narrowness into the world's far spaces,
as the small seed mysteriously extends
to the proud body of the giant oak.
(Tr. Adam Bittleston)

These are the words of Johannes from the ninth scene of *The Portal of Initiation*, which describe this situation. From rocks and springs he hears the words: 'O man, experience thyself!' And he is aware that these voices are indicating to him that he himself

is the one who is weaving and wafting out there in rocks and springs, in clouds and mountains, in the trees and in rain and sunshine. The human self is spread out into the world of awakening nature, and this sixth verse is like a summons to acknowledge and experience this: O man, know yourself in your whole being.

> I feel world being in me,
> and I must find myself in every world.
> I see my soul
> through my own power given life to me;
> I rest within myself.
> I gaze on rocks and springs;
> they speak the language of my soul.

Thus my imprint's truthfulness becomes an experience. Here the true experience of spring commences, which not only consists in one person finding himself lovingly in another person but that he conceives of himself as being spread out in the weaving of the world.

But now from the pre-Easter aspect of the year there sounds the song of the alto into this state of expansiveness:

> 47. There shall arise from out the womb of worlds
> The bliss of growth, fostering joys of sense;
> My force of thinking may it find,
> Armed with the forces of the gods,
> Which live a quickening force in me.

This sounds a note of warning to the soul. It speaks of how the bliss of growth seeks eventually to overwhelm this soul, but that at this point the highest level of the soul's systolic process must take place. 'The force of thinking ... armed with the forces of the gods' is the systole that with a sense of urgency stands over and against the expansive diastole of the self, outspread as it is in powers of time and space.

Now the soul is experienced here as a heart, just as light came

to be experienced in the fifth verse as a cycle. There we had light from the spirit's depths and the heights of worlds; here we have systole and diastole interwoven as soul in this cycle of light and functioning as a heart.

Here, however, there sound forth again the voices of the baritone and the soprano, filling out and accompanying what was initially manifested in the two-part song. From the end of August the baritone sings:

> 21. I feel a power unwonted, bearing fruit,
> Gather its strength and lend myself to me.

And in the contrary direction the soprano strikes up from the middle of November:

> 32. I feel my proper strength, a fruitful scion,
> With gathered power bestow me on the world

This again has to do with the experience of the self, both in the world and also in the human soul. The diastole of spring-time, after Easter but before Whitsun, and the systole of the time before Easter are now complemented by an experience that unfolds in the period of autumn before and after Michaelmas.

Out of the ripeness of summer there appears the now again contracting diastole, bringing its godly gifts to the human ego out of the widths of space. This is the 'power unwonted' that is felt and which restores human beings to themselves.

In November, however, this has already been transformed: it has passed through the soul — functioning as a heart — and become 'my proper strength,' which now turns its steady inner light to the dying surroundings.

In these four verses the heartbeat of the soul in the course of the solar year of the earth comes to expression. The soul expands to a cosmic diastole. It brings back what it has been enabled to receive in the realm of the gods. This gift is transformed and is directed to the world — though now it changes the world into that thinking which is armed with the forces of the gods.

The first six steps leading from the innermost regions of the soul into the divine expanses have now been taken. A decisive point in the journey has been reached here, and it requires us to pause. For it is the week of the Ascension, and something needs to be said about this.

The four verses associated with Ascension week lie at a quite definite point in the cycle of the year. For the verse that is opposite to the verse for the Ascension falls during the last days of February. This is the time when Lazarus was raised from the dead by Christ.

The baritone verse — at the end of August — is the week of the beheading of John the Baptist. And the November verse marks the time when the Solomon Jesus child was born. In the yearly cycle the following picture emerges:

Ascension	Raising of Lazarus
Beheading of John	Birth of the Solomon child

Intermingled with this is the St John's–Christmas threshold. Initially only this combination comes to general awareness; but we shall learn to feel how the diastole of the human soul which has become one with the earth's surroundings, how this is an event which points towards the unique great Ascension. This was when the Christ became the Lord of the earth. He entered into the earth's surroundings, penetrated and spiritualized it and thenceforth became 'the Lord of the Ascension forces on earth.'

Since then the human soul has been received in this week with a loving gesture into the now Christ-imbued substance of the earth's surroundings. 'My imprint's truthfulness' will be seen as the living Christ, for it is he who works and weaves in the 'powers of time and space.'

This is one of the great turning-points in the course of the

soul's year, and the following verse calls a 'halt' in the journey and inhibits one from going further.

'Know well,' it calls, 'know well, O man, thou must find thyself on earth.'

Sixth Sunday after Easter

7 May 19–25 (the week before Whitsun)
My self threatens to break away
Through strong enticement of the light of worlds.
Now rise, my boding power,
Assume in strength your rightful throne,
Replace in me the might of thinking
Which in the senses' show
Is like to lose itself.

With this verse a wholly new element is introduced into the soul's path through the course of the year. It is the seventh week and a quite special time, for these are the days between the event of the Ascension and the festival of Whitsun.

In his lectures on the Fifth Gospel, Rudolf Steiner describes how the disciples were going about during this time in a sort of dream state, not wholly imbued with the lucidity of waking consciousness but filled with an infinite, barely describable sorrow: their Master had left them.[5] He who had been by their side for forty days, teaching and instructing them, had now gone away; the One who was indispensable to their very existence had left them.

Something of the echo of this experience weaves in every human soul in this special week. The self, which had poured itself out into the expanses of the periphery through all the previous week, giving light and horizon to the soul, is now so strongly enchanted by the light of worlds that it would seek wholly to surrender itself to this light. However, this brings a danger: it could abandon the soul in a state in which the disciples — who were then healed by the miracle of Whitsun — found themselves. Our soul should, rather, seek to recognize

this. For not only is the self given up to the light of worlds but thinking, too, tries to lose itself in the ever strengthening glory of the senses.

Now the soul summons forth a new power from within, a power that emanates from its ancient roots: its intuitive faculty of boding.

> Now rise, my boding power,
> Assume in strength your rightful throne

Where thinking wants to cease its activity, boding — the intuitive faculty — comes into its own. What is boding, this sense for what is to come? It is not thinking, nor is it feeling; rather is it a soul faculty lying between thinking and feeling. Boding resides at the point where wakeful thinking merges into dreamy feeling. It feels, but it does not know, and yet its feeling is beyond what is usual for knowledge.

Because the self wants to lose itself in an upwards direction and thinking by reaching outwards, the ancient faculty of boding awakens at the threshold between thinking and feeling and helps the human soul in its present crisis. Boding is like a medicine that is proferred to the soul.

Now, however, the alto raises its voice and sings:

> 46. The world threatens to stupefy
> The inborn forces of my soul.
> Now rise from spirit-depths
> In all your radiance, memory.

This is the counter-picture from the days of the following February. The world becomes too strong, too overwhelming, and a different soul faculty is now called forth — the power of memory. Thus there is a kind of equivalence here between boding on the one hand and memory on the other.

Memory, too, is an ancient soul faculty which came into being at the time when boding was increasingly becoming less prominent. At that time, in the early part of Atlantis, when the power

of memory was being gradually bestowed upon human beings, boding was fading away. It did not disappear but remained in the ground of the soul as a faculty which could be accessed. Memory is directed towards the past, whereas boding points towards the future. And what had been boding in pre-Atlantean times, will in future times have the significance of memory.

Boding comes out of humankind's past and looks into the future. Memory leads into humankind's future, while gazing into the past.

The human being today as a thinking being stands between these two. Around the time of the change that takes place at Whitsun and St John's Tide, boding can again be experienced.

Once this has been recognized, two further voices can be experienced which begin to blend into this two-part song of boding and memory.

The soprano strikes up in something of a despondent mood in the middle of November, speaking of the death of the world:

33. Now first I feel the world,
Which, reft of my indwelling soul,
Would as a frozen waste ...
That in itself could look for death alone.

And as a counter-voice the baritone of August is heard, not despondent but with a note of despair:

20. Now first I feel my being —
Which, torn from world existence,
Within itself must quench the self ...
Must kill the self-enclosed self.

Again the theme is death — in the former case it was the death of the world, and now it is the death of souls, which is like extinction.

Thus these four verses, each of which stands in a quite distinctive position in the yearly cycle and which together form a cross — the only real cross — of verses bearing the gravest of warnings.

The human soul stands here in a place of probation, and it has the task of passing this test. It is a kind of rite of passage which has been inserted here in order that the further journey through the year may be embarked upon consciously. In verses 7 and 46 it is a question of a too rapid crossing of the abyss between soul and world:

> 46. The world threatens to stupefy
> The inborn forces of my soul

> 7. My self threatens to break away
> Through strong enticement of the light of worlds

Both times there is a 'threatening' element. The world crosses the abyss and overwhelms the soul. The ego rushes into the arms of the world and, by threatening and taking insufficient heed, abandons its bride, the soul.

The temptation that comes to expression in verses 20 and 33 stands as a contrast to this:

> 20. Now first I feel my being —
> Which, torn from world existence

> 33. Now first I feel the world,
> Which, reft of my indwelling soul

Here it is not a matter of an over-hasty crossing of the abyss but its opposite. The abyss seems so wide and immense that soul and world remain completely separated from one another and the soul comes inevitably to believe that it remains far from the world and the world far from the soul.

Thus in these four verses a dark warning makes its presence felt over the course of the year. The warning becomes a probation, and the soul is challenged to cultivate quite specific qualities. Here in verse 7 it is the faculty of boding that is to be awoken.

Whitsun

8 *May 26 – June 1*
The senses' might grows great
Bonded with the gods' creating;
It thrusts the force of thought
Down to the drowsing of a dream.
When godlike being
Will join in union with my soul,
Then human thinking
Must bow in peace to dream existence.

Once the probation of the seventh verse has been withstood, a threshold is crossed and the Whitsun of the year is reached. With this eighth verse it has arrived. But what has been achieved here? Into which realm have we come? We have reached the sphere that will henceforth lead to St John's Tide. It is the sphere that descended upon the disciples on the first Whitsunday and became manifest in the form of tongues of fire. It was then that the Johanine world-conscience came down to the disciples. For us it remains in the periphery, but holy Whitsunday is the gate through which this realm can be entered.

The soul's attention is drawn to this when the change that takes place in its sensory and mental faculties is indicated — namely, that the power of the senses increases, whereas the strength of thinking diminishes. 'I must decrease,' says thinking, 'but you will increase,' referring to the senses.

And then comes the explanation, which makes it clear that something new is to be expected — the union between the human soul and the divine being. What befell the disciples on Whitsunday in the cenacle — that the Holy Spirit descended upon them — is here indicated, in preparation for the coming

weeks of experience. It does not happen at this particular point, but the human soul is enjoined to prepare itself in humility, so that it may come about in the coming weeks.

But what is most significant is the opening of the door to that sphere which can be called the realm of warmth and fire of the John spirit. The human soul strives to reach it, for it is in this holy sphere that the process when 'godlike being will join in union with my soul' takes place.

And now the counter-song of the alto voice adds its note to the sound of the tenor, soaring upwards in a mood of devotion. This is the first indication of what will happen if the soul accomplishes the process referred to in the eighth verse.

45 *February 9–15*
The power of thought stands firm
Bonded with the spirit's birth,
On the dull spurrings of the senses
Raying the fullness of its light.
When plenitude of soul
Will join in union with the life of worlds,
Then must the senses' revelation
Embrace the light of thinking.

The Spirit's birth is spoken of here as something that has happened. But the senses need renewal and illumination, and this happens through the light of thinking. So the thinking that undergoes a darkening process in the eighth week is renewed again through the Spirit's birth that takes place then and will restore the dulled senses to their former radiance.

Both verses are wholly in the sensory and mental domain, the one aspiring towards St John's and the other leading away from Christmas.

The eighth verse opens up a perspective of the event of St John's Tide. Verse 45 concludes the review of the Christmas period. This is the character of these two transitional weeks in the soul's year.

But now the tones of baritone and soprano merge into the singing:

19. To wrap the new-conceived germ
 In memory's secret folds
 Be now my striving's master aim

34. To feel through selfhood new uprisen
 The treasured dower of old
 Stir secretly to life within

In both cases here there is a reference to what was secretly 'new-conceived' at St John's and what during the time before Christmas begins to come to life as secret treasure. This essence within the human soul that is veiled in secrecy is that spirit-seed which the divine forces implanted into human beings at St John's Tide. Year by year this 'fund' is entrusted to the soul, whose task is to administer and increase it.

It is the treasure in the field, it is the seed, it is the kingdom of God that is revealed to us and which is the object of all our striving.

The sounding together of these four verses furnishes an insight into this world where the spirit of God begins to be active in human existence.

A note concerning dates

The time between Whitsun and St John's Tide is variable, since the Whitsun festival which is linked to Easter Sunday moves together with the Easter festival. It is possible for Whitsun to be quite close to St John's, or fairly far away from it. The variation is approximately four weeks, and the festival can be any time between the second week in May and the second week in June. So how do we deal with the verses affected by this shift of dates?

I said at the outset that the Easter verse is the verse of the week that begins with Easter Sunday. The following verses correspond to the subsequent weeks until with the eighth verse we reach the festival of Whitsunday.

Rudolf Steiner inscribed verse 12 with the mood of St John's Tide, and it should be assigned to the week in which June 24 falls.

So it follows that verses 9, 10 and 11 should be equally divided into the time-span between Whitsun and St John's. At St John's the sequence is restored and one can again follow the cycle of the year.

Attempts to adjust the verses in a different way to the course of the year seem to me to be unjustified.*

* Karl König's suggestions for setting the dates of the Calendar verses are included on p. 439.

Trinity

9 June 2–8
Forgetting all my separateness of will,
The warmth of worlds, the summer's harbinger,
I feel it flood my spirit and my soul.
To lose myself in light
The gaze of spirit now demands,
And powerfully prophetic boding cries:
'Lose, lose your self, yourself to find.'

The human soul is prepared by the eighth verse for what is to take place at St John's Tide. In this Whitsun verse it was indicated that thinking needs to be silent. If one takes what is to come into account and through what is expressed in the counter-verses to this verse, one can become clearly aware of what is being 'secretly conceived.' The soul watches and waits.

The new verse reverberates into this receptive attitude and gesture, reaching upwards to where the warmth of worlds, proclaiming the summer, streams down to the earth. The soul senses the power of this warmth; it gives itself to this warmth and thereby experiences that it must give up its separateness of will for it.

Just as in the fifth verse it experienced itself weaving in the light, so does it now feel itself being imbued with warmth, not only in a bodily sense but through its soul-spiritual activity. This experience becomes an invitation to give oneself up totally and unreservedly to the world of the light: 'to lose myself in light.' These words ring out like an imperious order! Nevertheless, within them also sounds the soft voice of that sense of premonition, or boding, that has been awakened and was commended to

us in the seventh verse. This boding quality now imparts hope and courage to the hesitant soul:

> Lose, lose your self, yourself to find.

This means: 'If you do not dare face up to the adventure of death, you will not awaken to the other life.' 'Dying and becoming' is something that is gently, but energetically called for. Widen yourself, human soul, you are filled with the warmth of the universe that has bowed down to the earth. Now be emboldened to achieve the highest task of all: renounce yourself.

This call is heard by the soul every day anew, and on a daily basis it learns by degrees that this act of surrendering or renouncing is a process of giving oneself away in love. The old wealth that one has received is sacrificed in order that something new can come in its place.

It is now up to the human soul to replicate what the seed has to experience in the earth at springtime — to sacrifice itself so that the new plant can grow from it.

In confirmation of this the alto casts its voice over from the coming winter and sings:

> 44. Grasping new spurs of sense,
> Mindful of spirit-birth fulfilled,
> Clearness of soul outpours
> Into the wildering teeming life of worlds
> The will creative in my thinking.

There is hardly a counter-verse that is so remote in its diction from its twin as this one. It can be recognized only through the contrast and not through the similarity; for 'forgetting' is balanced by 'grasping.' 'Spurs of sense' are contrasted to 'separateness of will,' and the creative will in thinking takes the place of 'lose yourself.' Through this, however, certainty and confidence are granted to the soul. Once St John's and Christmas have been and gone, it seems to say, your present courage will have truly found its fulfilment.

But now two new indications come through the ringing tones of baritone and soprano. The baritone sings:

> 18. Can I expand my soul
> To grapple to her being
> This word of worlds in germ conceived?

And the soprano sings:

> 35. Can I then the being know
> That, known, it find itself again
> In the soul's urgence to create?

Here again there is a reference to what was accomplished at St John's — though now with absolute clarity. It is referred to by name and is called the 'germinal word of worlds.' This 'word' brings life to the soil of the soul and stirs its 'urgence to create.'

Now these four voices are intermingled, mutually illumining and enhancing one another. The spirit and soul nature that is filled with the warmth of worlds as St John's Tide approaches, sounds together with the 'germinal word of worlds,' with the 'soul's urgence to create' and with 'clearness of soul.' This is a fourfold path, which comprises the following distinct stages:

> First stage (verse 9):
> Let your spirit-soul be permeated by the warmth of the universe.
>
> Second stage (verse 18):
> Know that you may receive the word of worlds in germinal form.
>
> Third stage (verse 35):
> The word of worlds stirs within you and prepares you for soul creativity.
>
> Fourth stage (verse 44):
> Out of the seed the spirit is born within you. Clearness of soul can fill you.

All this is like a stimulus to the soul to find the courage to follow the call of this week. Warmth of worlds shimmers through one's soul-spiritual nature, which has already been loosened at this time. The wakeful life of insects is buzzing in this warmth of worlds. They have lost themselves, developed from caterpillars into dying pupae and have now awakened as imagos. Strive upwards, human soul , be full of confidence:

Lose, lose your self, yourself to find.

The tenth week

10 *June 9–15*
Far into summer heights
The sun lifts up its shining sphere,
It draws my human yearning
Into its own wide spaces,
While inwardly a feeling stirs
In dim prophetic boding:
'Hereafter you shall know —
A god, a god has touched you now.'

Anyone who attentively studies the aural interplay of any particular set of four verses in the course of the year will now have the important experience that the counter-verses move more and more closely together, so that around St John's Tide and around Christmas they have come close as happens at Easter and Michaelmas.

Now the experience of the world's wide bounds increases ever more in its strength and power, and the soul is led into an ever greater ascent. An additional aspect is the proximity of the counter-verse, which now comes in the month of July and therefore seems to be pointing towards the event that is awaited.

The sun is ascending far into summer heights. Light increasingly overwhelms the soul, and night and darkness are thrust back. The song of the birds can be heard almost continually, for when the last bird falls silent in the late evening, the first one begins to sing again. Thus the light of evening and the light of morning reach out their hands to one another.

The widths of space are filled with light and brightness, with sound and joy, and the soul's feeling extends outwards and

upwards into the world's expanses. In this reaching outwards a premonition, or boding, awakens, a feeling that beats a rhythm softly on the ground of the soul's foundations like a muffled drum, constantly repeating, speaking and proclaiming:

> A god, a god has touched you now.

Eichendorff expressed something similar in poetic words:

> Once men's loud enjoyment quietens:
> The earth with all its trees,
> It rustles as in dreams
>
> What the heart barely recalls,
> Times of old, a gentle sadness,
> And, like summer lightning flashes,
> Shudders quiver through the breast.

Human feeling is spread into the cosmic expanses, and in this broadening of the soul it begins — tenderly but nevertheless intimately — to approach what can be called the feeling of the divine world. The soul breathes from God's breast, and it feels his breath, and the divine participates in human feeling. This intimate, wholly hidden but nevertheless accessible encounter is what now takes place.

But the alto begins to sing and intones the words:

> 43. Sunk in its wintry depths
> True spirit-being quickens into warmth.

The power of the spirit's warmth makes itself manifest in the cold depths of winter, in hardening:

> Through the heart's force it gives
> To the world's show and seeming
> The mighty gift of being,
> And strengthens, maugre worlds of cold,
> In human inwardness the fire of soul.

It is the week when Paul's conversion at Damascus is celebrated — when the Risen One appeared to Saul, who had been persecuting him, and revealed himself as the 'unknown God.' From this point onwards humankind passes through the Damascus experience, which will in our time come to have an ever-growing significance.

This contrast and yet at-one-ness of feeling:

> A god, a god has touched you now

and

> And strengthens, maugre worlds of cold,
> In human inwardness the fire of soul.

is the contrast and the at-one-ness of the soul which — in devotion to the universe — breathes the breath of the Godhead but which also brings forth an inner fiery strength, confirming itself in full concentration as a spirit amidst outward worlds of cold. Both forces are related to Paul — the conception of the new Adam and the preserving of the old Adam.

The singing of the baritone and soprano rings out into this ever-waxing systole and diastole of the soul:

> 36. Speaks from my being's depths
> Surging to revelation,
> In secret wise the word of worlds.

and

> 17. Now speaks the word of worlds
> Which through the senses' door
> I may draw deep into my soul

Here again, as in the previous verse, explaining and interpreting what is seeking to come: the word of worlds in the soul's inner being.

This word of worlds is prepared in the encounter of the divine with the human soul — this word of worlds from whose power the fire of soul will be engendered in our inner being.

It is a soul-spiritual task to prepare for this conception. To know this is a cognitive necessity.

And so this week becomes a further step in preparation for the coming experience of St John's Tide. The human soul rests upon God's breast, spread out in the far widths of space, and in the rhythm of its heart there rings out the verse:

> Hereafter you shall know —
> A god, a god has touched you now.

With this a reference is made to the word of worlds, which will proclaim itself in the soul's inner being in the month of August (verse 17), knock at the door of birth before Christmas (verse 36) and finally radiate within human beings as fire of soul after Christmas in order to breathe life into, to thaw the world's coldness; and it can bring about in mighty self-fulfilment what may be called the most sublime experience of our present times: the experience of Christ's appearance in the etheric region of the earth.

All this should pervade the human heart as one communes with this tenth verse of the Soul Calendar, for in it is revealed the gate to the sacred time of St John's Tide.

The eleventh week

11 *June 16–23*
In this the sun's high hour
Be yours its herald wisdom to embrace.
Surrendered to the beauty of the world
The self aware of self shall deeply own:
The I of man can lose itself
And find itself within the I of worlds.

This verse has three aspects. It is a summons to the human soul, strong, admonishing and nevertheless full of supporting love. The soul can feel itself to be standing at a threshold, and the threshold guardian comes to meet it with his hands raised and says:

It is for you to hear and understand the tidings that I have to bring to you in this, the sun's high hour.

See, you have surrendered yourself to the periphery. The world's revelations of beauty are filling you, and in this experience you shall know:

You can cross the threshold, but you must recognize that it can be a matter of both winning and losing, for you are approaching the holy domain of the I of worlds. Here you can find yourself, but you can equally well lose yourself here.

This is a transcription of what the threshold guardian has to say to us who now stand at this threshold; for the door that was reached with the previous verse and at which we have knocked has now been opened. 'Enter,' we are summoned, and we stand in an attitude of waiting at the threshold. Shall I dare? asks the human soul. Can I do it? Will I not surrender myself completely if I cross?

These considerations and questions are now, however,

explicitly stated in the verse. The summons comes to the soul initially from without; it must itself be silent and simply listen to the words that are being addressed to it. These words are serious in their meaning; and the soul will need the same seriousness in this week to meet the demand.

That which in the verse for the previous week sounded forth like a dark drum roll has now been transformed, and the summons rings out like horns:

> The I of man can lose itself
> And find itself within the I of worlds.

In the background, however, as though sounding from the approaching St John's Tide and proclaimed by dark trombones, there sound forth the words of the St John imagination:

> Substances are densified,
> Errors are judged and rectified,
> Hearts are sifted.[6]

The human heart feels that all its mistakes, all its errors must be laid out and justified in full view on approaching the threshold.

Now from the winter time the counter-verse is intoned, sung by a hesitant alto voice:

> 42. In this dark wintertide
> To manifest her proper force
> Shall be the soul's imperious urge;
> Herself to haunts of darkness guiding
> To feel in new forebodement
> Through warmth of heart the senses' revelation.

These are courageous words of encouragement that are addressed to the soul. It loses heart in the cold wasteland, and its attention is directed to the coming revelation of the senses.

In the week before St John's, however, there is a serious warning. And the soul feels: in winter, too, I shall lose heart, just as I am at a loss in not being able to decide.

But now comes some unexpected help. Soprano and baritone attribute confidence, joy and courage to the soul.

The soprano sings the pre-Christmas song:

37. With joy to carry spirit light
Into the winter night of worlds

And the baritone proclaims:

16. Sternly my boding heart demands:
'Cherish within the spirit's dower ...'

Now the soul knows that it must have the courage to take the step across the threshold. Only if devotion is great enough, confidence firm and faith sufficiently alive will the spirit's dower be received; it will be transformed and ray out as the light of spirit at Christmas time.

Thus it is the reference to the spirit's dower and to the spirit light, hidden in the depths of the soul and resurrecting within it, which gives the soul the certainty to follow the trumpet call. Yes, my errors will be judged and rectified; I acknowledge them. Hearts will be sifted — for otherwise the course of human history cannot develop further. Substances are densified, so that the spirit can reveal itself within matter.

Thus the human soul, armed with these words of encouragement and with the exhortation, is now confronted by the voice demanding that it accomplish the great risk of working on oneself:

Lose, lose your self, yourself to find!

Mood of St John's Day

12 *St John's Tide. June 24*
The world's bright loveliness
Constrains me in my inmost soul.
'Set free the godlike gifts you own
To wing their way into the universe,
Your narrow self forego,
And, trusting, seek that self again
In universal light and warmth.'

Now the week of St John's has come. The one high-point of the soul's year has been reached, and the following three weeks are devoted to the soul's inner encounter with the spirit weaving in the heights of sense.

The world has become a revelation. The mysteries of existence lie out there in the open. The human soul has plunged into these revelations in the same way that an insect, a bee, dives into the calyx of the flower; it has immersed itself and is therefore full of life and warmth-bestowing substance. The human soul becomes a bee — a bee such as is also referred to in the old mysteries, when it served in the sacrificial rites in Ephesus, Eleusis and Samothrace.

The world becomes a mystery temple, for the sky has become lower and the earthly depths have risen up towards it. In this way the holy of holies is made manifest. The earth lifts itself up as an altar, and the heavenly world sinks down to meet it. And the holy Trinity can be perceived in the communion that is taking place: the heavenly Father, the earthly Mother and, in the middle, the Son whose sphere of activity is love.

This is 'the world's bright loveliness.' The brightness is the glory of what has unfolded, the fullness and the revelation of all existence.

So overwhelming is this wondrous display that the human soul is so shaken to its very depths that it answers to the call,

> Set free the godlike gifts you own
> To wing their way into the universe.

The words 'set free' are so fitting here. The spirit of its own life has been born out of the soul's depths; it is a birth that is taking place.

Over the course of the preparatory weeks a power of confidence has been streaming into the soul, and now with this same confidence it releases its own being and it knows: I want to seek and find myself in the light and warmth of the world. This 'own being' becomes a bee that emerges from the honeycomb of the soul and rises up into the light-filled world of the sun's warmth, in order to win for itself a new life in the archetypes of the flowers and plants.

Just as fire flares up from the pile of wood and thousands of sparks rise steeply upwards, so does the self draw itself up to the region where heaven and earth meet.

> It was as if the sky
> Kissed the earth in silence,
> That it could only dream
> Of heaven in blossom's shower!
> And my soul it outstretched
> Its wings to far expanses,
> It flew through silent lands
> As if it homewards sped.

This is what Eichendorff felt when he was writing this poem as one of his spiritual songs. The silent lands are the heavenly house of the Father, to whom the Prodigal Son returns repentant. And the Father receives him and gives him a bountiful feast as a godly dower, although he knows that, once the son has been provided with food, he may perhaps return to desolation and solitude far away as a stranger. All this should pass through the soul in the week which represents a high-point of the soul's year.

From beyond Christmas, however, in the voice of the alto, the following words sound from a distance, and in a wholly different way; and yet it is as though it were the very essence to which all that we now experience is aspiring:

41. The soul's creative power
Strives from the heart's deep ground:
'Kindle your godlike gifts
For rightful work in human life,
Fashion the self
In human love and human deeds.'

Here the surrounding world has disappeared. The human being who has become strong in himself stands there powerfully and awake.

'The world's bright loveliness' has been transformed into 'the soul's creative power.' 'Constraining' has become 'striving' and 'my inmost soul' the 'heart's deep ground.' Instead of 'your narrow self forego' we have 'fashion the self,' and 'universal light and warmth' have become 'human love and human deeds.'

Thus the whole tension between world and human beings has been bridged. Dying and becoming have been split apart here. Die into universal light and warmth, O man! But then grow towards human love and human deeds.

This bridge begins to shine like a rainbow and begins to sound forth out of the colours. The voice of the soprano sings the eternal 'Ave,' the greeting to Mary, and the baritone sounds the ancient 'Eva,' the paradisal Eve mood.

The Ave runs as follows:

38. I feel the spell dissevered
In the soul's womb freeing the spirit child

whereas the Eva sounds:

15. I feel the spirit's weaving
Spell-bound within the world's array

This refers to the two great events which, now that we have arrived at an experience of St John's, will take place in the soul's year: the conception that is shortly to follow and its fulfilment at Christmas.

St John's is like a threshold which, if it is crossed, brings different and further experiences with it.

Once the threshold is crossed, the human soul is confronted by a twofold experience. To this we shall now turn.

High-point of the year

13 *June 30 – July 6*
Am I then in the heights of sense —
So kindles in my depths of soul
The truth from spirit worlds of fire
The gods themselves proclaim:
'Seek through your boding power
And find in spirit ground
Your spirit brotherhood.'

The high-point of the year has now come. Although St John's Day is a culmination, the two weeks that follow tower above it, for the process whereby the soul gives itself up to the world of the senses' glory is now complete.

The thirteenth and fourteenth verses form a unity. They relate to one another like the two countenances of a Janus head. The one looks back to the foregoing period since Easter, while the other looks towards Michaelmas. It is as though the top of the mountain has been reached, and a twofold descent now begins: at once into the past but also into the future.

Here one can clearly experience how the voice of the tenor ceases; it hands its task over to the baritone, which begins singing from the fourteenth verse onwards. But at present it is a duet; what we hear is a two-part song between tenor and baritone.

A similar process takes place on the other side of the year. For verses 39 and 40 similarly belong together, with soprano and alto likewise forming a unity. So it is a special time.

In the ordinary way of reckoning the cycle of the year, the middle of the year is reached in this thirteenth week. The 182nd and 183rd days clasp their hands, just as during verse 39 the transition from the old to the new year comes about. It is the turn of

the year, because it is the summer solstice. Since the beginning of the year 182 days have passed, and it will take the same number of days until the next New Year.

The human soul is extended far out into the universe. It is spread out between the heights of sense and the depths of soul. The human being has surrendered itself to the beauty and the miracle of existence. In the depths, however, a new world is as though opened up. The soul's foundations are manifesting themselves and these words flare up from within them:

> Seek through your boding power
> And find in spirit ground
> Your spirit brotherhood.

Gottfried Gretler, a Swiss poet, has expressed this in different words, albeit less exact but nonetheless true and wholly appropriate:

> Thee I thank, my Lord and God,
> For this blessed summertime.
> It came as thy light's painful gift,
> And found me all prepared.
>
> Thee I thank that, with thy light,
> My blood thou dost imbue,
> That with its fiery golden glow
> Thou shinest in my veins.
>
> As a sacred fire I burn
> Before thy countenance,
> And all my vanity's trumpery
> Thy godly light consumes.

This divine light, consuming the vanity within the soul, is the word of truth spoken by the gods which now begins to flare up in the grounds and depths of the soul. It can be experienced as a mighty lightning flash, followed by the thunder of the word. The

thunderstorms now rumbling in the outer world are merely a reflection of what is occurring within the soul.

Summoned and addressed by the gods, we hear their voice sounding like the trumpet call:

> Seek through your boding power
> And find in spirit ground
> Your spirit brotherhood.

This call reverberates in the soul and is not intended only for this particular moment. It is a summons which reaches into every area of life, in order to awaken the human spirit, in order that it may listen to what is being said:

> Seek through your boding power
> And find in spirit ground
> Your spirit brotherhood.

Not in the world of the senses, not in our own soul or in the here and now, but solely in the spirit realm will we find our origin and our destiny.

To seek 'bodingly,' to exercise our faculty of having premonitions, means to seek in ways where our own angel is the guide. For premonitions 'are angels who can surely guide us here' says Novalis.

What rang out in the week after Whitsun as a first call:

> 9. And powerfully prophetic boding cries:
> 'Lose, lose your self, yourself to find'

is now pronounced by the words of the gods themselves. 'O man, you can find yourself only if you have the courage to find yourself in spirit brotherhood.' If this is expressed and felt right into the particulars of life, the tenor's task has been fulfilled; he has sung his song to its end since the trumpet thrust of the gods' truth-bearing words has echoed through the human soul. This quality of *per-sonare,* this sounding through has a personality-forming aspect if heard in the right way.

Now the baritone begins its first song as a leading voice. It sounds forth as a soft, hesitant answer, uncertain in its beginnings, in its mood. As a true contrast to the forsaken heights of the tenor, the equally — but differently — forsaken voice of the baritone now wrests itself free:

14. Surrendered to the senses' revelation
I lost my being's proper urge

This sounds confused and helpless — surrendered to the senses' glory but without inner guidance and leadership. The quality of independent egohood has gone. The higher I has dissolved into the infinite diversity of the surroundings and has for the moment lost its central earthly focus, the lower I. And it begins to understand:

And felt, in dreaming thoughts bemused,
My selfhood stolen away.

The senses' glory has also woven a mantle of thoughts and, hence, robbed the self of its waking consciousness. In this week not only their own being but also their self has eluded human beings. The world has taken possession of humans.

The baritone voice has in its confused way to profess allegiance to this; everything is decided not only in a dream state but in one of abandoned desolation, of non-being and aimlessness. But in this chaos there sounds like the call of horns, the courage-bestowing words:

But waking presses on me still
World-thinking in the senses' glow.

These words resound like the rushing wings of a new hope — as in the fairy tale, when the mute queen bound to the stake, flames already reaching her, and the seven ravens suddenly appear proclaiming her release. Now the baritone has again found its proper, powerful voice; its sound has become firm and it knows that it can henceforth be certain of what will follow.

The beating of the wings becomes ever more powerful and settles, full of promise, around the soul and spirit nature. We should feel this as intensely as possible, in the knowledge that, with this world-thinking, the beat of the spirit is engirdling our soul.

And from the distance, delicately and yet powerfully, the soprano rings out and sings:

> 39. Surrendered to the spirit's revelation
> I win the light of universal life ...
> And in me, from the thinker's power,
> Leaps into wakefulness the sense of self.

This is how it will be! From what rushes towards me as world-thinking, which does not as yet belong to me, my own thinker's power will develop, and from this a knowledge of my own self will be born.

With this the countenance turns its gaze towards autumn. It looks down from the top of the mountain into the valley and begins its journey. A few steps further the tenor, who had been standing here, also begins his descent, but on the other side and towards Easter. And in the distance the voice of the soprano can be intuited and then dimly heard. It, too, is on the move, making its way from afar towards autumn, and at Michaelmas they — the baritone and the soprano — will meet.

While beyond Christmas, far, far beyond the mountains, the alto makes her way towards the following Easter, communicating to her brother tenor.

This is the view that has now been gained. As it stands at the summit of the year, confused but nevertheless gathering courage again, the soul begins its descent into the earthly world.

The week of enchantment

15 *July 14–20*
I feel the spirit's weaving
Spell-bound within the world's array,
In drowsiness of sense
It wraps my selfhood in —
But all to dower that self
With strength, which cribbed and impotent
Mine I shall never give itself.

It is now indeed summer: still, stifling hot summer. An endless peace, full of the power of ripeness, permeates the natural world. Quietness pervades human activity — there is a fullness, a power and a sense of security. Theodor Storm expressed this in the following description:

The wind sings a lullaby,
The sun gazes warmly down,
Ears of corn now bend their heads,
Berries red swell on the thorn,
Farmland bears its bounties rich —
Young woman, what is on your mind?

The soul has come to be like this contemplative young woman; both experience:

I feel the spirit's weaving
Spell-bound within the world's array,

In his third symphony, Gustav Mahler composed an entire movement in this mood and wrote above it: 'Pan is sleeping.' Nature has wholly surrendered itself to the power of the heavenly forces, given over to a state of sleep. The human soul expe-

riences something similar. The noon-tide of the year has come; the earth Mother, the old sphinx is abroad and

> In drowsiness of sense
> [She] wraps my selfhood in

The light flickers and shimmers over everything. It shines and sparkles in the grass and above the blossoms, through branches and leaves and in the wafting air. Colours come and go, and one's eyes are wholly immersed in this interplay of light and radiance.

It is the same with warmth. It pervades and pulses through everything. It broods over our thinking and envelops our will, and the *dolce far niente* attitude becomes ever more dominant in us. We can feel that the soul is bathed in light and warmth rather like an embryo that is developing its sheaths in the womb.

The soul has become a child — an embryo — and the human being speaks:

> But all to dower that self
> With strength, which cribbed and impotent
> Mine I shall never give itself.

Surrounded by the powerful maternal forces of the natural world, the soul senses its childlike nature; for this moment in the year it has become nothing but a created object. But it knows that it is a thing of creation, and it accepts this with humility; for only if it allows itself to be fructified by the spirit, who is the spirit of the world, will it be able to give birth to the spirit child in the depths of winter.

As soon as this is intuited, that is, when the voice of the angel in the soul enables it to understand this, the soprano begins to sing its soft, tender song from out of the depths of the spirit, which are the depths of the heart:

> 38. I feel the spell dissevered
> In the soul's womb freeing the spirit child:

The holy word of worlds
Has in the heart's clear light
Begotten heaven's own fruit of hope

And now the soul knows that this is the distant proclamation of what will come about at Christmas tide, if the drowsiness of the senses is accepted with a capacity and willingness for devotion.

Percival, too, was once a child. Then he was naive and vague. But only because he was like this could he rise to a state of *saelde,* of bliss, to the heart's clear light of spirit. In the meantime, long years of wandering and searching lay before him.

Twenty-three weeks lie from here to the Christmas festival. If the human soul has the feeling that it will now discard its fool's attire and wants to don the armour of necessity during the transition to midwinter, this journey can become a Percival path.

In this week when we have within us only an attitude of devotion, the spirit of the world endows us with its own being. It reaches out to us; it gives us manna every day anew, without which we cannot live. The great meal takes place of which we are able to have a foretaste. Conrad Ferdinand Meyer has had a glimpse of this:

The spirit spoke: look up! It was in a dream.
I raised my eyes. In radiant clouds above
I saw the Lord breaking bread for the Twelve
And speaking words full of boding and love.
Far above their heads he invited the earth
With a gesture that expressed love for all.

The spirit spoke: look up! The blue of the air
A boundless meal extends where'er I look,
Springs of life have gushed forth in abundance,
No cup has stretched forth now in vain,
All folk are blessed with ample sheaves of corn,
No place was empty, and none need go without.

Thus the sheaves of the heavenly forces now bend down to human souls, they fill and fructify them, and no place remains empty, and no one needs to live in want.

The wings of world-thinking rustle with powerful beat around the soul. But world-thinking bears the word of worlds and offers it to the meal as heavenly bread. But then a youth, a boy, appears beside the soul; he holds five barley loaves and two fishes in his hand. He is the new spirit of John, who always accompanies and leads the souls of human beings to this place where the meal of the Holy Grail may be received.

And so this week, and the verse accompanying it, is a quite particular multiplication sign in the course of the year. Outwardly it is the drowsiness of a dream; inwardly, however, it represents the highest blessing for all: renewal and fulfilment.

The week of boding

16 July 21–27
Sternly my boding heart demands:
'Cherish within the spirit's dower,
So shall the gifts of God grow ripe
In the soul's soil maturing,
And selfhood reap their fruits.'

The great event, the conception of the word of worlds in the womb of the human soul, has taken place. The high-point of the year has passed; the change of direction is beginning, and a muted stillness, like the foretaste of evening, takes hold of us as a mood. The days become imperceptibly shorter; the first autumnal gusts of wind can be heard in the dusk. One or another leaf begins to become yellow, and although the sun still warms and shines in its full strength, a breath of coldness is beginning to rise up out of the foundations of the earth.

Thus one's mind turns inwards. No longer is there a surrendering to sensory experience; at the foreground of one's experience is the growing loss of light and warmth. A first listening quality enters again into the central focus of our self. This is the command of boding, of premonition; it is the voice of the angel. It says:

Cherish within the spirit's dower!

What we have received we should now make our own by protecting it within ourselves, so that it can grow and develop.

What we have received is like the wealth that we should not bury; it is that with which we may work and create.

What we have received is the pearl; it is also the seed which was scattered; it is the treasure in the field; it is everything that

Christ Jesus calls the heavenly kingdom in his discourses. It is the mustard seed, which is the smallest of all seeds on the earth; but when it germinates, it grows and becomes so great 'that the birds of the air can make their nests in its branches.'

So it is the time of the parables that have become part of us and through which the different levels of existence can become apparent to us.

In this verse the mystery of all parables is contained in seed form, and in this week of the year we should become increasingly conscious of this.

> So shall the gifts of God grow ripe
> In the soul's soil maturing,
> And selfhood reap their fruits.

The sower went through the land at the high-point of summer, scattering his gifts. Now that this has happened, the human I becomes conscious of this and experiences that a seed has been cast into its soul. Human individuals can take it in, but they can also leave it uncultivated, on the path, among thorns and on the stony ground of their existence.

However, from the other side of the year, in a mood of presentiment and in a high soprano voice, there joyfully ring out these words of anticipation for the approaching Christmas time:

> 37. With joy to carry spirit light
> Into the winter night of worlds —
> For this my striving heart is fain,
> That, kindling, seeds of soul
> Strike in the soil of worlds,
> And sounding through the dark of sense
> God's word illumine all that is.

Here is fulfilled what is given as a promise in the present week. For the kindling seeds of soul have now arisen in their fullness from the seed of God, and the human being may carry spirit light into the darkness of worlds. The seed has germinated

and has borne manifold fruit. So what was once properly sown is coming to fulfilment.

In all this there sounds the earnest, recent warning to the soul challenging it to cross the threshold. Because of this warning the human I made the decision to immerse itself in the widths of space and, hence, to become the spirit ground in which the seed can be planted. It sounds:

> 11. The I of man can lose itself
> And find itself within the I of worlds.

These words are now heard as though it had been the ploughshare that impressed itself upon the self and prepared it for sowing.

From the time beyond Christmas, however, the alto can be heard:

> 42. In this dark wintertide
> To manifest her proper force
> Shall be the soul's imperious urge;
> Herself to haunts of darkness guiding

For the power of spirit sowing can so strengthen the soul that it can break through the darkness of winter — even the gloom of the earth's winter, in whose darkness it will remain unless the 'kingdom of God' can be transformed through the grace of the word of worlds, received as a new seed, and be brought once more to fruition.

The week of the call

17 July 28 – August 3
Now speaks the word of worlds
Which through the senses' door
I may draw deep into my soul:
'Fill full thy spirit's depths
With my world wideness,
To find hereafter me in thee.'

Now the seed of the word of worlds which has gained entry to the human soul begins to manifest itself. 'Now speaks the word of worlds' — but before this happens we are told in what form this seed has reached the inner regions of the soul:

Which through the senses' door
I may draw deep into my soul:

The word of worlds has entered our inner being through the various senses, through sight, sound, smell, etc. What Rudolf Steiner called the stream of cosmic nutrition constantly enters into us through the senses, and it may reasonably be supposed that the word of worlds found its way into us around St John's Tide together with this stream of nutrition. The word of worlds, however, entered into the ground of our souls, whereas the stream of cosmic nutrition itself enters the foundations of our body.

This stream comes from the sun realm of light, and at the time of high summer it brings with it those life, or etheric, forces which begin to be active in the inner regions of the soul as the power of the word. Thus this word also begins itself to make a statement, and it speaks as follows:

Fill full thy spirit's depths
With my world wideness,
To find hereafter me in thee.

The spirit depths of the human soul need to be filled with world wideness. But what is this world wideness? The answer is given by the pre-Christmas counter-verse, which says:

36. Speaks from my being's depths,
Surging to revelation,
In secret wise the word of worlds.
'Fill full your task in life
With this my light of spirit
To offer up the self through Me.'

What are now, in the time after St John's, the spirit's depths will then become the fulfilment of our tasks; so that *the spirit's depths* are transformed into the *task in life.* However, the world's wideness becomes the light of spirit, because it was the light of worlds which entered into the soul through the gates of the senses.

Thus the world's wideness is that light which has entered into us and shall imbue the depths of our spirit in order to become the light of spirit which will subsequently illumine the aims in our work. In this way what has now been conceived will be born.

It was conceived through the senses, but it will be born through the limbs which implement the aims of work. This light of worlds from the upper regions passes through the human heart in order to ray out into the limbs.

Then when this has been accomplished, the challenge of this week will have been met:

To find hereafter me in thee.

This last phrase is equivalent to St Paul's continual expectation that our highest aspiration should be, as he says, 'Not I, but Christ in me.'

Hence the voice of the alto is added to this group of verses, sounding the words of the week at the end of January which is the Damascus week:

> 43. And strengthens, maugre worlds of cold,
> In human inwardness the fire of soul.

The tenor proclaims something similar; for as though in a premonition it describes all of this when it concludes the verse leading up to St John's with these words:

> 10. 'Hereafter you shall know —
> A god, a god has touched you now.'

Thus in these four verses there is the one great demand — initially as a proclamation, then as a demand and finally as a fulfilment: that the human I should surrender itself in order to become the bearer of the word of worlds, thereby filling the spirit depths of its existence to the point where the aims of work can ray forth in this light, and the fire of soul in our innermost being becomes this eternal light which continues to shine in all darkness and all decline.

In this week the call for this sounds through the word of worlds itself within the soul. That the soul hears this word and begins to respond to it is the theme of the verses of the coming weeks.

The eighteenth week

18 *August 4–10*
Can I expand my soul
To grapple to her being
This word of worlds in germ conceived?
I do forebode I strength must find
To found and form my soul
A garment worthy of the spirit.

The word of worlds has gained entry into human depths of soul through the sphere of the senses. It will stream into the limbs, which are borne by the spirit, in order to be reborn in the aims of work.

Between conception and birth lies the time of this transformation, which is spoken of in the verse for this week. How can it come about that this change takes place worthily?

This is the question that the human I poses itself:

Can I expand my soul
To grapple to her being
This word of worlds in germ conceived?

It is an inner listening, a real effort to keep quiet and listen, that needs to happen now. The words, 'Behold, I am the Lord's handmaid, let it be according to thy word,' express the attitude of soul which is alone appropriate here. It should also be said: Can I open the ear of the soul out of humility to such an extent that I can listen to the tender voice of the word of worlds? For only in the element of listening and hearing can that connection arise of which the I is speaking here.

How otherwise would we be able to encounter the word if we did not incline our ear towards it in an attitude of listening?

If this inner surrender has been achieved, the voice of the angel speaks again within us, for a 'boding' note is sounded:

I do forebode I strength must find
To found and form my soul
A garment worthy of the spirit.

To fashion 'my soul' so that it is 'worthy' — this is a message that the angel whispers to the I. 'Become worthy,' he says, 'then you can adorn yourself like the bride that the spirit birth awaits.'

For this, however, it is necessary to find the strength which can bring such a condition about. This requires not brute force or strength but an inner power of resolve.

The compelling power, the restriction which forever cramps the soul into the corset of its habits needs to be loosened. The expansiveness of the festive as opposed to the restrictions of everyday life would have to be cultivated in many moments of life. In this way that dress is woven which may be spoken of as a garment for the spirit.

This festive expansiveness is acquired if the soul is granted access to beauty and takes in the written word, music, colour and form in ever greater measure. By this means a substance is woven into the form that prepares the germinal word of worlds in the soul.

Opposite to this verse there stands another, sung by the soprano. It is the verse accompanying the first week in Advent. If the awakening presentiment of the approaching time of Christmas is present, we hear these words:

35. Can I then the being know
That, known, it find itself again
In the soul's urgence to create?
I feel the power entrusted me
My own self humbly to insert
A living member in the self of worlds.

Here the humility that has been acquired becomes modesty, and the self, which has emerged from the intermingling of the I with the word of worlds, knows itself as a part and member of the self of worlds.

Humble listening has been transformed into modestly ordered activity. All this was prepared when these words sounded forth in the ninth week:

> 9. Forgetting all my separateness of will
> The warmth of worlds, the summer's harbinger,
> I feel it flood my spirit and my soul.

For the warmth of worlds was at that time woven as a kind of cosmic under-garment into separateness of will, and the call, 'Lose, lose your self, yourself to find,' was able to ring out.

This will be completed when clarity of soul has been achieved in verse 44 and the awakening manifold sense-impressions and phenomena can be imbued with form and order.

The nineteenth week

19 *August 11–17*
To wrap the new-conceived germ
In memory's secret folds
Be now my striving's master aim:
Gathering strength to waken
Force of my own within me,
Emergent, it shall give myself to me.

The word of worlds has entered into the human soul through the sphere of the senses. This was the first step.

The soul now tries to transform itself in humility, so that it may become worthy of the influence of the word of God. That is the second step, and it was brought before us in the previous week.

Now, in the week of the third step, something further comes about. This is

To wrap the new-conceived germ
In memory's secret folds

The new-conceived germ has now become to such an extent part of our being that the life of memories may be woven around it as its sheaths. This power of memory is a part of our life of will; it represents the germinal memory pictures that the will has created out of the world of ideas. Thus former experiences which have been reshaped by the will are offered up to the word of worlds as a garment. This is 'now my striving's master aim.'

The under-garment of humility is thereby covered with a shimmering, radiant garment of memories, and these feeling and will aspects of our existence make, or rather dedicate, their contribution to what was 'secretly conceived.'

The result of this process is also characterized in the form of a promise:

> Gathering strength to waken
> Force of my own within me,
> Emergent, it shall give myself to me.

The gathering of one's inner being and the self-development of one's own I are here undertaken as a promise. In order to understand this more closely, it is important to see this as the third precondition to be added to the two previous ones.

The first one was (and this was the word of worlds itself):

> 17. Fill full thy spirit's depths
> With my world wideness,
> To find hereafter me in thee.

The second one stated (and this is expressed by the human I):

> 18. I do forebode I strength must find
> To found and form my soul
> A garment worthy of the spirit.

In the third, that of the present week, it is likewise the human I which is speaking, but it does not speak in its own name but objectifies itself as 'it.' The human I has conceived the word of worlds and says of it what two weeks previously it proclaimed with its own word, 'I.'

Thus now the word of worlds is no longer speaking but is, rather, hearing what the human ego has to express about its future working within it. This word of worlds will by degrees bring the human ego closer to the higher self.

In this way the three steps in the receiving of the word of God into the inner regions of the soul have been accomplished.

Now from the last week in November, the week preceding Advent, the voice of the soprano sounds forth and sings:

34. To feel through selfhood new uprisen
The treasured dower of old
Stir secretly to life within
Shall, waking, pour into my human deeds
A tide of universal powers,
And so, maturing, grave me in existence.

This is, again, the result of that garment of memories which served as a sheath. It streams into life's *outward* (human) *deeds* and has the effect of moulding or graving me in existence as well as enabling me to be creative in my work. The I, which has now found itself, multiplies itself in its activity amidst the surrounding world of which it forms a part.

In the background of both these verses, however, there sounds the Whitsun song of the tenor:

8. The senses' might grows great
Bonded with the gods' creating

and the counter-song of the alto:

45. The power of thought stands firm
Bonded with the spirit's birth

In this way there comes to expression what this quartet of verses is about: it has to do with the birth of the spirit, which is to be united with thinking so that it can work towards the perpetual protection of the ego as self in the world:

34. ... grave me in existence

and

19. ... it shall give myself to me.

The twentieth week

20 August 18–24
Now first I feel my being —
Which, torn from world existence,
Within itself must quench the self,
And building on itself alone
Must kill the self-enclosed self.

The receiving of the word of worlds into the soul has been accomplished. The 'new-conceived germ' has been spread throughout the inner being, and now something completely new arises.

Human beings now confront what is going on in such a way that they begin to assess themselves and from this arrive at the judgment that they must quench and kill themselves.

Now, in the second half of August, when the fields have been harvested, when the first breath of approaching autumn is passing over the fields, when the first stubble covers the earth — at this hour this strange feeling comes over the human soul: Everything has come to an end; the harvest has been brought in. All that I have achieved must be laid down like a sacrifice so as not to stand in the way of the advent of the word of worlds. Not I, but the word of worlds in me shall enter into activity.

Just as the harvested fields lie fallow so that later on the plough may have a new resource with which it can work, so will the soul relate to the harvested field so as to surrender itself anew to the plough of the word.

Now first I feel my being —
Which, torn from world existence,

Human beings have become strangers in the world; they feel themselves to be far from world existence, separated from everything that was previously connected to them.

Thus the field of stubble bereft of ears of grain is no longer given up to heavenly forces, since the ear is lacking as a mediator; earth and heaven are separated from one another. The human individual is similarly cut off from the world, for the word now lives in him and has distanced him from ordinary world existence.

However, it is this that becomes the new feeling for one's own being, so that the state of being 'torn from world existence,' and the 'quenching' and 'killing' of 'the self' create something entirely new.

> Now first I feel my being —

For here the new life is gained through dying.

And now the counter-verse sounds forth from the November side of the year:

> 33. Now first I feel the world,
> Which, reft of my indwelling soul,
> Would as a frozen waste
> Unfold its feeble life,
> Create itself anew in human souls,
> That in itself could look for death alone.

What comes to expression here is a newly gained feeling of the world which stands in contrast to the feeling of my own being that has now, in August, been acquired. On the one hand one's inner being must be surrendered in order to arise anew. On the other, the world must be recognized as 'a frozen waste,' if it does not include the participation of the soul.

The world must unite with the soul if it is to experience an enlivening process. If it does not do this, it would die and — left to itself — find only death.

On the other hand, the self must die, pass through death, in order to awaken a new existence within itself.

We find this same thought in the introductory words to the Children's Service:

> That leads the living into death that it may live anew,
> That leads what is dead into life that it may behold the spirit.

However, both these verses are embedded in another duality, one of which has already been surveyed:

> 7. My self threatens to break away
> Through strong enticement of the light of worlds.

and the other:

> 6. The world threatens to stupefy
> The inborn forces of my soul.

The rescued self must be surrendered in order that a new feeling of self can arise.

The world that has been renewed by the soul will later on rise up in a threatening way in order to help the self towards a new trial.

Now, however, in the harvest month of August, it needs to surrender itself so that the word of worlds which has been conceived can develop on the foundation of the newly attained feeling of self. In the world without is the harvest; within there is emptiness. Outside there is fullness, and inside a sense of loss.

Distance, strangeness and emptiness need to be experienced if the hope is to arise that the light of the spirit will shine in the darkness.

The twenty-first week

21 *August 25–31*
I feel a power unwonted, bearing fruit,
Gather its strength and lend myself to me.
I sense the germ maturing,
The while my boding weaves a web of light
Within me for my selfhood's power.

Through the creating of an inner emptiness the space has now arisen where what has been 'newly conceived' can unfold. Because human beings have brought their own light, which shone egotistically, to the point of extinction, the light of worlds begins to shine within them. This is as yet experienced more as a feeling, not as light but as the first breath of new life and activity that begins to arise within the realm of the soul.

As in the approaching autumn something new begins to weave through the earthly surroundings. It manifests in the changing of colours and in breaths of wind and warmth; thus it is the first delicate indication of something which was not formerly present and which begins to appear within humans. Outwardly the blue of the sky becomes deeper and more opaque; distances become clearer and what is close by becomes more transparent. A first cool wind pervades the morning and evening, and sometimes it forms eddies which play with the hay and the first fallen leaves.

This first premonition of autumn, which is accompanied by the rapid changes in birdsong, has its counterpart in the soul. Something new is announcing itself here too.

I feel a power unwonted, bearing fruit,
Gather its strength and lend myself to me.

As it awakens, the power of the word of worlds works upon my 'quenched' being. With a fructifying and swelling gesture, it fills what initially had to be killed. Now, however, my I calls out:

> I sense the germ maturing

For the fructifying gesture enables it fully to expand.

> The while my boding weaves a web of light

The angelic 'boding' quality of the higher self hovers with a sense of joyful participation around the ripening process within the soul, so that my selfhood's power can fill itself anew, better and also more beautifully than ever before.

For the higher self and the lower ego together form that pair of siblings, the twins, from whom selfhood must constantly be forged. However, on one occasion in the year this selfhood receives the strength and blessing of the word of worlds; at this point the lower ego must be quenched and the higher ego participate like a godparent in the baptism which the self now has to undergo.

This process is completed as many weeks after Michaelmas as the number of weeks that now precede Michaelmas. Then we hear what is proclaimed with a strong sense of inwardness by the soprano:

> 32. I feel my proper strength, a fruitful scion,
> With gathered power bestow me on the world,
> I feel the essence of my being
> Grow strong in clarity
> To trace life's web of destiny.

The self has emerged newly strengthened. The autumnal mood without has enabled it to mature, and now it can clearly experience itself in the web of threads of destiny. A new saviour arises for the dying natural environment in the human self, which has been fructified by the spirit of worlds.

Now there arises a contemplation of the experience in which the soul had participated in the week of Ascension:

6. There has arisen from its separateness
My self — to find that self
As worlds made manifest
In powers of time and space.

At that time the old self was lifted out and above itself and found its home in the higher ego, experiencing itself in the widths of the world. The tenor within us has this year already sung this song.

From the coming spring, however, there sounds forth from the alto:

47. There shall arise from out the womb of worlds
The bliss of growth, fostering joys of sense.

In this bliss of growth the first signs can be discerned of the word of worlds and the light of worlds which live in all creation. They manifest themselves as a sun, summoning all that exists to new becoming.

Thus the human I can now be grasped in its threefold being. To begin with it is the 'higher ego.' As such it stands at the gate of birth and death, but it does not enter the earthly world. It becomes an eternal godparent to what is manifested in the body as the lower ego. This lower ego works in the domain of the body as a shadow-picture of the higher ego; it pervades the senses and limbs. However, this lower ego would be in danger of an early death if it did not experience fructification by the light-filled sound of the word of worlds every year at St John's.

The self, which holds the balance between the lower and higher ego, emerges ever and again from this annual baptism. It is the self which maintains self-consciousness in its uprightness; it is the self which creates knowledge from among sensations; it is the self which intones the bodily sheaths as their personality.

Hence in this verse we encounter the formulation: *mir mich selbst* (in the second line, approximately rendered in the English translation as 'myself to me'). What are being referred to here are

the higher *(mir,* 'to me') and lower *(mich,* the 'my' of 'myself') ego, which engender the self. But the germ is the renewing of the self, which — following its annual baptism by the spirit of worlds — identifies with the life of autumn and winter.

The twenty-second week

22 September 1–7
Light from the worlds' wide bounds
Unfolds in me its life of power,
Changing to light of soul,
Illumining my spirit's depths,
That fruitage to set free
Which, when time runs, shall ripen
The self of man from out the self of worlds.

Again we enter directly into the world of the light, of which we already had an intimation in the fifth verse. At that time we had a sense of the presence of a cycle of light, as we called it, and experienced the human soul as a heart — the light-filled heart of this cycle.

At that time — in the spring — it was the 'light from spirit's depths' which summoned the soul forth into the expanses of the world in order that it might be prepared for communion with the spirit-word. Now, at the beginning of autumn, something different is happening. It is the 'light from the world's wide bounds' which has surrendered itself to the human soul. Formerly the soul was reaching out into these expanses in order to unite with the light streaming out of the depths of spirit. Now it is different: the soul has experienced its fructification by the spirit. It humbly awaits what is to happen; and the light from the widths of the periphery now pervades this soul. The light-filled heart now receives the stream of the light of worlds into itself. In the spring it had been a streaming out; now it is an in-streaming, for the light is entering the heart, the human soul.

This whole verse has something thoroughly autumnal and inward about it and must be felt as such. Out in the natural

world summer is drawing to its close. Beauty is waning and life is dying. The light that is wresting itself free from nature is seeking a new home. Like the birds, which have left for the south, light now streams into the human soul in order to undergo a transformation there.

In the world without it has summoned the plants from their earthly roots, it has called forth blossoms and caused the fruits to ripen. All this has happened, and now the same light can go to where it is 'at home.' It returns home to the human soul. This 'homecoming of light' is the autumnal theme of this verse.

However, it undergoes a transformation in the soul and becomes a light of soul and, as such, shines into the spirit-depths of the human being.

Rudolf Steiner once spoke of how with every breath of air, we take not only air but also light into ourselves and that we transform this light within us and make it our own as we do any other substance: we digest it, that is, we make it an integral part of our self.[7]

This happens to a particular degree in autumn. For now this light of worlds which has become light of soul encounters the germ formed within the human being, and from this germ fruits ripen, 'the self of man' is won over the course of time 'from out the self of worlds.' It is with this immense hope that we may approach autumn and winter.

From the time after Michaelmas there sounds the voice of the soprano, singing of the same light that now — after its transformation in the soul — rises up from the spirit-depths of our being, in order to turn outwards again and to flow back whence it came.

Thus in this verse 22 the cycle of light has arrived at that point in the year where the great arc of worlds is transmuted into the small and narrow human arc. Light comes from the world expanses to the focal point of the soul. It is the crossing-point of a lemniscate, where the big loop turns into the little one. It is also a complete change of mood; for autumn is beginning to draw near

and the soul has the task of becoming strong in humility in order to be prepared for the coming of winter.

The poet Georg Trakl put this into these words:

> There tower around him the sky's cool blueness
> and the dwindling light of autumn,
> The quiet house and the legends of the forest,
> Measure and law and the moonlike paths
> of the departed.[8]

All this lives in the verse for this week. For the human being receives the grace of the light; the light of worlds wafts over the spring-like field of the soul, which bears the seeds that want to ripen as fruit.

The softness of this evening light, the rich colours of its rays — all this streams into the inner regions of the soul in an intimate mood of loving readiness. The compelling need here is to receive it, recognize and experience it, while not rejecting it.

O man, take heed! The light of the world-wide spaces, it lives in you. Take hold of it lovingly.

The twenty-third week

23 September 8–14
Subdued to autumn's mood
The spurrings of the senses die away;
Veil upon veil, the mist
Dims the still radiant light.
In the wide spaces I discern
The autumn's sleep of worlds;
Summer to me
Has yielded up itself.

With this verse autumn makes its initial entry into the changing face of nature. The human soul, whence this verse has been wrested, has been wholly given over to the surrounding world. It is as though it had momentarily forgotten itself and had become wholly immersed in the natural processes taking place before its eyes.

In hardly any other verse is this devotion to the world so absolute as it is here. The events taking place in the world without are described very simply and yet most beautifully, and it is as if the dim veils of mist can be smelt.

Many memories rise up in the soul through these verses: the sharp fragrance of the last hay as it is cut, stacked and brought in from the meadows and slopes; the tender violet of the meadow saffrons which now begin to appear over all meadows and, in their nakedness, proclaim the melancholy of autumn; the rapidly drifting clouds, which break up and become veils of mists that linger in the trees and in valleys; the last ringing of the cow bells, which soon fades away and falls silent, because a deep stillness pervades the world.

All this is the autumnal self-surrendering of the senses. For

the 'light from the world's wide bounds' has now begun to enter into the human soul, and wherever it disappears 'veil upon veil' of mist dims the continuing radiance of the last of summer's glory.

In those places where the light steals away, the waters springing from the depths of earth condense as breath that envelops the world in veils of mist. The revelations of summer are withdrawing, for the creative energies of light are pervading the soul.

Human beings stand abandoned amidst the harvested fields. They alone remain upright in all the fading and departing that surrounds them. 'Where are you going, O world?' calls the heart. 'Will you completely vanish from my field of vision?'

The departing summer speaks like the friend in Mahler's *Song of the Earth:* 'I am going for a walk in the mountains'; and the melancholy of this song, the mood of an inevitable parting, pervades our whole existence.

This is the beginning of autumn's winter sleep, extending into the widths of space.[9] But behind this knowledge, at the inner core of this mood of parting and solitude, the soul hears the gentle bubbling up of a new spring. It says:

> Summer to me
> Has yielded up itself.

For this is hope and a new beginning, amidst all that is dying. Although summer seems to be disappearing, its true being is now within me; and whereas its outward sheath is fading, I keep the seed of its fruit within my self.

And the counter-voice of the soprano rings out and sings jubilantly:

> 30. Warmed in the sunshine of the soul
> Ripe fruits of thinking thrive,
> To sureness of a self aware
> All feeling is transformed.
> I joy to feel the spirit stir

Of autumn's watchfulness,
Winter shall wake in me
The summer of the soul.

This is what the counter-verse expresses. The threshold of Michaelmas has drawn the dying revelation of light inwards, and it has become 'sureness of a self aware.' Now an inner watchfulness emerges from the outward wintry sleep or sleep of worlds, and the approaching winter enables the summer of the soul to unfold.

The element of surrendering to the surrounding world that lives in this verse becomes a total devotion to the inner world of the soul in the counter-verse from the time after Michaelmas which has just been cited.

And the voice of the tenor recollects from the springtime:

4. 'I feel my being's very being,'
So speaks the feeling soul
Which in the sunlit world
Unites itself with floods of light.

While from the coming pre-Easter time the alto sings with full confidence:

49. 'I feel your strength of life, O worlds,'
So the clear voice of thinking cries,
Mindful of its own spirit's growth
Through the dark world-nights achieved

In both these verses what is taking place is again an encounter between self and world, between inner being and outer being. Thus in these four verses it is not the light-cycle itself that is being referred to but the heart of the human soul in its activity as the centre of its circulation — as the meeting-point between world and humans in the time before and after Easter. In the time after Michaelmas there is the sense of standing wholly on one's own feet. Thus the verse of the present week has the

quality of a complete diastole. The soul has surrendered itself to autumn, it has given itself over to the melancholy of parting, in which, however, lies the source of the song of promise:

> Summer to me
> Has yielded up itself

begins to sound forth. In this mood, as we anticipate the promise with courage, we can move on to the next verse.

The twenty-fourth week

> 24 *September 15–21*
> Unceasingly itself renewing
> The soul grows self-aware;
> In new self-knowledge vivified
> The spirit of the world strives on,
> Creating from the darkness of the soul
> What sense of self matures as fruit of will.

In this verse the gate granting a preview of the approaching time of Michaelmas opens up. Just as in the verse for the previous week the world of nature as autumn approaches was characterized, so does the present verse reveal the advent of the Michaelmas festival.

The human sense of self stands at the foreground of experience — not as it pertains to a personal destiny and an individual existence but, rather, his awareness of his existence as a human being on the earth in the present period of humankind's history.

It is a process of becoming aware that needs to happen here, as is indicated in the verse through the three instances where the word 'self' appears:

> Unceasingly it*self* renewing
> ...
> In new *self*-knowledge vivified
> What sense of *self* matures as fruit of will

A threefold experience of self-consciousness is referred to here. In the first part of the verse it is the soul-being that grows self-aware. In the second part it is the spirit of the world that finds itself in self-knowledge and, in this finding of itself, engenders sense of self as the fruit of will.

It is, however, the human soul which is initially conscious of itself and thereby gives the spirit of the world the possibility of experiencing its self-knowledge. From this it fashions the fruit that is formed as a result of this process.

A threefold process is involved here: the first act takes place within the human soul; the second act is in the sphere of the spirit of the world; and the third act is the result that accrues from the first and second acts.

In the well-known Michaelmas lecture of October 5, 1923 Rudolf Steiner speaks about this task of developing self-consciousness for the time of Michael.[10] He says:

> In the time when outer nature is dying, man must set the power of self-consciousness over and against consciousness of nature ... If, under the impulse of anthroposophy, a person enters thus into an enjoyment of nature, a consciousness of nature, but then also awakes within himself an autumnal self-consciousness, a picture of Michael with the dragon will stand majestically before him, revealing in picture-form the overcoming of nature-consciousness by self-consciousness when autumn draws near.

In these words lies one of the elements behind this verse. The approaching time of Michaelmas calls forth in the human soul what was merely felt in verse 21, raising it now to consciousness. The first two lines of that verse were:

> I feel a power unwonted, bearing fruit,
> Gather its strength and lend itself to me.

But now we have:

> Unceasingly itself renewing
> The soul grows self-aware.

What happens here is a twofold reflexive process, making a self-perception of the soul possible. Just as an eye looking at itself

in the mirror has an awareness of itself, so the soul is now called to self-consciousness through renewing itself perceptively. Once this happens, an enlivening process takes place in the spirit of the world, which now — by working back upon the soul — begins to transform the seeds enabling 'sense of self to mature as fruit of will' which were the fruit of summer.

The more intimately we engage our feelings with a study of the meaning of this verse, the clearer do the concealed images become that derive from the same source as Goethe's *Fairy Tale of the Green Snake and the Beautiful Lily.* For this 'self-renewing' of the human soul is the sacrifice of the Green Snake, which crumbles into pieces in order to make the bridge possible and gives its jewels over to the river. The river, an image of the spirit of the world, foams up allowing the temple to rise to its surface. This is the 'sense of self maturing as fruit of will' in our inner being.

The counter-verse, sung by the soprano, rings forth in the time after Michaelmas:

29. To light in me the lamp of thinking
And fan with inner force the flame,
Illumining life's story
From the world spirit's well of power,
For me is summer's heritage,
Is autumn's peace and winter's hope to be.

Here what in the present verse is formed only to an initial, rudimentary degree has fully come about. The 'sense of self maturing as fruit of will' lights up fully and powerfully in the inner being as a renewed thinking. It thereby becomes the temple in which the spirit can incarnate and manifest itself. Hardly at any other time does the call in Goethe's Fairy Tale, 'the time is at hand!' sound forth so loudly and audibly.

The time is at hand, O man, for you to begin to perceive yourself in such a way that you become conscious of your self. Then the world spirit can also manifest in you and thereby achieve the

purpose of its mission. But where the human soul and the spirit of the world join together in matrimony, there arises the seed whence a new kingdom, the kingdom of God, will grow.

The two connected verses that sound forth in the tenor and in the alto in the time before and after Easter also point towards this relationship of the human soul to the spirit of the world.

The tenor sings:

> 3. Speaks to the universe ...
> The waxing I of man.[11]

And the alto proclaims:

> 50. Speaks to the human I ...
> The bliss of growth in world existence.

At the other side of the year, around Easter time, both entities are still such that they can be exchanged purely through the world of language. Now, at Michaelmas, this needs to happen more inwardly and strongly, and this should be felt.

What sought to be expressed around Easter in the element of the word has now entered into the sphere of thinking and should experience its resurrection there. This resurrection can take place only if the germ of the self, fashioned out of the meeting between the higher and lower self (verse 21), is now grasped and understood as such in self-knowledge.

The week before Michaelmas

25 September 22–28
My self, now made my very own,
May shine abroad its inner light
In dark abysms of space and time.
A slumber seizes nature's being,
But the deep hidden soul shall waken,
And waking carry sunny gleams
Into cold winter's tides and streams.

In this verse individuals who have become conscious of their self raise themselves to their full worth. A sublime play of gestures unfolds in the sounds of these words and enables them to experience their position in the world of existence.

As in the verse for the previous week our position in the present age came before our soul, so in the verse for this week our place within the world as it is is indicated. 'Man and the earth' is the basic theme. Its first melody breaks out with the words:

> My self, now made my very own,

Here we stand, inwardly listening and devoted to our own mission, as a being of the natural world who has been enabled to raise ourselves above ourselves. In this way we may belong to 'ourselves' (be 'made my very own') and not only to the world.

Out of this inwardly directed listening, however, a new gesture arises; for now it sounds forth:

> May shine abroad its inner light
> In dark abysms of space and time.

It is as though we were stretching out our arms and standing

like a living cross amidst nature. In the oldest church in Rome, Santa Maria Antiqua in the Roman Forum, there is a fresco representing the Crucified One as though standing on a cross with horizontally extended arms. This is an allegory of how human beings stand in this week amidst the natural world — wakeful, spreading light. Into the dying world around them they send the light in which they have through grace been able to partake and which they can inwardly experience as the 'self.' In this attitude the soul awakens to the spirit, and this process of awakening pours light into the darkness of approaching autumn.

Now, however, this world that surrounds us becomes visible to us and we know:

> A slumber seizes nature's being,

Although I am a being of nature, I am not only this. What follows applies to me:

> But the deep hidden soul shall waken,
> And waking carry sunny gleams
> Into cold winter's tides and streams.

This takes the Michaelic character of this week a step further in comparison to the experience of the previous week. For by letting our light stream outwards, we now experience how the world of nature is sinking into a condition of sleep. A gentle mood of dying, a steady dimming and darkening, is weaving through the natural world. However, this only becomes visible through our own inner light beginning to shine outwards. We then awaken to the knowledge: I must bring an inner awakening to meet this outward sleep. Yes, this knowledge goes beyond this point. In a lecture given on Easter Sunday 1923, Rudolf Steiner spoke about this:

> Easter thought: He has been laid in the grave; He is risen. Michaelmas thought: He is risen and can confidently be laid in the grave.

> The first thought, the Easter thought, pertains to the Christ; the second thought pertains to the human being. It pertains to the man who directly comprehends the power of the Easter thought, comprehends how when spiritual knowledge enters into the earthly life of the present, in which his soul-spiritual is dying away, his soul can resurrect, so that he becomes living between birth and death, so that in the earthly life he becomes inwardly alive. The human being must through spiritual knowledge comprehend this inner resurrection, this inner awakening; then will he confidently be laid in the grave. Then he may be laid in the grave, through which he otherwise would fall prey to those ahrimanic powers who work within the earth realm at the time of the winter solstice.
>
> And the festival which contains this thought: He is risen and can confidently be laid in the grave — this festival must fall in the time when the leaves are beginning to turn yellow and fall from the trees, when the fruits have ripened, when the sun has received that power which brings to maturity what in the spring was budding and sprouting, full of the forces of growth, but which also brings withering and the inclination to seek again the inner part of the earth, when what is development on the earth begins to be a symbol of the grave.[12]

Thus it is not only the case that an inner awakening needs to be brought as a counterpoint to outward sleep. It is even essential to counter outward death with an inner resurrection. But this resurrection quality must be acquired at the time of Michaelmas, so that the death that is approaching can no longer have power over the human soul.

The radiant power of this verse therefore stands like a sign-post on the road that leads to Michaelmas.

The baritone sings within us:

> But the deep hidden soul shall waken,
> And waking carry sunny gleams
> Into cold winter's tides and streams.

And now, as if in answer, the voice of the soprano strikes up and sings:

> 28. Quickened anew within
> I feel the vastness of my being,
> And power is mine to shed clear rays of thought
> From the soul's sunlike potency
> Solving life's riddles

What in the present week merely shines is in the corresponding week of Michaelmas to become an illuminating light of thoughts which is capable of deciphering the riddles of the world of things.

While from the time before and after Easter the alto intones the words:

> 51. The spirit of the world beholds
> His mirrored image in the eye of man

and the tenor:

> 2. The worlds of spirit find
> Anew their offspring, Man

What is in the first instance a matter of finding something, is now something that has been found. The spirit of the world has entered into the human spirit, which has given it a dwelling-place.

In this way the Holy Spirit may become active through human beings as the good.

Now the sky takes on this special blue of autumn, where human beings can find their inner clarity and peace as though reflected. Now the lark rises high up into the sky, and its song

rings clearly through the rarefied air and bears the communion of a created being up to the heights of heaven.

Now the leaves may fall, for out of sorrow arises the confidence that death can be countered by inner awakening.

Light emerges from the realm of the soul and streams into the growing darkness. 'Death, where is thy sting? Hell, where is thy victory?' (1Cor.15:55).

Mood of Michaelmas

26 Michaelmas. September 29
Nature, thou soul of motherhood,
I bear thee in the essence of my will,
That will whose fiery strength
Tempers my spirit's edge
That it beget such sense of self
As may bear I in me.

Now the soul enters the hallowed week of Michaelmas. For the last time the voice of the baritone rings out; it is filled with the inner power of radiance which it has brought from the time and the yields of summer, and like a ripe fruit it lights up now in the fullness of perfection. A verse sounds forth which has not only become of the highest quality in its sound but which harbours important revelations in its verbal content.

In the verse of the previous week the soul experienced itself in the gesture of the cross. Out of this gesture it has found resurrection forces in itself and with this attitude it has passed through the forecourt of the temple of Michaelmas time. It sounds now in the holiest of holies of this temple, and the revelation in which it is to share is contained in the verbal content of this verse. In the previous week the gaze of the soul was directed outwards; now the soul looks into its own existence and finds that in a part of its self it has become a dwelling-place of nature.

It experiences:

Nature, thou soul of motherhood,
I bear thee in the essence of my will,

O man, you are embedded with your will in the domain of nature. In your will you are as if one with the creative forces of

the world, enveloped and incorporated into everything that is active in the world. The rumbling of thunder and the flashing of lightning, the blowing of the wind and the moaning of the storm, the trickling of the rain and the heavy weight of stones, the softness of snow and the surging of waves — all this is both around and within you. In so far as you are a being of will, you are one with these creative forces. You are that.

This is the gist of the first two lines of this Michaelmas verse. But they also say that motherly forces hold sway in the kingdom of nature. 'Nature, thou soul of motherhood' is what the Greeks revered in the Eleusinian mysteries as the being of Demeter, the great, all-powerful goddess of the whole earth. This is what the soul now experiences. It feels itself taken up into the starry cloak of the eternal mother in whom the working of the father ground is manifested.

Behind these opening words there sounds another verse, from the Foundation Stone Meditation:

> Soul of Man!
> Thou livest in the limbs,
> Which bear thee through the world of space
> Into the ocean being of the spirit:
> Practise Spirit-Remembering

And later on come these words:

> For the Father Spirit of the heights holds sway
> In depths of worlds, begetting being.

These words in all their mighty depths sound forth as though a whole choir of powerful organ notes had arisen behind the song of the baritone. The ancient ground of the world rings out in the full majesty of its existence. In an earlier time the priest Zachariah was struck mute amidst this ringing in the Temple around Michaelmas. The birth of John was proclaimed to him out of the trombone tones of the Michaelmas choir.

Once this has been recognized in deepest trepidation, the soul goes a step further:

> That will whose fiery strength
> Tempers my spirit's edge

Out of the fiery forge of the will there now arises an upward moving energy: beams of light radiating upwards from the will's wealth of natural resources, working formatively and creatively into the world of thoughts. There the spiritual impulses (my spirit's edge) are illumined and guided by this light.

This picture is the human, earthly reflection of what is described as a cosmic imagination in Chapter 12 of the Book of Revelation. The woman clothed with the sun, with the moon beneath her feet, pregnant and crying out in her labour pains, is the fiery forge of the will. From her the light radiates upwards: 'She brought forth a male child, one who is to rule all the nations with a rod of iron; and her child was caught up to God and to his throne.'

Here appears the iron staff as the will-forces tempering the impulses of my spirit (my spirit's edge). From the mother the child is born.

Again the curtain behind these words opens up, and a new sign resounds:

> Soul of Man!
> Thou livest in the beat of heart and lung
> Which bears thee through the rhythm of time
> Into the realm of thine own soul's feeling.
> Practise Spirit-Awareness

And then:

> For the Christ-Will in the encircling round holds sway
> In the rhythms of worlds, bestowing grace on the soul

The upward striving spiritual impulses reveal themselves now not as the world mother working in the fire of the will but as

the holy cosmic Virgin passing above the clouds and holding the child in her arms. This child is, however, taken away from her; it is transported to the highest throne and works upon earthly evolution from this region of the world. But the holy virgin goes down to the earth, just as in the Greek mysteries Persephone left her mother. The sphere of activity of the Son, who bestows grace on human beings through the rhythms of worlds, is revealed behind this cosmic drama.

The Michaelmas experience now goes a stage further and leads to the words:

> That it beget such sense of self
> As may bear I in me.

What the spiritual impulses in their upward orientation have now achieved appears in the soul as a reflection of that child to whom the cosmic Virgin gave birth. This child is taken up into heaven — with an iron staff, with the sword of Michael, for the child is Michael himself; and this child will conquer the heathen human forces in such a way that a presentiment of an angel consciousness awakens within him. This is the sense of self that can bear 'I in me.' The dawning of the spirit in the realm of the soul, as a conscious experience, begins.

With this a third aspect sounds forth:

> Soul of Man!
> Thou livest in the resting head,
> Which from the grounds of eternity
> Opens to thee the world-thoughts.
> Practise Spirit-Beholding.

To this is added:

> For the world-thoughts of the Spirit hold sway
> In the being of worlds, craving for light

This awakening sense of self in the inner being is the answer to the craving of the world-thoughts. They are searching for a

seat, a throne where they can settle, just as every bird needs a nest where it can focus its earthly existence.

The nest of the birds of the world-thoughts is the self that has been fashioned in the inner being. It is the eternal light that every human being is able to kindle within them and is ready to carry them through all perils and trials. The sword of Michael has caused the light to burst into flame.

Here Triptolemos* has awakened within the soul, and the human being is received into the realm of the hierarchies. This is the new experience of Michaelmas.

* Triptolemos was one of the demigods in the mysteries of Eleusis and received Demeter when she came mourning the loss of her daughter Persephone. The young goddess was eventually returned to her from the Underworld, and Demeter in her munificence, instructed Triptolemos in the art of agriculture, and gave him a winged chariot drawn by serpents so that he might travel the world to give his arts.

The beginning of autumn

Now in the following week there sounds the counter-verse. For the first time a female voice takes the leading role in the yearly cycle. The soprano sings gently and softly, almost timidly in comparison to the brassy power of the departed baritone, and there is nothing in this counter-verse that seems to approximate the verse for Michaelmas. There are probably no other two closely related verses in the Soul Calendar which seem at first to be so different. This new song rings out tenderly and tentatively, softly and as though hovering in the air:

> *27 October 6–12*
> To dive into my being's depths
> Stirs up a yearning in me, boding well,
> That self-exploring I may find
> Myself the gift of summer sun,
> Which lives in autumn's mood
> A warm seed life
> Of thriving forces for my soul.

What does this say in contrast to, and yet in harmony with, the foregoing Michaelmas verse? What does the end of summer hand over to the beginning of autumn? No contrast can be felt here, not a mutually complementary element such as verses 13 and 14 or verses 52 and 1 bring with them. A different mystery is in evidence here. For this verse 27 is like a seed.

It is that seed within our being of which verse 26 tells us. This last verse of summer, and, indeed, of the whole previous six months since Easter, is like a fully ripened fruit. Michaelmas has revealed this fruit, and now the new seed appears within it, which speaks:

> To dive into my being's depths
> Stirs up a yearning in me, boding well

For it is new land which the spirit-germ, or seed enters here. It has only just been created and can be found in the sheath of the soul. It awakens to its existence and now begins to find itself in self-exploration as the gift of summer sun. Now the seed comes to know its own existence. It knows that it was born out of the forces of summer, that it has been transplanted into the realm of the soul and now needs to recognize itself for what it is.

It has become 'thriving forces.' What has been raised by way of spiritual impulses out of the fire of will becomes the thriving forces of the soul.

Now we recognize the stages of this stream of becoming in the course of the year. A new seed has arisen within the soul. The self has been born anew and from now on, through the second half of the year, it will try to develop. It has emerged from the fruit which came to a revelatory maturity through the power of Michael.

But another verse sounds forth, one that is just as tender and has a similarly germinal effect:

> At the turning-point of time,
> The Spirit-Light of the World
> Entered the stream of earthly being;
> Darkness of night
> Had held its sway

What formerly took place in the dark times of the earth will henceforth happen in the inner regions of the soul under the power of Michael. For the spirit-germ, the self, which is a reflection of this Michael being, will be illumined by the Sun of Christ and begins to develop and grow in its light.

The more conscious this seed is of itself, the more graciously will the Sun of Christ shine upon it. For it is in the growing darkness of autumn and winter that the dawning of his Spirit-Sun begins. The self, which has now arisen, has to find it.

Second Sunday after Michaelmas

28 October 13–19
Quickened anew within
I feel the vastness of my being,
And power is mine to shed clear rays of thought
From the soul's sunlike potency
Solving life's riddles,
And granting many a wish fulfilment
Whose wings had drooped with hope foregone.

Once the seed of the spirit has been released from the shell of the soul's fruit, a new path in the yearly cycle begins. The voice of the soprano sings, high, bright, often like a bird song that penetrates the stillness of the landscape.

The warming light of the spirit-germ pervades the inner regions of the soul and fills the abodes of thinking with an awakening radiance.

The course of the counter-verses now runs forwards from Michaelmas to Christmas and backwards to St John's Tide. At the same time the counter-voice at Easter begins proceeding to the festival of St John's, whereas the Palm Sunday voice goes back from this point towards Christmas. This is how it looks:

St John's Tide
Tenor *Baritone*
Easter Michaelmas
Palm Sunday Autumn
Alto *Soprano*
Christmas

Thus accompanied by the strains of the soprano we make our way towards Christmas, and the counter-voices interweave their contributions into the overall harmony.

The spirit-germ itself now begins to speak, like a being that on the morning of its birth gains a sense of itself and the miracle of its existence — just as a bird confirms its own existence through the resounding of its song:

> Quickened anew within
> I feel the vastness of my being

Thus it rings out, full of inner joy, full of gratitude and creative power. For now the sun of the soul begins to rise above the horizon of the world; it sends forth rays of thoughts, like arrows of light, illuminating the world around it and filling it with their substance of ideas.

Who does not remember October days when the dying world accompanies the lighting up of the inner birth of spirit! These are days when we wander through the gardens, filled with the inner certainty that we can decipher many of life's riddles, filled with the firm intention of beginning new, untackled tasks. This verse, which gives expression to what takes place within our soul during this week, is akin to experiencing the lighting up of an inner creative power, just as the bird feels the beauty and expansiveness of its song. It is not the sorrow of autumn that is experienced here but the radiant light of an inner spirit-birth.

But what do these words mean:

> And granting many a wish fulfilment
> Whose wings had drooped with hope foregone?

Is hope a quality that causes wings to droop? Is it not always a bringer of strength? If hope remains merely hope, if it never comes to fulfilment, it does indeed have a laming effect, and the wish sinks down to the earth. But in this week, old, unfulfilled wishes can find fulfilment, for the year is now rounding itself off. Georg Trakl gave expression to this mood:

With new-found power the year now ends
'Midst golden wine and fruit of gardens.
The woods they hold a wondrous stillness,
Companions of my solitude.[13]

The soul's spirit-wakening takes place in this context. And now the voice of the baritone resonates once more amidst this inner joy, as it sings:

25. My self, now made my very own,
May shine abroad its inner light
In dark abysms of space and time.

And we feel that when we experienced this roughly three or four weeks ago it was still dark, as it were, in comparison to the brightness which is now able to rise up out of the soul. Formerly there was still a summery natural light; whereas now this light is a new-born light of heaven. As soprano and baritone stand with regard to one another, so do these two different experiences of light relate.

While from the early days of Easter the tenor sings:

2. Into the utmost fields of sense
The force of thought resigns its separate life.

The alto voice speaks from the pre-Easter time, complementing this:

51. Into the inmost life of man
The senses pour their wealth

And the tenor continues:

2. The worlds of spirit find
Anew their offspring, man,
Whose seed in them
But his soul's harvest
Must in himself be found.

So every year anew the spirit-germ, or seed, is to be sought and found in the worlds of spirit. It is incorporated in the soul in the cosmic heights of St John's Tide and comes to fulfilment as a fruit in the time between St John's and Michaelmas. Then the seed is liberated and begins as such to shine forth within the soul.

This lasts for a while, until the spirit of the worlds begins once more to be manifested in the time before Easter; for then the alto sings:

51. The spirit of the worlds beholds
His mirrored image in the eye of man,
That eye which from that spirit
Must still renew its power.

At this time the newly arisen seed passes away after Michaelmas and leaves its achievements behind in the soul's treasure of memories. From now until Christmas and from Christmas until the week before Easter, step by step it works within the human being towards this moment of the year as a new self, as an image of the sun and of the light.

Let us now try to trace its influence with our fullest devotion.

Third Sunday after Michaelmas

29 October 20–26
To light in me the lamp of thinking
And fan with inner force the flame,
Illumining life's story
From the world spirit's well of power,
For me is summer's heritage,
Is autumn's peace and winter's hope to be.

The spirit-germ continues to radiate forth, and it is as though crystals and minerals are beginning to shine amongst rock faces — as if the stone were beginning to glow from within. Thus the soul is imbued and pervaded with light, and the colder and gloomier the world becomes outside the brighter the inner light shines.

The human soul feels itself to be stronger than the light as the world grows darker, and it knows that this light is needed for the new creation of the world. It embraces everything that it has received from the earth's past with gratitude. But all this must fade away again in the course of the future: the wax needs to be drawn out of this past and candles of the future moulded from it, so that they can be lit with the spark of human freedom — this is what the soul feels to be its immediate task. It thereby finds itself again in its historical position in earthly evolution and joyfully becomes aware of itself as a member of the world as a whole. Thus it recognizes itself as a bearer of this spiritual seed, which has been proffered to it out of grace. Hence it can say:

Illumining life's story
From the world spirit's well of power,

Not only what has been individually experienced matters here, but the experience of humankind since the beginning of Creation recalled in the soul.

It extends far back into the earth's past and also on into what it will become in the future. But this

> For me is summer's heritage,
> Is autumn's peace and winter's hope to be.

Past, present and future arise here not as abstract periods of time when nothing much happens but as full and creative entities. And the soul rises to the experience that, wherever it may be, the past bears the experience and the outer garment of summer. Everything that is past is filled with the warmth of memory. The past is what has been fulfilled, as summer also is, even if it is present; so it has more past within it than any other present.

Autumn, on the other hand, is always the present, for it is the spirit-present, the time for presence of mind: it is the time for decision and resolve. These are neither of the past nor of the future, but manifest solely in the present.

Winter, in contrast, always has the element of hope — that what is not here may come, that what has come may go. It bears the future within it, as it includes Christmas. Winter is always a seed, that is in in the process of becoming.

However, the soul experiences itself now as the point of intersection of these circles of time. Summer passes through it as the past, autumn as the present and winter as the future. They bear within themselves the three Christian virtues of faith (past), love (present) and hope (future), and so the human soul can play its part in them.

Hence this soul within which the light of the spirit radiates forth becomes the bearer of fixed point in the flow of time — a point of radiance illumining the darkness of events.

What has taken place here was proclaimed in the counter-verse for the week before Michaelmas:

24. Unceasingly itself renewing
The soul grows self-aware;
In new self-knowledge vivified
The spirit of the world strives on,
Creating from the darkness of the soul
What sense of self matures as fruit of will.

This has now happened. The spirit of the world has over the course of time taken hold of the human soul and has caused light to ray out in its darkness. What was proclaimed before Michaelmas has come to fulfilment after Michaelmas through the power of Michael.

The voices of tenor and alto, however, reach across from the period of the year around Easter, and they too point towards the time-processes of growth and decline, of creating and dissolving.

The spring period after Easter reaches right into the ancient past, and the tenor sings:

3. Speaks to the universe,
Itself forgetting
And mindful of its primal form
The waxing I of man.

The vista of the pre-Easter period, however, leads into the future, for the universe reveals itself to the human I with the words:

50. To you my life transporting
Unbanned from its enchantment
I reach my own true goal.

Thus the human I, mindful of its origins, and the universe, with its words concerning the earth's ultimate goal, are looking in opposite directions here.

In these four verses the whole life of time can be discerned. They are an expression of the experiences of the soul that related particularly to the course of time.

We need to develop a feeling for the tapestry of time that is woven in these weeks. There we find what underlies these verses as an archetypal picture, something arising from that primal source which, in the verse for this week, is called 'the world spirit's well of power.'

The soul's journey through the year

Conclusion of the first version, entitled On the Calendar of the Soul, *September 21–23, 1952*

The question that one may ask at the conclusion of these studies could be put as follows. Is there an archetypal picture of this soul's journey through the year in our bodily organization? An event which, like point and counter-point, like fugue and counter-subject, continually keeps on happening, with a greeting when there is an encounter and immediately a leave-taking when the greeting occurs? Is there a fourfold coming and going that can be experienced in the same, virtually eternal harmony of coming together and parting?

This organ is formed in the human heart; for there is a fourfold stream of blood that flows to and from the heart. Like the soul, which in the context of the yearly cycle receives and then again releases this stream and, hence, becomes the heart of the ever-changing seasons, so the physical heart receives into itself the ebb and flow of the blood's tide.

The heart has four chambers. From the left ventricle the heart reaches out into the circulation of the body in the youthful forces of the tenor. There it broadens until it is lost in the infinitude of the many capillaries. From there it is gradually transformed into the steadily flowing baritone forces of the venous blood and returns to the right atrium of the heart.

This is the path leading from Easter week into the heights of St John's Tide and thence through the changes of summer back to autumn.

Between the right atrium and the right ventricle there is a threshold which in the heart takes the form of a triple valve: this is the threshold of Michaelmas, which has to be crossed. From

here the blood streams as the self-overcoming soprano up into the lungs, where it meets the spiritual air of winter. Here in the lungs the transformation occurs: the blood is renewed and streams in the power of the alto back into the left auricle.

This is the path that leads from Michaelmas to Christmas and from there through winter back to the heart. In the left auricle there is again a threshold, that of the double valve; this is the time leading through death to the Resurrection at Easter.

Rudolf Steiner spoke about these mysteries of the cycle of the year within human beings and the world on December 29, 1922, saying the following words:

> The purely external mode of scientific observation does not reach the stage where the investigation can say: in the being of man you must hear sounding together what can only be heard as separate tones in the flow of time. But if you develop spiritual hearing, the tones of summer and winter can be heard ringing simultaneously in man, and they are the same tones that we hear in the outer world when we enter into the flow of time. Time becomes space. The whole surrounding universe also resounds to us in time: expanded widely in space, there ring forth what resounds from our own being as from a centre, gathered as it were in a single point.

And Rudolf Steiner concludes this lecture with these words:

> Living together with the course of cosmic existence becomes [for man] a ritual, and the cosmic ritual comes into being in which man can have his place at every moment of his life. Every earthly ritual is a symbolic image of this cosmic ritual.[14]

Thus every mass or communion service is a fourfold event, because it is a reflection of that cosmic ritual which the human soul learns to celebrate step by step when it endeavours to use the Soul Calendar as a guide.

The Metamorphosis of the Cross

Osterstimmung

Tenor

5.–11. April

1.

Wenn aus den Weltenweiten
Die Sonne spricht zum Menschensinn
Und Freude aus den Seelentiefen
Dem Licht sich eint im Schauen:

Dann ziehen aus der Selbstheit Hülle
Gedanken in die Raumesfernen
Und binden dumpf
Des Menschen Wesen an des Geistes Sein.

A

Michaeli-Woche

Bariton

27. Sept – 3. Oct.

26.

Natur, Dein mütterliches Sein
Ich trage es in meinem Willenswesen.
Und meines Willens Feuerkraft
Sie stählet
meine Geistestriebe
Daß sie gebären
Selbstgefühl
Zu tragen mich in mir.

Z

Sopran

4. Oct – 10. Oct.

27.

In meines Wesens Tiefen dringen
Erregt ein ahnungsvolles Sehnen,
Das ich, mich selbst betrachtend finde,
Als Sommersonnengabe
Die als Keim
In Herbstesstimmung
Wärmend lebt,
Als meiner Seele Kräftetrieb

A

52.

Wenn aus den Seelentiefen
Der Geist sich wendet zu dem Weltensein
Und Schönheit quillt aus Raumesweiten

Dann zieht aus Himmelsfernen
Des Lebens Kraft in Menschenleiber
Und einet, machtvoll wirkend
Des Geistes Wesen mit dem Menschensein.

Z

Karwoche

28. März – 4. April

Alto

2. 12.-18. April

Ins Äußere des Sinnesalls,
Verliert Gedankenmacht ihr Eigensein.

Es finden Geisteswelten
Den Menschensprossen wieder,
Der seinen Keim in ihnen,
Doch seine Seelenfrucht
In sich muss finden.

B

Tenor

Herbst

25. 20.-26. Sept.

Ich darf nun mir gehören
Und leuchtend breiten Innenlicht
In Raumes- u in Zeitenfinsternis.
Zum Schlafe drängt natürlich
Wesen.
Der Seele Tiefen sollen wachen
Und wachend tragen Sonnengluten
In kalte Winterfluten.

Y

Bariton

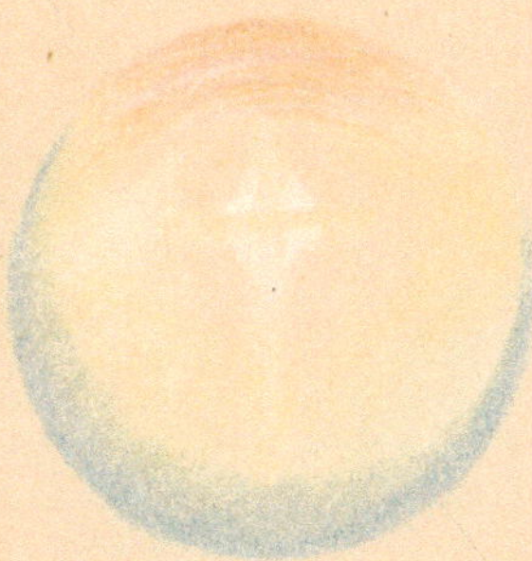

28. 11-17. Oct.

Ich kann im Innern neu belebt
Erfühlen eignen Wesens Weiten.
Und krafterfüllt Gedankenstrah
Aus Seelensonnenmacht
Den Lebensrätseln lösend spenden
Erfüllung manchem Wunsche l
Dem Hoffnung schon
Die Schwingen lähmte.

B

Sopran

51. 21-27. März

Ins Innere des Menschenwesens
Ergießt der Sinne Reichtum sich.

Es findet sich der Weltengeist
Im Spiegelbild des Menschenauges,
Der seine Kraft aus ihm
Sich neu erschaffen muss.

Y

Alto

3. Fastenwoche

Frühling

3. 19. – 25. April

Es spricht zum Weltenall,
Sich selbst vergessend
Und seines Urstands eingedenk
Des Menschen wachend Ich:

In dir, befreiend mich
Aus meiner Eigenheiten Fessel
Ergründe ich mein echtes
Wesen.

C

Tenor

24. 13. – 19. Sept.

Sich selbst erschaffend stets
d Seelensein sich selbst gewahr.
er Weltengeist er strebet fort
In Selbsterkenntnis
neu belebt.
nd schafft aus Seelenfinsternis
Des Selbstsinns
Willensfrucht.

X

Bariton

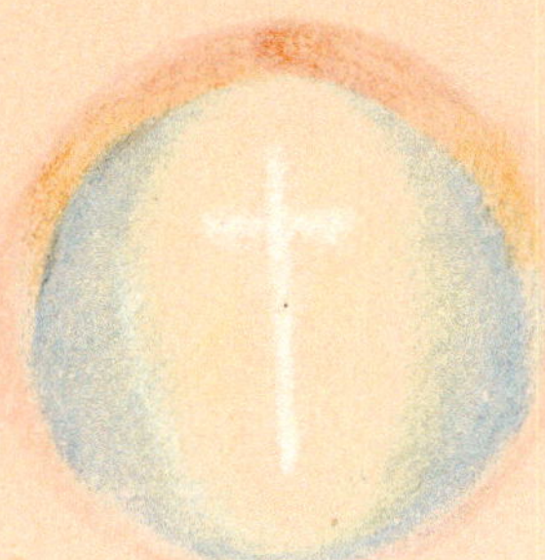

29. 18.–24. Oct.

Sich selbst des Denkens Leuchten
Im Innern kraftvoll zu entfachen,
Erlebtes sinnvoll deutend
Aus Weltengeistes Kräftequell
Ist mir nun
Sommererbe.
Ist Herbstesruhe
Und auch Winterhoffnung.

C

Sopran

50. 14. – 20. März

Es spricht zum Menschen-Ich
Sich machtvoll offenbarend
Und seines Wesens Kräfte lösend
Des Weltendaseins Werdelust:

In dich mein Leben tragend
Aus seinem Zauberbanne
Erreiche ich mein
wahres Ziel.

X

Alto

2. Fastenwoche

4. 20. April – 2. Mai

Ich fühle Wesen meines Wesens
so spricht Empfindung
Die in der sonnerhellten Welt
Mit Lichtesfluten sich vereint.

Sie will dem Denken
Zur Klarheit Wärme schenken
Und Mensch & Welt
In Einheit fest verbinden.

D

Tenor

23. 6. – 12. Sept.

Es dämpfet herbstlich sich
Der Sinne Reizesstreben.
In Lichtes Offenbarung mischen
Der Nebel dumpfe Schleier sich.
Ich selber schau in Raumesweiten
Des Herbstes Winterschlaf.
Der Sommer hat an mich
Sich selber hingegeben.

W

Bariton

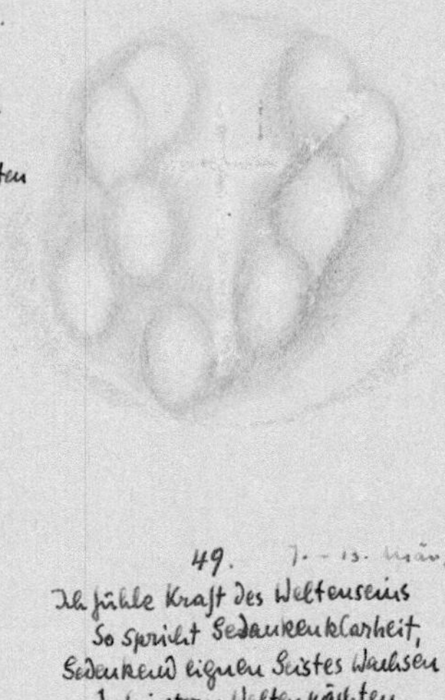

30. 25. – 31. Oct.

Es sprießen mir im Seelensonnenlicht
Des Denkens reife Früchte.
In Selbstbewußtseins Sicherheit
Verwandelt alles Fühlen sich.
Empfinden kann ich freudevoll
Des Herbstes Geisterwachen.
Der Winter wird in mir
Den Seelensommer wecken.

D

Sopran

49. 7. – 13. März

Ich fühle Kraft des Weltenseins
So spricht Gedankenklarheit,
Gedenkend eignen Geistes Wachsen
In finstern Weltennächten.

Und neigt dem nahen Weltentage
Des Innern Hoffnungsstrahlen.

W

Alto

1. Fastenwoche

5. 3. – 9. Mai

Im Lichte das aus Geistestiefen
Im Raume fruchtbar webend
Der Götter Schaffen offenbart:
In ihm erscheint der Seele
Wesen
Geweitet zu dem Weltensein
Und auferstanden
Aus enger Selbstheit Innenmacht.

E

Tenor

22. 30. Aug. – 5. Sept.

Das Licht aus Weltenweiten
Im Innern lebt es kräftig fort.
Es wird zum Seelenlichte
Und leuchtet in die Geistestiefen
Um Früchte zu entbinden
…e Menschenselbst aus Weltenselbst
Im Zeitenlaufe
reifen lassen.

V

Bariton

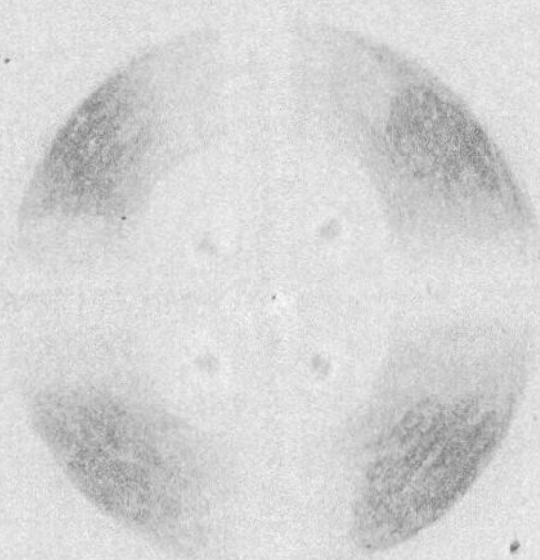

31. 1. – 7. Nov.

Das Licht aus Geistestiefen
Nach außen strebt es sonnenhaft.
Es wird zur Lebenswillenskraft
Und leuchtet in der Sinne Dumpfheit
Um Kräfte zu entbinden
Die Schaffensmächte aus Seelentrieben
Im Menschenwerke
reifen lassen.

E

Sopran

48 28. Feb. – 6. März

Im Lichte das aus Weltenhöhen
Der Seele machtvoll fließen will,
Erscheine,
lösend Seelenrätsel,
Des Weltendenkens Sicherheit,
Versammelnd seiner Strahlen Macht,
Im Menschenherzen
Liebe weckend.

V

Alto

Himmelfahrt-Woche

6. 10. – 16. Mai

Es ist erstanden aus der Eigenheit
Mein Selbst findet sich
Als Weltenoffenbarung
In Zeit- u Raumeskräften.

Die Welt sie zeigt mir überall
Als göttlich Urbild
Des eignen Abbilds Wahrheit.

F

Tenor

21. 23. – 29. Aug.

Ich fühle fruchtend fremde Macht
Sich stärkend mir mich selbst verleihen.
Den Keim empfind ich reifend
Und Ahnung lichtvoll weben
Im Innern an der Selbstheit Macht.

U

Bariton

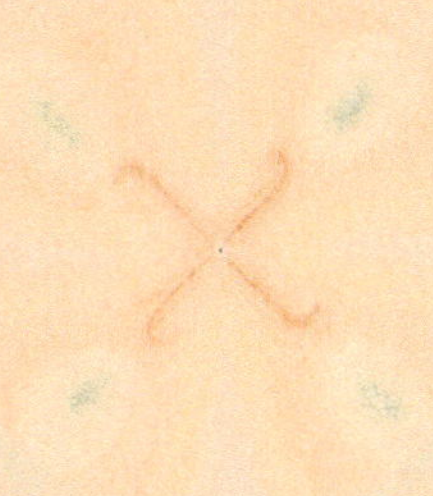

32. 8. – 14. Nov.

Ich fühle fruchtend eigne Kraft
Sich stärkend mich der Welt verleihn
Mein Eigenwesen fühl ich kräftend
Zur Klarheit sich zu wenden
Im Lebensschicksalsweben.

F

Sopran

47. 21. – 27. Feb.

Es will erstehen aus dem Weltenschoße
Den Sinnenschein erquickend Werdelust.
Sie finde meines Denkens Kraft
Gerüstet durch die Gotteskräfte
Die kräftig mir im Innern leben.

U

Alto

7. 17. – 23. Mai

Mein Selbst es drohet zu entfliehen,
Vom Weltenlichte mächtig angezogen.
Nun trete du mein Ahnen
In deine Rechte kräftig ein,
Ersetze mir des Denkens Macht,
Das in der Sinne Schein
Sich selbst verlieren will.

G

Tenor

20. 16. – 22. Aug.

So fühl ich erst mein Sein
Das fern vom Welten-Dasein
In sich, sich selbst erlöschen,
Und bauend nur auf eignem Grunde
In sich,
Sich selbst ertöten müßte.

T

Bariton

33. 15. – 21. Nov.

So fühl ich erst die Welt,
Die außer meiner Seele Miterleben
An sich nur frostig leeres Leben,
Und ohne Macht sich offenbarend,
In Seelen sich von neuem schaffend,
In sich
Den Tod nur finden könnte.

G

Sopran

46. 14. – 20. Feb

Die Welt, sie drohet zu betäuben,
Der Seele eingeborne Kraft.
Nun trete du, Erinnerung,
Aus Geistestiefen leuchtend auf
Und stärke mir das Schauen,
Das nur durch Willenskräfte
Sich selbst erhalten kann.

T

Alto

Carnevale

Pfingsten

8   24.–30. Mai

Es wächst der Sinne Macht
Im Bunde mit der Götter Schaffen.
Sie drückt des Denkens Kraft
Zur Traumes Dumpfheit mir herab.
Wenn göttlich Wesen
Sich meiner Seele einen will
Muß menschlich Denken
Im Traumessein sich still bescheiden.

H

Tenor

19.   9.–15. Aug.

Geheimnisvoll das Neu-Empfang'ne
Mit der Erinn'rung zu umschließen
Sei meines Strebens weitrer Sinn.
Es soll erstarkend Eigenkräfte
In meinem Innern wecken
Und werdend mir mich selber
geben.

St

Bariton

34.   22.–28. Nov.

Geheimnisvolle das Alt-Bewahrte
Mit neu erstandnem Eigensein
Im Innern sich belebend fühlen:
Es soll erweckend Weltenkräfte
In meines Lebens Außenwerk ergießen
Und werdend mich
Ins Dasein prägen.

H

Sopran

45.   7.–13. Feb.

Es festigt sich Gedankenmacht
Im Bunde mit der Geistgeburt.
Sie hellt der Sinne dumpfe Reize
Zur vollen Klarheit auf.
Wenn Seelenfülle
Sich mit dem Weltenwerden einen will
Muß Sinnesoffenbarung
Des Denkens Licht empfangen.

St

Alto

9. 31. Mai – 6. Juni

Vergessend meine Willenseigenheit
Erfüllet Weltenwärme sommerkündend
Mir Geist s Seelenwesen.
Im Licht mich zu verlieren
Gebietet mir das Geistesschauen
Und kraftvoll kündet Ahnung mir
Verliere Dich
Um Dich zufinden.

i

Tenor

18. 2. – 8. Aug.

Kann ich die Seele weiten,
Daß sie sich selbst verbindet
Empfang'nem Welten-Keimesworte?
Ich ahne, daß ich Kraft muß finden
Die Seele würdig zu gestalten
Zum Geisteskleide sich zu bilden.

S

Bariton

1. Advent-Sonntag

35. 27. Nov. – 5. De

Kann ich das Sein erkennen,
Daß es sich wiederfindet
Im Seelenschaffensdrange?
Ich fühle, daß mir Kraft verliehen
Das eigne Selbst
Dem Weltenselbst
Als Glied bescheiden einzuleben.

i

Sopran

Lichtmess

31. Jan. – 6. Feb.

44.

Ergreifend neue Sinnesreize
Erfüllet Seelenklarheit
Eingedenk vollzogner Geistgeburt
Verwirrend sprossend Weltenwerden
Mit meines Denkens
Schöpferwillen.

S

Alto

10. 7. - 13. Juni

Zu sommerlichen Höhen
Erhebt der Sonne leuchtend Wesen sich.
Es nimmt mein menschlich Fühlen
In seine Raumesweiten mit.
Erahnend regt im Innern sich
Empfindung dumpf mir kündend
Erkennen wirst du einst
Dich fühlte jetzt ein
Gotteswesen.

K

Tenor

2. Advent-Sonntag

17. 26. Juli - 1. Aug

Es spricht das Weltenwort
Das ich durch Sinnestore
In Seelengründe durfte führen:
Erfülle deine Geistestiefen
Mit meinen Weltenweiten
Zu finden einstens
mich in dir.

R

Bariton

36. 13. - 19. Dez.

In meines Wesens Tiefen spricht
Zur Offenbarung drängend
Geheimnisvoll das Weltenwort:
Erfülle deiner Arbeit Ziele
Mit meinem Geisteslichte
Zu opfern
Dich durch mich.

K

Sopran

Damaskus-Tag

43. 24. - 30. Jan.

In winterlichen Tiefen
Erwarmt des Geistes wahres Sein
Es gibt dem Weltenscheine
Durch Herzenskräfte Daseinsmächte.
Der Weltenkälte trotzt erstarkend
Das Seelenfeuer im Menscheninnern.

R

Alto

11. 14.–20. Juni

Es ist in dieser Sonnenstunde
An dir
Die weise Kunde zu erkennen:
An Weltenschönheit hingegeben
In dir dich fühlend zu durchleben
Verlieren kann das Menschen-Ich
Und finden sich im Welten-Ich.

L

Tenor

3. Adventsonntag

16. 19.–25. Juli

Zu bergen Geistgeschenk
Im Innern,
ebietet strenge mir mein Ahnen.
Daß reifend Gottesgaben
In Seelengründen fruchtend
Der Selbstheit
Früchte bringen.

Q

Bariton

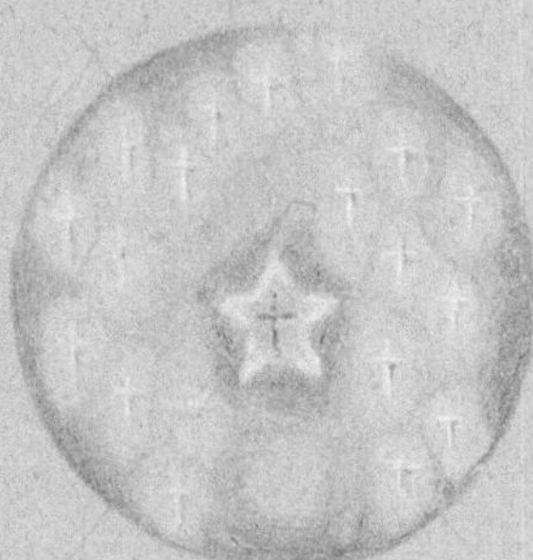

37. 13.–19. Dez.

Zu tragen Geisteslicht
In Weltenwinternacht
Erstrebet selig meines Herzens Trieb.
Daß leuchtend Seelenkeime
In Weltengründen wurzeln
Und Gotteswort im Sinnesdunkel
Verklärend alles Sein durchtönt.

L

Sopran

42. 17.–23. Jan.

Es ist in diesem Winterdunkel
Die Offenbarung eigner Kraft,
Der Seele starker Trieb,
In Finsternisse sich zu lenken
Und ahnend vorzufühlen
Durch Herzenswärme, Sinnesoffenbarung.

Q

Alto

Johanni-Woche

12. 21.-27. Juni

Der Welten Schönheitsglanz
Er zwinget mich aus Seelentiefen
Des Eigenlebens Götterkräfte
Zum Weltenfluge zu entbinden.
Mich selber zu verlassen,
Vertrauend nur mich suchend
In
Weltenlicht
&
Weltenwärme.

M

Tenor

4. Advent-Sonntag

15. 12.-18. Juli

Ich fühle wie verzaubert
Im Weltenschein des Geistes Weben.
Es hat in Sinnesdumpfheit
Gehüllt mein Eigenwesen,
Zu schenken mir die Kraft
Die ohnmächtig sich selbst zu geben
Mein Ich
In seinen Schranken ist.

P

Bariton

38. 20.-26. Dec.

Ich fühle wie entzaubert
Das Geisteskind im Seelenschoß.
Es hat in Herzenshelligkeit
Gezeugt das heil'ge Weltenwort
Der Hoffnung Himmelsfrucht,
Die jubelnd wächst in Weltenfernen
Aus meines Wesens
Gottesgrund.

M

Sopran

41. 10.-16. Jan.

Der Seele Schaffensmacht
Sie strebet aus dem Herzensgrunde
Im Menschenleben Götterkräfte
Zu rechtem Wirken zu entflammen.
Sich selber zu gestalten
In
Menschenliebe
und
Menschenwerke.

P

Alto

Sommer

(Schwellen-Erlebnis)

13. 28. Juni – 4. Juli

Und bin ich in den Sinneshöhen,
So flammt in meinen Seelentiefen
Aus Geistes Feuerwelten
Der Götter Wahrheitswort:
In Geistesgründen suche ahnend
Dich geistverwandt zu finden.

N

Tenor

Winter

(Ich-Geburt-Schwelle)

(Erwachen)

14. 5. – 11. Juli

… Sinnesoffenbarung hingegeben
…or ich Eigenwesens Trieb.
Gedankentraum erschien
…äubend mir das Selbst zu rauben,
Doch weckend nahet schon
Im
Sinnenschein
mir
Weltendenken.

O

Bariton

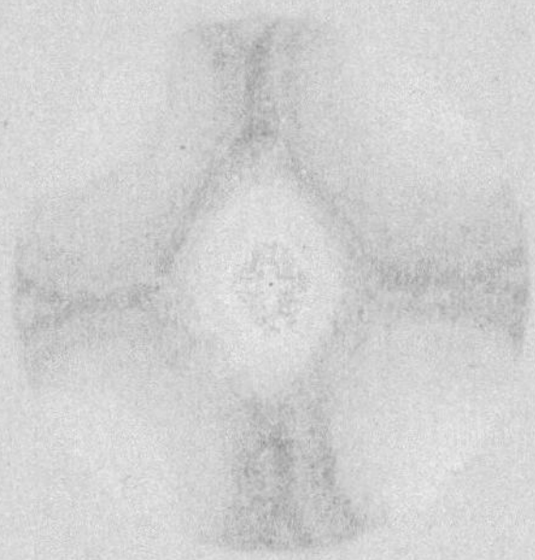

39. 27. Dec. – 2. Jan.

An Geistesoffenbarung hingegeben
Gewinne ich des Weltenwesens Licht.
Gedankenkraft sie wächst,
Sich klärend mir mich selbst zu geben
Und weckend löst sich mir
Aus
Denkermacht
das
Selbstgefühl.

N

Sopran

Epiphanie

40. 3. – 4. Jan.

Und bin ich in den Geistestiefen,
Erfüllt in meinen Seelengründen
Aus Herzens Liebewelten
Der Eigenheiten leerer Wahn
Sich mit des Weltenwortes Feuerkraft.

O

Alto

Essays on the Calendar of the Soul

The Word 'Boding' *(Ahnung)*

In his translation of the *Calendar of the Soul,* for the German word *Ahnung* A.C. Harwood used the word 'boding' or 'foreboding' in the original neutral sense by which we still say 'it bodes well' or 'it bodes ill.'

'Boding' is a strange word. It expresses an elusive feeling, which in certain — and usually rather special — moments of life, touches our daytime consciousness. This feeling is sometimes so powerful that it condenses into a mood in which anxiety and fear may be mixed. It is then a boding of an approaching ill, the boding of a coming sickness and much else.

But a foreboding may also flit quickly by, overpowered by the daily rush of thoughts and impressions, and reappear in the soul only when that which was foreseen has happened. What is this 'boding' in the realm of the soul? Is it feeling, will, mental image? Is it an emotion like anger or fear?

Boding is also an awareness of conditions and circumstances that are not clearly apprehended. As well as misleading, mood-dependent self-deceptions, there are bodings which bring intuitively-sensed objective realities into consciousness. One may also have a boding of the solution of a task or a problem, and yet still not reach the answer.

Thus the awareness of boding belongs in a region of our experience which may be characterized as a kind of pre-consciousness. Boding is not an unconscious experience, yet it is not conscious either, nor is it similar to dreaming. It is a condition which indicates to us something which is present, but which we cannot yet apprehend with clear consciousness. It is an activity which indicates to the soul something that nevertheless remains hidden from it.

In the verses of the Calendar of the Soul, the word 'boding' and the words connected with it are used in a number of places. They appear nine times in the fifty-two verses: seven times in the period between Easter and Michaelmas, but only twice during the other half of the year. This difference is most significant, since the time of year when the sun is increasing in strength is the season when the soul, because it can be overwhelmed by the excess of growth activity in nature, all too easily loses its self-consciousness. In this way, the clear day-time consciousness can easily be damped down, and boding can appear.

Thus verse 7, in which the word 'boding' appears for the first time, begins by pointing to this danger:

> My self threatens to break away
> Through strong enticement of the light of worlds.

There follows immediately a plea:

> Now rise, my boding power,
> Assume in strength your rightful throne,
> Replace in me the might of thinking
> Which in the senses' show
> Is like to lose itself.

This verse belongs to the Whitsun season of the month of May. The world is in full blossom. The fresh green of spring is embroidered with the brilliant colours of flowers; perfumes are wafted through the air, and the eye is overwhelmed by the beauties of the world. Thinking loses itself 'in the senses' show,' and consciousness becomes dim and dreamy. Now another soul-faculty — boding — is summoned to replace thinking. Boding is urged to assume in strength its rightful throne. It thus becomes a positive faculty, which can be active in the soul in place of thinking. When thinking begins to falter, boding is summoned to replace it.

Two weeks later, in the period after Whitsun, the soul is still more closely united with nature. The outer warmth has

penetrated into the soul and taken hold of the human will. Verse 9 says:

> Forgetting all my separateness of will,
> The warmth of worlds, the summer's harbinger,
> I feel it flood my spirit and my soul.

Then, when the soul has been bid lose itself in the light, there follows:

> And powerfully prophetic boding cries:
> 'Lose, lose your self, yourself to find.'

Boding has established itself as a guiding power in the soul, and it now proclaims to the human self the secret of 'dying and becoming.' This is a secret to which thinking can point, but whose real significance is accessible only to boding.

These two verses, which are so closely connected with the Whitsun experience, indicate the true task of boding. It is a special faculty of the soul, which can be substituted for thinking. These powers enable judgments to be made, and bring insight. Indeed, they bring higher insights than thinking can. For 'dying and becoming' is one of the primal secrets of human life here on earth.

'Boding' appears again in the next verse, the tenth; the sun has become more powerful and has carried human feeling with it into the wide realms of light. The word now characterizes a feeling which strives to convey to the soul an awareness of a mighty event:

> 10. While inwardly a feeling stirs
> In dim prophetic boding:
> 'Hereafter you shall know —
> A god, a god has touched you now.'

An event is to be grasped through boding which later in the year, when the thinking-power has returned, can be consciously apprehended. The Divinity has taken the human soul to its

breast; the self rests in the arms of God, and feels his breath. Boding it must feel and experience what can only later become knowledge. Thus in this feeling, woven through with boding, the soul experiences a kind of understanding which will only gradually transform itself into comprehension.

But the power of boding has not only the ability to replace thinking; it can also penetrate the feelings, so that they convey to the soul the awareness that 'A god, a god has touched you now.' Subsequently, when St John's Tide is past and the self is spread out and expanded in the fiery breath of summer, in verse 13 the voice of that divine being speaks, which has taken us up to its breast:

> Seek through your boding power
> And find in spirit ground
> Your spirit brotherhood.

Boding is now not merely a cloud which expands the feelings. It becomes a lamp which illumines the path before the questing self into spiritual depths, and strives to proclaim a further secret to it: 'Thou art spirit! Know thyself as a spirit in spirit-depths.' At this point we have reached the summit of the year. The process of 'dying and becoming' is complete; the marriage between nature and the soul has occurred, and the self sets forth to return to the earth. It bears with it the gifts it has received. But it must learn to understand how to care for these properly. Therefore verse 16 says:

> Sternly my boding heart demands:
> 'Cherish within the spirit's dower,
> So shall the gifts of God grow ripe
> In the soul's soil maturing,
> And selfhood reap their fruits.'

The soul must not immediately squander the gold of the heavenly wisdom like the Will o' the Wisps, but rather, like the Green Snake, guard and nurture it inwardly, until it shines

quietly. 'Sternly my boding heart demands' that this be done. Here, boding becomes a gesture. It adjures the soul to remember most earnestly the command, 'Guard and keep what has been given to thee.'

The soul grasps this challenge. It begins to recognize what it means to be allowed to bear these divine gifts; it says in verse 18:

> I do forebode I strength must find
> To found and form my soul
> A garment worthy of the spirit.

Boding's gesture is bravely taken up, and with the approach of autumn, man speaks for the first time, 'I do forebode.' Previously, boding was given to him. But now he has made it his own, has united himself with a part of its being, and has himself begun to *be* it. He can now say, 'I do forebode.'

Before the light of summer passes and becomes light of the soul towards the end of August when the corn is ripe and the fruits are swelling, boding completes the path it began to tread as support for the soul at Whitsun.

It has returned with the soul to earth; the soul has grasped a part of it, but it lives as a blessed grace within the soul, where the divine gifts are to ripen. Verse 21 says:

> I sense the germ maturing,
> The while my boding weaves a web of light
> Within me for my selfhood's power.

The germ of selfhood is enfolded in the light-filled veils of boding, so that it may grow ripe, to appear at Christmas as the spirit child 'in the soul's womb.' We now see revealed the seven stages of boding's progress from Whitsun to the approach of autumn:

1. It appears first, rightly by replacing thinking (verse 7).
2. Filling the soul, it proclaims to the self the law of 'dying and becoming' (verse 9).

3. It prepares the feeling-life for the experience of the Divinity (verse 10).
4. It illumines the path into the spiritual depths for the questing self (verse 13).
5. It accompanies the soul back to the earth, and warns it to cherish the gift of the gods (verse 16).
6. The self takes hold of boding, speaking, 'I do forebode' (verse 18).
7. Now boding can surround the growing self with light (verse 21).

Like a loving guide or a wise companion, boding has joined forces with the soul and accompanied it during its journey through the summer season. The path led from Whitsun to Michaelmas. The human self passes across the bridge of light and beauty, of devotion and self-surrender. Boding accompanied it, as friend and guide, as the archangel Raphael once accompanied the young Tobias.

During the first week of autumn, immediately after Michaelmas, the soul begins its journey inwards. Like Persephone, it descends into the Hades of its own depths, and this striving awakens a new feeling:

27. To dive into my being's depths
Stirs up a yearning in me, boding well.

The longing filled with the power of boding to find oneself 'as gift of summer sun,' has begun to work as a germinating seed within the soul. It is like a final sunset glow of that boding which was the companion and guide of the soul. It now manifests as a longing, which endeavours to prepare the way for the I to its higher self.

Then, for many weeks, the Soul Calendar does not speak of boding. The path of thinking and understanding is followed leading in the Holy Nights, to the birth of the self:

39. And in me, from the thinker's power,
    Leaps into wakefulness the sense of self.

Verse 39 belongs to the turn of the year. Not until the end of January is boding mentioned again, when the first signs of the approaching awakening of nature are hesitatingly suggested, when the world is still frozen, yet within the soul the first delicate hints appear of the coming revelation in the sense world:

42. In this dark wintertide
    To manifest her proper force
    Shall be the soul's imperious urge;
    Herself to haunts of darkness guiding
    To feel in new forebodement
    Through warmth of heart the senses' revelation.

In this verse, the germ of what will replace thinking at Whitsuntide begins to grow once more, in the realm of the heart's warmth. It senses the approach of the increasing powers of the sun. For now, although it is cold, the days begin to lengthen, and the growing light awakens the power of boding which is to become the soul's support in the weeks of summertime.

Just as the sunset glow of boding can be contemplated in verse 27, so in verse 42 the dawn of boding is heralded. In between lies the night of winter, which for the soul became bright spirit day.

2

It is one of the marvels of the Calendar of the Soul that in every verse each word is exactly in place, in accordance with its meaning and significance. Each word is so formed that it literally incorporates the process which it describes. The new word-creations which appear there are necessary because precision demands them.

The word *Ahnung* (boding) has a Central European origin. It appears as a verb in Middle High German in the form *anen* before the end of the twelfth century,

> ... and it spread widely, without being common, as is still in general the case ... A magical-religious origin is probable, though unproven, since the first traces of it already convey the present meaning, 'to have a dark premonition.' The personal form *ich ahne,* (I forebode) did not appear before 1350; reflecting the new view of the world, men now carried the premonition within themselves.[1]

This reference to the history of the word *Ahnung* is of great significance. It shows that the expression arose in the late Middle Ages, and had the same meaning as today. The genius of language gave birth to this word at the same moment that the last traces of clairvoyant faculties left the human soul. In the lectures *Occult History,* Rudolf Steiner gave a full account of this significant period of human evolution. He showed that the year 1250 has a unique historical significance, because it stood in a polar relation to the Atlantean flood. During the Atlantean catastrophe, in the eighth and seventh millenia before the Mystery of Golgotha, the Spirits of Form worked into the kingdoms of nature, and the face of the earth underwent mighty changes. During the thirteenth century, in contrast, changes were wrought on the human spirit: not nature, but the soul underwent a profound transformation. Rudolf Steiner said:

> This year 1250 is indeed a significant and historic year. It falls in a period which may be characterized as follows: The men of the time felt impelled to express in precise terms how man looks up to the divine beings standing above the other hierarchies; how he attempts to form some relationship with them; how they are experienced, to begin with, as a unity, first through Yahweh,

> then through Christ; and how the aim of all human knowledge is to unveil the Mystery of Jesus Christ ... Thus we see that this year is the starting point of a great effort to work out in a precise form what had previously only been believed and divined in foreboding: the starting point of scholasticism. But it was also the starting point of those revelations which manifested through Agrippa of Nettesheim, for example, and which found their profoundest expression in the whole of Rosicrucianism.[2]

This new revelation came to human souls from which the last traces of atavistic clairvoyance had been lost. On another occasion, Rudolf Steiner said about this time:

> The significance of the year 1250 for the spiritual evolution of humanity is revealed with special emphasis in the light of the following fact derived from clairvoyant research: Even individuals who had achieved high levels of spiritual development in previous incarnations, if they were born again around AD 1250, were compelled to experience a complete darkening of their perception of the spiritual worlds for a period of time. Individuals spiritually enlightened to a high degree were as though cut off from the spiritual world and could only know something of it through memories of earlier incarnations. It is thus apparent that from then on, it was necessary for a new element to enter the spiritual guidance of mankind. This element was the true modern esoteric path.[3]

It is at this moment of history, when the old clairvoyance is transformed into a new spiritual knowledge, that the little word *anen* appears. It is similar to the event Rudolf Steiner describes when, in the brief interval between Aeschylus and Euripides, the Greek word for 'conscience,' *synoida,* was first uttered.[4]

At that time, conscience was born in the human soul. In place of the pursuing Furies, there appeared for the first time

the warning voice within. Towards the end of the fifth century BC, the birth of conscience began. Sixteen hundred years later, a new province of the soul is opened to human experience: *Ahnung* (boding) appears.

The Latin words *divinare* and *praesagire* denote a different experience. The Augurs looked ahead and pronounced on the future, but did so out of states which they owed to a sibylline clairvoyance. But towards the end of the Middle Ages, *Ahnen* emerged, not out of a somnambulistic state, but in wide-awake daytime consciousness, and began to direct human awareness to a higher source of guidance.

Conscience appeared first in the evolution of the human soul, to replace the goddesses of revenge. Later, boding was born, which directs attention to the guidance of destiny. Even when the soul is cut off from all spiritual perception, and finds itself isolated and lonely in the world, conscience speaks within as warning, and the dawning light of karma works within as boding. Then, at the beginning of the fifteenth century, which ushers in the consciousness soul age, the human soul says: 'I do forebode.' With this, a new Christian experience is born in the soul, teaching it the secret of 'dying and becoming.'

Who is it that the soul experiences in the power of boding? Or who is it whose being is sensed when it approaches the boding soul? Is it destiny itself, or the higher self, which leads the soul from one life to the next?

Rudolf Steiner once described the connection of that higher being, the angel of the human individual, with the human soul:

> When we consider modern man, we must recognize that his astral body consists in fact of two parts: That which he has already transformed and is now ruled by his I, and that which his I cannot yet control. This second part is still filled with lower forces, it must still be imbued with, and penetrated by higher beings ... these beings ... are the angels, the Spirits of Twilight.[5]

It is into this realm of the angels that the soul gazes when it forebodes, and, boding, is directed to forthcoming events. The Spirit of Twilight is that guiding helper and helping guide, who leads the soul from incarnation to incarnation until it has achieved complete sovereignty of its astral body.

On the same occasion, Rudolf Steiner added:

> Whether one says that man gazes upwards to his higher self, which he must come to resemble ever more closely, or alternatively that he looks up to his angel as to a high ideal, is from a spiritual point of view exactly the same.

Thus boding is a becoming-conscious-of, a looking-up-to, one's own angel. It is like a perception of one's own higher self, which guides and leads us. At one time, the Germanic peoples could still perceive how the angelic and archangelic beings worked into the human soul. Rudolf Steiner said:

> The ancient gods, who were active before these beings took hold of the human soul ... the divine beings, who were active in the very distant past, in ancient Atlantis, were called the *Wanen*. Mankind then moved on from the Atlantean age and beheld the weaving of the angels and archangels, who were called the *Asen*. They were beings who as angels and archangels concerned themselves with the human I, which now awoke to the first, lowest stage of its development.[6]

Later, like the *Wanen* earlier, the *Asen* become invisible to human consciousness, and knowledge based on sense perception obscured spiritual vision. Then *anen* arose in the human soul. The path of divining opened up, which leads to the guiding spirit of the human individual.

Thus the realm of boding appears again and again in the Calendar of the Soul. It transmits to the soul the experience of the spiritual guidance, and helps the soul to encounter, during the season of increasing light, the divine beings to which

it owes its self. These are the beings described in *An Outline of Occult Science* as Exousiai, the Spirits of Form. It is the angels who lead us into the realms of these Spirits of Form. It was the Exousiai who in AD 1250 gave human beings the mighty inspiration which has already been described. At this time, the word *anen* arose.

If the relevant verses of the Soul Calendar are now considered again, this insight can help us towards real understanding.

In verse 7, boding enters, replacing thinking, and assumes 'in strength its rightful throne.' Here, at Whitsuntide, the self lifts up its gaze to its own angel, to the Spirit of Twilight.

In verse 9, this spirit (the power of boding) proclaims to the lower self the secret of its existence: 'Lose, lose yourself, yourself to find.'

Verse 10 indicates to the soul a still higher truth. The angel warns: 'Hereafter you shall know, / A god, a god has touched you now.'

In verse 13, the angel goes before the ego-being, so that it may apprehend itself as a spirit in the realm of the spirit.

Returning earthwards, the angel warns the soul to cherish within it the spiritual gift it has received from the divine Word. This occurs in verse 16.

Two weeks later, there appears the statement, 'I do forebode.'

18. I do forebode I strength must find
To found and form my soul
A garment worthy of the spirit.

The self now grasps its exalted task; it embarks on the path which leads through trials and tribulations, and will eventually enable it to become an angelic being.

Finally, a few weeks before Michaelmas, in verse 21, the angel, 'weaving in light,' enfolds the germ of the growing self. With this, the guide has completed his task of renewal of the I for the present year, which has been achieved in seven steps.

Thus what we feel as divining is revealed as our experience

of the angels. It is not a vague feeling, but an experience of the breath of that higher being which leads our earthly self through births and deaths. This experience begins at Whitsuntide, and intensifies until the climax of summer, when the earthly self and the angels, intimately united at the divine breast, listen to the cosmic word. This renews and enlivens the human self, and strengthens it for the autumn and winter period. Thus the cycle of the seasons becomes a sacred ritual, with St John's Tide a communion at the world-altar, to which angelic divining, foreboding, leads the human soul.

In a lecture on the spirituality of language, Rudolf Steiner said that the voice of conscience which sounds in our soul arises because it is renewed each night from out of the realm of the Exousiai and the Kyriotetes.[7]

But this occurs only when the soul can encounter the archangels through the spirituality of language. If language dries up and loses its spirituality, the meeting and contact with the realm of the archangels during sleep does not occur.

> They [Exousiai and Kyriotetes] must bring that which we, united with the archangels, have previously achieved through the spirituality of language, into the instincts and desires of the physical body, which otherwise resists us: There it flames up as the voice of conscience.

Just as the human spirit, through the meeting of the soul with the archangels, is impressed with the voice of conscience each night out of the realm of the Exousiai and Kyriotetes, so do the angelic beings lead the earthly human self in summertime up into the same spiritual region. There, enfolded by its angel, the self may hear the universal word, and carry its enlivening forces back into earthly life. This brings about the experience of boding within the self, and sustains its connection with its angel, its higher self.

Conscience and boding are the two experiences of the soul

which can become a gateway and a window into the land of spiritual existence. Through the gateway of conscience, human beings hear the voice of warning; through the window of boding, they behold their higher being.

The Winter and Christmas Verses

In the essay on the word 'boding' an attempt was made to demonstrate how closely the meaning of a single word depends on its appearance at various seasons of the year and how the passage of such a word through the 52 verses can help towards understanding of the interdependence of nature and soul. The structure of the Calendar is extraordinarily artistic and is developed with spiritual precision.

Many other words disclose similar open secrets — forgetting and remembering, seeking and finding, attaining and preserving, beauty, and light and darkness of soul. A whole group of words might be enumerated which reflect some particular thread of meaning woven into the manifold and infinitely beautiful pattern of the Calendar.

One particular word, found in the verses for winter and Christmas, will now be considered. The significant thing about it is that it is not found in the verses for spring, summer and autumn, but only in those for winter. The word denotes something active throughout the whole of every year of our life; yet Rudolf Steiner found it suitable for use only in the verses for Christmas and winter: it is the little but comprehensive word, 'heart.'

It is not to be found anywhere between Easter and early winter, only appearing for the first time in the verse for the third Sunday in Advent:

> 37. With joy to carry spirit light
> Into the winter night of worlds —
> For this my striving heart is fain

Then the word appears in verse after verse with the most varied shades of meaning and context. It occurs seven times in all,

each time revealing a new aspect of its being and an unexpected picture of its activity and its life.

In the verse for Christmas we hear the sacred music of its inmost being, a sort of *Gloria in Excelsis:*

38. I feel the spell dissevered
In the soul's womb freeing the spirit child:
The holy word of worlds
Has in the heart's clear light
Begotten heaven's own fruit of hope,
Which, rising from the god in me,
Goes paeaning to the corners of the world.

It does not appear in the next verse, where another word takes its place. It occurs again, however, in verse 40:

Am I then in the spirit's depths —
So in the roots of soul profound
From out the heart's wide worlds of love
Illusion vain of selfhood fills itself
With powers of fire from the word of worlds.

The next verse also includes the word, displaying a new insight into its comprehensive reality:

41. The soul's creative power
Strives from the heart's deep ground:
'Kindle your godlike gifts
For rightful work in human life,
Fashion the self
In human love and human deeds.'

Closely linked is the following verse, which takes us well into the first month of the new year:

42. In this dark wintertide
To manifest her proper force
Shall be the soul's imperious urge;

Herself to haunts of darkness guiding
To feel in new forebodement
Through warmth of heart the senses' revelation.

Then comes the last verse for January, which may be regarded as an expression of what has since antiquity been associated with the day of Paul's conversion at Damascus, January 25. In its lines we find the inner strength and constancy of the heart's impulse:

43. Sunk in its wintry depths
True spirit-being quickens into warmth.
Through the heart's force it gives
To the world's show and seeming
The mighty gift of being,
And strengthens, maugre worlds of cold,
In human inwardness the fire of soul.

In February a new phase of the earth's course begins. The period of winter's introversion is passing and the outer world begins to reveal itself again to the senses. In verse 44 we have 'Grasping new spurs of sense,' but in this and the following verse there is no mention of the heart. The world makes its way into the soul and prepares for Easter. Then, shortly before Passion-tide, in the week covering the end of February and the beginning of March, the word, 'heart,' resounds once more. This is one of the four verses in the course of the year (5, 22, 31 and 48), which are closely connected with the 'light of the world,' and in it the word heart appears for the seventh and last time:

48. In light, that wills from heights of worlds
To stream amain into my soul,
May sureness of world thinking
Shine out, to solve the riddles of the soul,
Massing the power of its rays
And waking love within the hearts of men.

This seventh mention of the word 'heart' is like an echo. The soul in spring and summer turns to experiencing the world; it moves outward through the gate of the senses and begins to concern itself with creation's coming into being, ripening and fading away.

Only just before Christmas does the heart's inner quality become so powerful that it can once again give expression to this inwardness.

Of the 52 verses of the Calendar, then, these are the seven in which the word heart occurs — all between verses 37 and 48. Here is a common sign, to be seen in the winter and Christmas verses.

2

Following step by step the path along which the heart and its qualities are described, we find opening before us a prospect of the organ of the heart in its inner formation and its wide significance for us.

The first step is the waking endeavour of the heart's urge to carry spirit-light into the night of winter being. Here the heart is quite specifically described as 'mine' — 'my striving heart is fain' (verse 37). A feeling of joy streams through the soul as it approaches the threshold of the twelve Holy Nights.

Then follows the actual Christmas verse: from the newly experienced joy 'the heart's clear light' shines forth. A radiant light of the heart surrounds the birth of the 'spirit's child.' A cry of joy rings out, and in the glory of the light the word of worlds is born. Christmas is fully come; the period of the twelve Holy Nights begins.

After this there is a gap in the process of the heart's transformation. Verse 39 does not mention it: the soul is surrendered to the spirit's revelation and experiences the 'light of universal life.' What has happened is that the radiance of the heart's clear light has become an eye, by which the light of the world can be perceived.

But the heart is more than an eye: it is also transformed into

an ear when, from its 'worlds of love' the 'powers of fire from the word of worlds' begin to resound in the soul. This experience marks the end of the twelve Holy Nights. The heart has become an inner sense organ, which, seeing and hearing, has experienced the light of the world's being and the 'powers of fire from the word of worlds.'

Now the inner human being is, as it were, new-born. He bears this power of renewal within himself; it rests on the foundation of his own heart:

41. The soul's creative power
Strives from the heart's deep ground

In this fourth transformation it is no longer the heart's urge to spread light in the winter darkness of the world, but to take up the work of earth and strive to

Fashion the self
In human love and human deeds.

With this the first of four stages of metamorphosis is concluded. The joyful urge of the heart at the later Advent period had transformed itself into the heart's clear light at the time of the Christmas mystery, and as a result the inner sense was born which, thanks to the heart's 'eye' and 'ear,' had enabled the soul to experience the winter revelations of the twelve Holy Nights. Finally this experience has created the power necessary for the renewal of its activity within human life.

But immediately a challenge appears to test the power of what has been newly won. In the darkness of winter (verse 42) warmth of heart must prepare the sphere in which coming sense-experiences may be won in advance. Out of this warmth the power of being (verse 43) streams into the world of winter and strengthens the power of endurance in our inner being:

43. And strengthens, maugre worlds of cold,
In human inwardness the fire of soul.

Warmth of heart and the heart's force have endured: winter's grip and the cold without have been overcome because the heart has experienced its new birth. This is the path of inner development, which the heart takes from before Christmas till the end of January. Now the heart again withdraws into the depths of its pure and hidden activity.

The heart is mentioned only once more. When the gracious light of the approaching spring streams down to earth, bearing with it on its wings the assurance of world-thoughts, the door to the secret chamber of the heart opens once more, 'wakening love' within. This is the message of verse 48, which is immediately followed by Passion-tide.

3

What are we to make of the Calendar mentioning the heart only during the winter? After all it goes on actively beating throughout the whole year.

In one of Rudolf Steiner's notebooks of 1924 there are some lines which remind us of the close connection of the sun in the heavens and the human heart: they end with this assertion:

> Looking upwards I can see
> In the sun's shining orb
> The mighty heart of the world.
> Looking inwards I can feel
> In the heart's warm beat
> The sun of man ensouled.[1]

Here the secret is distinctly and clearly stated, and it also appears in the Calendar during the year. The first verse for Easter speaks of the outward sun:

> 1. When from the worlds' wide bounds
> The sun speaks to the sense of man

Thereafter the sun is referred to again and again. Verse 4

speaks of 'the sunlit world'; in verse 10, for the beginning of June, the first lines run:

10. Far into summer heights
    The sun lifts up its shining sphere

And verse 11 speaks of 'the sun's high hour,' in which the human soul is summoned to the highest sacrifice. After this verse, which establishes the mood of St John's Tide, the sun is not mentioned again: human beings have lost sight of it, and 'the heights of sense' (verse 13) and 'the senses revelation' (14) have taken hold of their being: the 'drowsiness of sense' (15) spreads round them.

During this time, however, the word of worlds makes fruitful the human being. The Godhead, ruling in the word, renews the soul and from heaven a sound descends upon it. This new beginning shows itself in the light-garment of the outer glory veiling the sun's light. In the weeks following there is no mention of light or sun. Only at the beginning of September, when the heat of summer declines and autumn approaches, we read:

22. Light from the world's wide bounds
    Unfolds in me its life of power,
    Changing to light of soul

From now on the outer light is transformed into an inner light; it becomes 'sunny gleams' in the soul (verse 25), 'the gift of summer sun' (27), 'the soul's sunlike potency' (28), 'the summer of the soul' (30). Thus the heritage of summer wakes in the inner being and leads towards the 'soul's summer' in winter.

But there is still no mention of the heart. During the autumn the inner light is still only dawning. It illumines the soul, it streams into thinking and pervades the will. The human heart, however, is still silent, enfolded in the soul's light. It is quietly making ready for the mystery of Christmas.

Since St John's Tide the heart, which is the physical organ of the soul and spirit in the inner being, has become the cradle of the word of worlds. Then at Advent:

36. Speaks in my being's depths,
    Surging to revelation,
    In secret wise the word of worlds.

And now the springs of the heart break forth. It carries the light of spirit into 'the winter night of worlds' so that 'sounding through the dark of sense God's word' may 'illumine all that is' (verse 37). The light of the soul unites with the heart's clear light, and the holy word of worlds, 'heaven's own fruit of hope,' grows outwards 'to the corners of the world.' It becomes the creative power of the soul and appears manifest in the love and work of people so transformed.

The sun does not merely shine, it also resounds; its light does not merely radiate, it becomes wings for the thought and the word of worlds. For this reason when, for a moment, the year in its course holds its breath, stands still and in silence listens for the almighty power of heaven, it is possible for the human heart, which is the inner sun, to become an eye and ear of the world during the twelve Holy Nights. To this inner perception supersensible human beings awake, and the power of the spirit can stream through them. Here, in the words as they recur, the annually consummated birth and death of the soul encounter and are interwoven with the spirit of worlds. In summer the soul is led to the heavenly table and there offers itself up. It dies and in self-surrender is nourished by the bread of heaven, and is reborn. The word of worlds works on in it and in the heart becomes that fruit of heaven which illumines all humanity's doing. The heart becomes the cradle of 'the spirit child.'

Thus also in the verse quoted earlier the heart is addressed:

O heart, bearer of the soul,
The spirit power of your light
Charms life forth from man's
Inner depths unfathomable.

At Christmas this passes into the realm of inner revelation in space. It is the light originating in the spirit-light of the worlds, which warmed the hearts of the poor shepherds and illumined the wise heads of kings: it lives on as sound in the heart. Now heart and Christmas are one. Christmas is the heart of the world made manifest; the heart is the hidden Christmas of the growing human soul.

The Words 'Heights' and 'Depths'

In Rudolf Steiner's usage, the words heights and depths tend to occur in quite particular contexts, where they arouse in the mind, on being read or meditated upon, distinctive images and feelings.

Thus in the first mantric verses by him, in a lecture dealing with the signs and symbols of the Christmas festival on December 17, 1906, quoting words suited to the winter solstice, he said:

> The heights reveal
> The eternal word of the gods;
> The depths will preserve
> The treasure of peace.

These words remind us at once of the Christmas 'secret' announced by the angel to the shepherds. Rudolf Steiner gave a number of translations or paraphrases of this verse, for instance,

> The spirit of God reveals itself in the heights
> And it brings peace to men on earth
> In whose hearts good will abides[1]

and again:

> The divine reveals itself
> In the heights of the world's expanse,
> And peace will put forth shoots on earth
> For men who are of good will.[2]

In these verses we are concerned more specifically with words that have a special significance for Christmas, and they speak of the heights of heaven and the depths of earth. There is a further

metamorphosis in the Foundation Stone verses, given by Steiner when the General Anthroposophical Society was established on December 25, 1923. There we have:

> For the Father Spirit of the heights holds sway
> In the depths of worlds, begetting life.
> Spirits of strength!
> Let this ring out from the heights
> And in the depths be echoed:

and again:

> For the spirit's universal thoughts hold sway
> In the being of all worlds craving for light.
> Spirits of soul!
> Let this be prayed in the depths
> And from the heights be answered.

These examples make it clear that when Rudolf Steiner uses these words, heights and depths, in this mantric fashion, he is referring to the world of divine beings on the one hand and the existence of humanity on the other: in the last quotation the spirits of soul become the representatives of humanity when men strive for the spirit. In this way the mighty Foundation Stone verse becomes a transformation of the verses first quoted given in 1906.

All this furnishes contexts for the interpretation of similar usages in the Calendar, where, in comparison with other verses by Rudolf Steiner, the words occur with marked frequency. But they never occur alone without an accompanying adjective or at least closely associated with some other word indicating clearly which heights and depths are meant. Let us try to make this clear in detail.

2

The words heights and depths are used seventeen times in the Calendar in sixteen verses. Both occur in successive lines in verse 13. Heights by itself occurs only three times, in verses 10, 13 and

48. In contrast depths occurs fourteen times: five times as 'depths of the soul,' six as 'spirit's depths,' twice in 'the depths of my being' and once with reference to the 'depths of winter.' Heights occurs as 'heights of summer' (10), as 'heights of sense' (13), and as 'heights of worlds' (48).

After this statistical summary let us begin our detailed study with the use of the word 'heights' in these last three verses.

The word first appears in the verse for the second week in June, the tenth week of the sun's year, which prepares us for St John's Tide and begins thus:

10. Far into summer heights
The sun lifts up its shining sphere,
It draws my human yearning
Into its own wide spaces

The spirit-flight of the human soul mounts into the heights. The rising sun carries it upwards into the spheres of eternal light. Then in the following lines we have the 'feelings' of the soul:

While inwardly a feeling stirs
In dim prophetic boding:
'Hereafter you shall know —
A god, a god has touched you now.'

Three weeks later, when St John's Tide is over and the sun has passed the solstice, we have the 'heights' again, but in a different context:

13. Am I then in the heights of sense —
So kindles in my depths of soul
The truth from spirit worlds of fire
The gods themselves proclaim:
'Seek through your boding power
And find in spirit ground
Your spirit brotherhood.'

The words here employed are particularly important for our studies. The human soul, expanded in the heights of sense, drinks in the light and feels itself cradled in the warmth of the world. But out of the depths sounds forth a warning that the soul must experience itself in 'spirit ground' — we might equally well have had 'spirit depths' — in its 'spirit brotherhood.'

These heights of sense, both in verse 13 and in verse 10, where they appear as 'summer heights,' are not to be confused with those mighty heights mentioned in the verses for Christmas and also in the Foundation Stone. These are, rather, the heights of the world of senses, unfolding in a world flooded with the summer sun. This is more clearly indicated in verse 15:

> 15. I feel the spirit's weaving
> Spell-bound within the world's array.

It is this 'world's array,' or splendour, permeated with the spirit, which is referred to when the verse speaks of 'summer heights.'

To the heights spoken of in verses 10 and 13 two verses of the winter half-year correspond: verse 43 in the fourth week of January and verse 40 at Epiphany. Corresponding to 'Far into summer heights The sun lifts up its shining sphere,' we have:

> 43. Sunk in its wintry depths
> True spirit-being quickens into warmth

and to 'Am I then in the heights of sense,' we have:

> 40. Am I then in the spirit's depths —
> So in the roots of soul profound
> From out the heart's wide worlds of love
> Illusion vain of selfhood fills itself
> With powers of fire from the word of worlds.

In the one case wintry depths are related to summer heights; in the other spirit's depths are the polar opposite of heights of sense. Here are two pairs of opposites which we must later

discuss. But first we must seek some understanding of the meaning of 'the spirit's depths' and what region they characterize.

The word, 'heights,' occurs a third time; not in the summer verses, but at the beginning of March:

> 48. In light, that wills from heights of worlds
> To stream amain into my soul

This is in early spring, at the beginning of Passion-tide. The winter is passing away and a boding of the growing light gleams on the horizon of life. The first forces of life and growth become active; and then light breaks forth from the east, from 'heights of worlds.'

Verse 48 is balanced by verse 5 at the beginning of May, when spring has fully unfolded, Easter is past, all nature prepares for the fullness of Whitsun, and 'field and wood are greening and blossoming.' At this time the soul is thus spoken of:

> 5. In light, that from the spirit's depths
> Plays fruitfully through space
> And manifests the god's creating.

Here again we encounter the 'spirit's depths,' which are opposed to the 'heights of worlds.' Each time light is mentioned; light from spirit's depths and light from heights of worlds. There is thus a hidden rectangle in the Calendar of four 'light' verses closely interrelated, verses 5 and 48, just quoted, and verses 22 and 31 still to be discussed. In all four a hidden activity of the weaving of light in the world's space is referred to, a sort of rotation through the course of the year.

It begins with the heights of worlds in verse 48, passes on to depths of spirit in verse 5, continues as summer declines and ends at the beginning of autumn. Thus in the first week of September:

> 22. Light from the worlds' wide bounds
> Unfolds in me its life of power,

Changing to light of soul,
Illumining my spirit's depths

and at the beginning of November:

31. Light from the spirit's depths
Strives outward like a sun

Three times in these four 'light' verses we find the words 'spirit's depths': once soon after Easter, and twice just before and after Michaelmas. If we trace the orbit of this light we find it appearing in early spring (verse 48) from 'heights of worlds,' moving later, as the world of spring unfolds, into 'spirit's depths' (5), and appearing again at the end of summer from the 'worlds' wide bounds' (22): here it becomes the 'light of the soul,' which shines into the 'spirit's depths' and thereafter rises from those depths to shine like a sun.

By now its course has reached its end; it has been transformed into the force of will and assumes form in human works; it has become a creative force. Then again, in the days before Easter, it begins its course anew, moving from the heights of worlds into the realm of earth.

Here we find the activity of the world's light united with the spirit's depths. In autumn (verse 22) the human being becomes the mediator between light and spirit's depths; in spring, however, light streams forth from spirit's depths into all the realms of nature (verse 5). The realms of light and of the spirit's depths are mutually related.

There are three other points in the Calendar at which we find 'spirit's depths': verses 17 and 46 and at the Epiphany-tide verse 40, already discussed. Verse 17, for the end of July and the beginning of August, runs:

17. Now speaks the word of worlds
Which through the senses' door
I may draw deep into my soul:

'Fill full thy spirit's depths
With my world wideness,
To find hereafter me in thee.'

This is an important pronouncement, St John's Tide is past; the human soul has been fertilized by the world's spirit and now bears the treasure which it has been able to bring with it through the 'senses' door' into the ground of the soul. From this divine germ sound forth the words: 'Fill full thy spirit's depths / With my world wideness.' These are the spirit's depths into which, a few weeks later, light will make its way through human beings (verse 22). The human being as well as the world has some part in these 'spirit's depths.' The divine seed is planted there so that, during the autumn, the transformed light of the soul may shine upon it; and in the fourth week of October we read (verse 30): 'Winter shall wake in me / The summer of the soul.'

In the period before Christmas the seed has ripened and corresponding to verse 17 is verse 36:

36. Speaks from my being's depths,
Surging to revelation,
In secret wise the word of worlds.
'Fill full your task in life
With this my light of spirit
To offer up the self through me.'

The light streaming in during the days before autumn, which became the soul's light and shone forth on to the seed in the word of worlds, has been transformed by this seed into spirit's light and can now illuminate purposeful human work.

The same 'depths of being' appear earlier in the first verse after Michaelmas:

27. To dive into my being's depths
Stirs up a yearning in me, boding well,
That self-exploring I may find

Myself the gift of summer sun,
Which lives in autumn's mood
A warm seed life
Of thriving forces for my soul.

Here again the theme of the 'seed' appears. This 'gift of summer's sun' has begun to shine in the soul's inner being and from the depths of being gives its warmth to the approaching autumn. These depths of our being are the same as the 'spirit's depths' earlier discussed; the soul's light streams into them and in them 'the wide worlds' of the divine seed are active.

Finally, in the middle of February we have verse 46, which inwardly establishes what outwardly expresses itself in all the revelry and masked dances of Carnival:

46. The world threatens to stupefy
The inborn forces of my soul.
Now rise from spirit-depths
In all your radiance, memory.
Establish my beholding,
Which only through the force of will
Can hold itself erect.

The region of the depths of the human spirit is here described more exactly. From them memory is summoned to arise. It is the sphere of the 'life-tableau,' which begins to unfold itself immediately the threshold of death is crossed. According to Rudolf Steiner this region is the realm of the etheric body. The divine seed, granted to us every year in high summer, is implanted into this life-body, thither the soul's light radiates and thence the spirit's light arises at Advent.

But when the verses speak of 'depths of spirit' they refer also to the life-body of the earth. In this, in spring time, light plays fruitfully through space, manifesting the divine weaving at work. In verse 5 only is the world-ether spoken of as 'depths of spirit': in other verses (17, 22, 31, 40 and 46) it is the etheric body which

is meant — that part of ourselves which forms and maintains our life-tableau.

Over against these spirit-depths we have the heights of summer (verse 10) or of the senses (13) or of the worlds (48). In them is manifested what remains hidden from our physical eyes in depths of spirit — the creative world. The 'heights' of the Calendar reveal the secret which, though hidden, is active in the spirit's depths of the etheric forces.

The real bearer of these heights of sense and depths of spirit is light, which creates and maintains, and also renews, space, containing life within itself and radiating warmth. This is not the light seen by our eyes; it is the invisible creative light, active as the background of all that our senses perceive, which summons all the etheric forces to their activity. What the Calendar describes is the 'breath of light,' which weaves in and behind our sense-world: it finds expression in the words which speak of heights and depths. The breath of light and its course, which permeates the human being and the world, is revealed in these words.

3

This word, 'depths,' is used in yet another combination in the Calendar. It occurs five times as 'depths of soul'; in each of two successive verses (52, the verse for Palm Sunday and Holy Week, and verse 1, which begins the Calendar year on Easter Sunday), then later in verses 12 and 13, both of which fall in John's Tide, and finally in verse 25, which introduces us to Michaelmas.

Thus we meet depths of soul at three very important dates in the year — Easter, St John's Tide and Michaelmas. All fall within the first half of the Calendar's year, from Easter to Michaelmas; and they are not further mentioned during the darker part of the earth's soul-year. They occur again only in verse 52, for Palm Sunday, which begins:

52. When from the depths of soul
The spirit turns towards the life of worlds,
And beauty wells from the wide bounds of space.

These lines are like a breathing process: the human spirit turns outward; it breathes in again the beauty which speaks from the wide bounds of space. For some weeks it was tarrying in the depths of soul; now it is free to breathe in anew the world's breath. Then comes the beginning of the year:

1. When from the worlds' wide bounds
The sun speaks to the sense of man,
And joy from depths of soul
Grows one with light in gazing

As the human spirit strives outwards from the depths of soul, so the sun streams forth to meet him from the 'worlds' wide bounds.' The sun reveals beauty, and from man's side joy comes to meet it. The depths of soul are the source of joy; the wide bounds of space, filled with light, become the place whence beauty shines forth.

From now the sun climbs higher and higher in the heavens until, at St John's Tide, it reaches the solstice. Now there is a further mention of depths of soul:

12. The world's bright loveliness
Constrains me in my inmost [deepest] soul.
'Set free the godlike gifts you own
To wing their way into the universe'

Here again it is beauty which moves to meet the depths of inmost soul; but now its power is so great that we feels it as a sort of compulsion: it calls forth powerfully from us the divine that lives in us, and urges us to undertake a flight into the world, the unmeasurable realm of the spirit.

In the next week we hear the same call:

13. 'Seek through you boding power
And find in spirit ground
Your spirit brotherhood.'

These words are like a message written in fire. They are heard in the depths of our soul and we experience the compelling force of the divine world, which lies concealed behind all beauty:

Am I then in the heights of sense —
So kindles in my depths of soul
The truth from spirit worlds of fire
The gods themselves proclaim

Finally in the penultimate week of September, as Michaelmas approaches, comes verse 25:

25. My self, now made my very own,
May shine abroad its inner light
In dark abysms of space and time.
A slumber seizes nature's being,
But the deep hidden soul shall waken,
And waking carry sunny gleams
Into cold winter's tides and streams.

Here we have, not the compound word 'soul-depths,' but 'the deep hidden soul' — literally, 'depths of the soul.' They are to awake and pour forth their sun-forces: but these have their origin in that divine seed planted in the soul in high summer. We said something about this in reference to verse 17:

17. Now speaks the word of worlds
Which through the senses' door
I may draw deep into my soul

This ground, these depths of the soul are, as it were, the forecourt of those spirit-depths, which are active in the human being. Without, on both the near and the far side of our senses' door, is the world of appearance, of splendour, the region of the

senses' heights and the worlds' wide bounds. Behind this 'veil' spreads the ocean of the spirit's depths, the ether-ocean of the astral world. Thence the divine seed makes its way into us as the word of worlds. That word streams through the senses' door and is then taken up into the ground of our soul. There it presses on into the spirit-depths of our etheric being, where it is taken over by the forces which sustain our memories. Therefore we have in verse 19:

> 19. To wrap the new-conceived germ
> In memory's secret folds
> Be now my striving's master aim

The forecourt of this is the depths of the soul.

In Volume 1 of *The Riddles of Philosophy,* in connection with an account of J.G. Hamann's thought, Rudolf Steiner wrote:

> It is one of the facts of this present age that men of genius feel that we must make our way into the soul's depths in order to discover the point at which the soul is closely related to the eternal ground of the world.

That is the particular point in the depths of the soul where our thinking can make contact with world-thoughts, where for our feeling the keynote of the world sounds forth, where for our will the power of the life of worlds begins to awake. There lies the boundary between the conscious and the half-conscious experiences in the soul's inner being and the depths where the individual soul can make contact with the body's etheric ocean.

In the third lecture of the cycle, *Macrocosm and Microcosm,* Steiner describes this region of the inner being:

> When we awake, our attention is directed outwards and we can no longer observe our inner being. But what is it which we pass over at the moment of waking and which obscures the spiritual? It is something which thrusts

> itself between our sentient soul and our etheric and physical bodies. When we awake, what covers up these two last bodies is our sentient body, which interposes itself as a definite boundary between our inner and outer experiences.

He then goes on the describe how an unprepared experience of the physical and etheric bodies would be accompanied inwardly by a vastly enhanced sense of shame:

> The reason for this is that, at such a moment, man would feel how immensely further developed on the road to perfection are his physical and etheric bodies than his soul's being ... This feeling of shame would overwhelm the human soul so irresistibly that man would feel it permeating everything he might come across in the external world. He would, in fact, feel as if he were being annihilated by a fire: the sense of shame would act on him like a consuming fire.

Here, in a different context, the individual would experience that sphere of fire and warmth which are spoken of in verse 13 in connection with the depths of soul: 'So kindles in my depths of soul,' and in verse 25: 'And waking carry sunny gleams.' This fire is also the source from which joy from the depths of soul is continuously new-born. That is why all joy fills us with warmth and fire when it reveals itself in a genuine form.

We conclude then that the 'depths of soul' are the region of the sentient body, which marks the boundary between soul body and life body. It is where warmth and fire of soul originate.

4

Tracing through the texture of the Calendar the thread of the spirit's depths we were led to the activity of the breathing but invisible light, while the soul's depths led us to the region of

inner warmth and fire, which becomes the bearer of the divine seed implanted in the soul at St John's Tide.

This seed is described as 'word of worlds' (verse 17), as 'word of worlds in germ conceived' (18), as the 'spirit's gift' (16), as the 'gift of summer's sun' (27), and so forth. It then reappears at Advent and Christmas as 'word of worlds'; and in verse 40 its nature and being are spoken of as 'powers of fire from the word of worlds.'

It is thus light and warmth that have their home in the depths of spirit and of soul. The world-seed of the spirit-word is implanted in the human life body. Thus in verse 19 we have:

> 19. To wrap the new-conceived germ
> In memory's secret folds
> Be now my striving's master aim.

This has already been referred to; the etheric body is irradiated by the light and permeated by the soul's warmth and thus in the 'soul's summer' of autumn the new-conceived germ develops to be brought to birth at Christmas. Its fruit matures in the light of the Spirit's depths and the fire of the depths of soul.

From the twelve Holy Nights onwards, the new-formed 'word of worlds' penetrates earthly human activity in 'human love and human deeds' (verse 41). The awakened 'fire of soul within man' remains (43). The diagram overleaf summarizes what has so far been achieved. The circle marks the course of the year from one Easter to the next. Individual numbers indicate the verses in which the words 'depths' and 'heights' are found in various combinations. The three rectangles mark the hidden 'quadrature' of the Calendar. The 'light' quadrilateral is formed by verses 5, 22, 31 and 48; that of the 'heights' and 'depths' by verses 10, 17, 36 and 43; that of Easter-Michaelmas by verses 1, 25, 27, and 52 (verse 25 being brought forward one week).

A study of these figures discloses the hidden pattern of this light and warmth-structure within the Calendar. It is a pattern filled with the forces of joy and beauty.

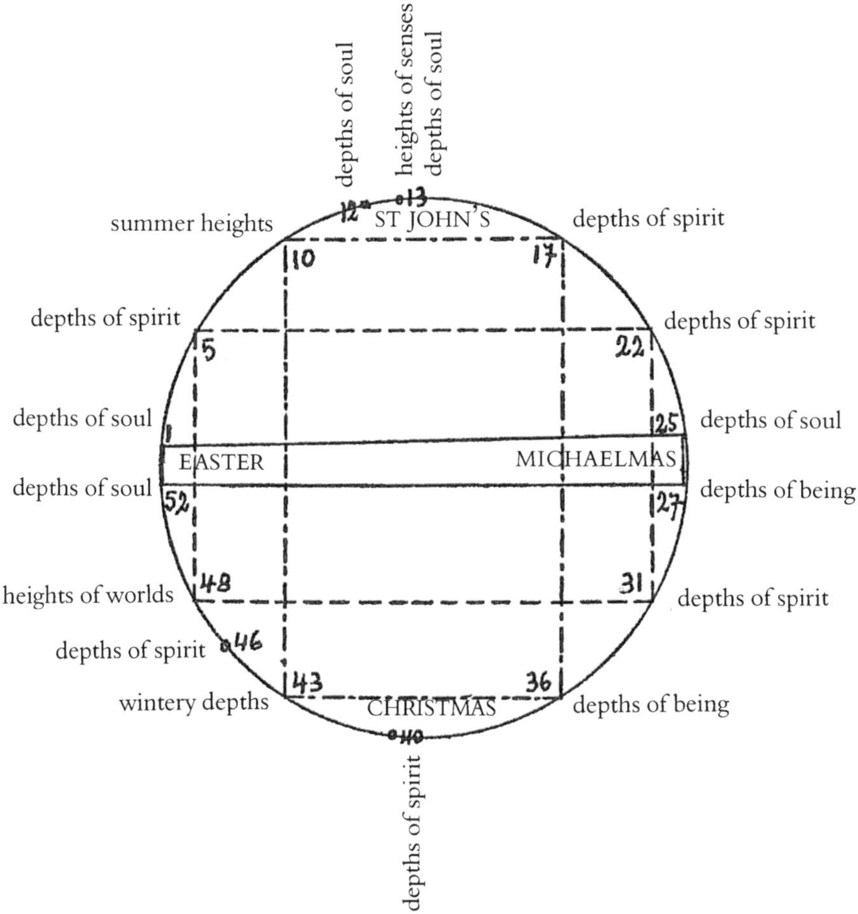

To conclude let us note a verse by Rudolf Steiner. It is from a notebook of November 1924, and contains in concentrated form what has occupied us here.

> Look into the realm of your soul
> And there you can perceive
> The force of light in world's expanse
> And divine working in the course of time.
>
> Look into the realms of the sun
> And there you will behold
> The spirit light of your own heart
> And the creating of your own soul's forces.

Thus man's soul may joyfully see
The heights of the world of stars
In the depths of the heart,
And man's eye may find
Deep in the heart the spirit's weaving
In the heights of the world of stars
Blessing him.

It is at this point that the bridge is built between the heights and the depths in the mantric Christmas verse quoted at the beginning of this chapter. Those heavenly heights and earthly depths are not the same as the summer heights and winter depths of the Calendar. But now the mantric verses and the verses of the Calendar dealing with the soul interlock, since in the heart's depths can be found the heights of the world of stars, from which is revealed the eternal word of the gods, and our eye can there find the power wielded by the Father God, active in depths of worlds, creative of being.

In human hearts weaves warmth; in human eyes shines light. Out of the depths of soul and spirit, the seed of the worlds' word is active, enabling human beings from the depths to make their prayer, which will be answered from the heights.

The Calendar is a marvellous work. The heights and widths of the world and the depths and ground of the heart's feeling are woven into it. Upwards and downwards it leads the soul to experience a meeting with the all-powerful creation of the world.

The Sense of Self

The underlying structure of the Calendar of the Soul reveals itself gradually to anyone who lives with it: they will very soon notice that there are two groups of verses in a polar relation to each other. One group takes us from Easter (verse 1) to Michaelmas (verse 26); the other from the week after Michaelmas (verse 27) to Palm Sunday (verse 52). One verse in each group complements a verse in the other, and cannot be properly understood without reference to it.

Verse 1 corresponds to verse 52, verse 2 to verse 51, and so on until we reach Michaelmas with verse 26 in polar relationship to verse 27. Thus between Easter and Michaelmas there is a kind of axis, if we may so put it, dividing the year into two antithetical halves. For instance verse 13 begins, 'Am I then in the heights of sense,' and the corresponding verse 40, 'Am I then in the spirit's depths.' Again verse 10 begins, 'Far into summer heights,' and the corresponding verse 43, 'Sunk in its wintry depths.' This polarity is basic to the structure of the Calendar and is related to the passage of the sun between the spring and autumn equinoxes.

There is, however, at right angles to this, a second axis, which stretches from St John's Tide to the twelve Holy Nights and bisects our 'horizontal' Easter-Michaelmas axis, so that we can distinguish four groups of thirteen verses each. We now have four interrelated groups, two complementing the other two.

Thus verses 1 and 52 correspond to verses 26 and 27, giving a group of four interrelated verses: and there is a similar correspondence between verses 2 and 51 and verses 25 and 28. The accompanying diagram makes this clear.

Without this fundamental picture in our mind we cannot properly understand the internal correspondence and mutual

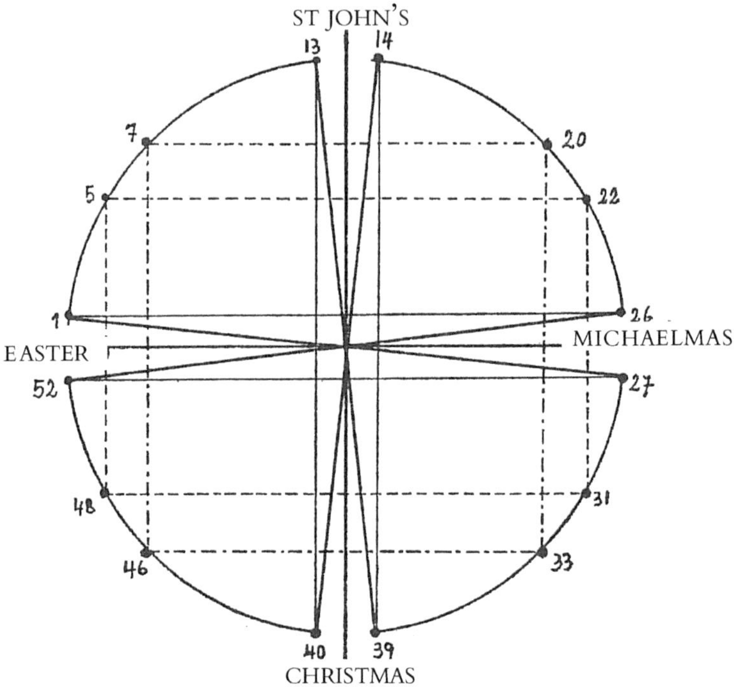

relationship of the weeks in the course of the year. Thus there are four verses about light (5, 22, 31 and 48); only if they are brought into relationship do they reveal a true picture of the interweaving of light's activity over the course of the year. Again, during four weeks in the year the powers of the tempter most markedly approach the human soul; and the four verses for them (7, 20, 33 and 46) occupy the central position in each of the groups of thirteen verses.

This structure forms the basis of the Calendar, as Rudolf Steiner made clear when he not only numbered the individual verses but also added a letter of the alphabet to each.* All this

* The letters have been omitted in this book, as the lettering differs in the German and English as well as in different editions of the Calendar. In any context, König always looks at the opposite verse, together with the mirrored ones.

gives us what might be called a 'dial' or 'clock-face' of the year's course. The diagram makes clear the position of each week in the course of the year, and also its relationship to the corresponding week.

The progress of the year is indicated by the movements of the 'hands' of this 'clock'; the verses themselves are at rest; the hands move through them like a wave. The nature of the hand is represented for us in certain words systematically employed. Just as the hands of a clock do not change as they move but acquire significance by their movement, so individual words (for instance, boding or foreboding) remain the same, but their meaning varies as the weeks progress.

The word we will first consider is 'sense of self' *(Selbstgefühl)* as Rudolf Steiner uses it. It occurs twice only, but each time at an important point in the course of the year, marking significant events.

2

We first come upon this word, 'sense of self' in the verse representing the Michael mood:

26. Nature, thou soul of motherhood,
I bear thee in the essence of my will,
That will whose fiery strength
Tempers my spirit's edge
That it beget such sense of self
As may bear I in me.

It appears a second time in the verse for the week after Christmas, covering the period of the twelve Holy Nights:

39. Surrendered to the spirit's revelation
I win the light of universal life.
The force of thought grows strong in clarity
To grant me selfhood,

And in me, from the thinker's power,
Leaps into wakefulness the sense of self.

Though they have not the same structural principle, the two verses appear at similar points on the 'clock-face' of the Calendar, the 'clockhand' is in analogous positions. The first, the Michaelmas verse (26), concludes the second group of thirteen; the second (39) concludes the third group of thirteen. In the Michaelmas verse a birth is foretold:

That it beget such sense of self
As may bear I in me.

in the second that birth has occurred:

And in me, from the thinker's power,
Leaps into wakefulness the sense of self.

We can see from the use of this single phrase how the hand of the clock moves forward in the course of the year.

But what does the compound word, 'sense-of-self,' really mean? It is one of the many new word-creations of Rudolf Steiner. We must try to feel our way into the meaning he gives it.

When we read these two verses with care, we find they contain another pair of almost identical expressions. In the Michaelmas verse (26) we read, 'As may bear I [or myself] in me;' in the winter verse (39), 'To give myself to me.' What is the meaning of these expressions?

In the Calendar phrases like 'you yourself,' 'oneself,' 'me myself,' are common. But in the connection in which they appear above they are to be found only in two other verses, 19 and 21, where there are two corresponding lines: 'Emergent it shall give myself to me' and 'Gather its strength and lend myself to me.'

These lines come in the second and fourth weeks of August. They refer us to the gift of the spirit which the soul receives at St John's Tide and must tend and nurture in the following weeks.[1]

Both refer to this activity of the soul:

19. To wrap the new-conceived germ
In memory's secret folds
Be now my striving's master aim;
Gathering strength to waken
Force of my own within me,
Emergent, it shall give myself to me.

21. I feel a power unwonted, bearing fruit,
Gather its strength and lend myself to me.
I sense the seed maturing,
The while my boding weaves a web of light
Within me for my selfhood's power.

Both verses describe an experience of the soul when it becomes aware of 'This word of worlds in germ conceived' (verse 18).

Sinking like a seed into the human soul, this gift renews and enlivens those forces leading to the birth of the spirit, which is to occur at Christmas. In verse 19 they are described as a 'force of my own,' to be aroused in my inner being, so that 'emergent, it shall give myself to me.' In verse 21 it is a 'power unwonted,' a foreign power, which shall 'gather its strength and lend myself to me.' But in each case we are concerned not only with the growth of the I, but with something more.

3

With the spirit's help, which the soul has received, the 'sense of self' is gradually enhanced; it is the meaning of this word which we are seeking. During the summer the spirit confers this gift on the inmost soul, but only on the basis of the experience of 'the I in me.' We must, then, consider what is the real meaning of experiencing the I in myself and of giving me to myself.

A kind of consciousness is here indicated, which goes beyond our everyday 'self-consciousness'; an experience having some

analogy with 'thinking about thinking.' The ordinary, earthly I becomes conscious of itself, so that the I divines the existence of a higher I, which has so far remained beyond its threshold. It is part of the process referred to in Rudolf Steiner's *Theosophy* in the section dealing with the Being of Man:

> Anyone trying to understand the essential nature of the human being by means of thinking is first required to come, through self-reflection, to a clear understanding of the difference between body, soul and spirit.[2]

This means that the self makes clear to itself something about itself: expressed in the first person, that I must make clear to myself something about myself, or even that myself should make something clear to me.

In these and similar phrases we are referred directly to a relation existing even in everyday consciousness between the I and the self — between which there is an abiding veil, pierced, whether gradually or suddenly, as the result of appropriate thinking, by the light of self-knowledge.

Western philosophy has always been aware of this condition. Thomas Aquinas, for instance, spoke of it thus: *Dicitu enim conscientia testificari, ligare vel instigare, vel etiam accusare, vel etiam remordere sive reprehendere.*[3] Freely rendered, this quotation may be taken to mean that, whereas the province of reason is knowledge, conscience cognizes the implications of rational knowledge.

It is interesting that philosophers have generally discussed this experience of the 'I in me' in relation to conscience. H. Plessner, for instance, calls it 'the positionality of the eccentric form, in which man can feel, as a basic datum, that he is both subject and object; and he designates it as the typically human form of life.'[4] For completeness we might add that it involves the possibility of our bringing into consciousness everything that we think or experience.

Jaspers gives an even clearer and more significant description of the condition:

> In my conscience I can stand at a distance from myself. I do not think of myself as a being, a form of existence, which is 'given' and merely unrolls itself before me. I take hold of myself and bring into existence what I am, so far as in me lies. Between my bare existence and my true self, which has not yet been fully revealed to me, my conscience appears before me as something real; and through it I am able to acknowledge, accept or reject what is to become part of my real being.[5]

We will not here discuss whether the reality appearing between my existing self and my real self, which is not yet fully revealed to me, can rightly be called conscience. It is enough for the present to take note of this 'something given,' of the fact that, in our ordinary life on earth, we are always in some relation to the light of that sun which shines down upon us, and is our self's being, our higher I. It is this experience to which, as I believe, phrases in the Calendar like 'I in me' refer.

4

Help towards understanding the real meaning of 'sense of self' may be found in something which Rudolf Steiner said in a lecture, in which he used this new word-coinage. Referring to the life between death and re-birth he describes how the human being lives 'immediately, in immediate contact, with spirit-beings. Then comes a time when he lives only in the revelation of spirit-beings, that is when they only reveal themselves to him.'[6] Human beings are not then living with spirit-beings who can be differentiated one from another: rather they live 'more or less pantheistically in a general world of spirit.' Then comes the description which is so significant for our problem:

> Whilst you are living in this general world of spirit, a stronger sense of self arises out of your inner being than

> you had before. Previously you were 'in your self' in such a way that you lived, to a certain extent, at one with the spiritual world, which you could experience in your own individuality. Now you feel the spirit-world as if it were no more than a general spirituality, but you feel your own self more strongly. There awakes an intensification of your individual self-feeling. And when this happens, the human being begins to feel the need for a new existence on earth.

Here 'sense of self' describes an 'awaking to one's self.' When the human soul passes out of a realm of experience, in which it has an individual sense of 'living with spirit-beings,' and finds itself face to face with a more general spirituality, it becomes more conscious of its own individuality: and as a result there is an immediate longing for the earth, a sense of the need for a new earth-existence.

This is something similar to what is described for us in the Calendar. In verse 39 we read:

> 39. Surrendered to the spirit's revelation
> I win the light of universal life.

Here the soul surrenders to a spirit-revelation and the experience is so powerful that the 'light of universal life' appears. But now, under the influence of Christmas-tide, the force of thought grows and brings the 'sense of self' to birth:

> The force of thought grows strong in clarity
> To grant me selfhood,
> And in me, from the thinker's power,
> Leaps into wakefulness the sense of self.

The 'sense of self' is the outcome of this power of thinking, which, in its clarity gives me back to myself. When the soul surrenders itself to the spirit-revelation, it experiences, by the power of its own thoughts, the awaking of the 'sense of self.' Clarified

and purified, there grows in the soul's inner being the feeling which gives me back to myself to be the bearer of the word of worlds as it is born within me. In the very next verse, Epiphany's, we read:

40. Am I then in the spirit's depths —
So in the roots of soul profound
From out the heart's wide worlds of love
Illusion vain of selfhood fills itself
With powers of fire from the word of worlds.

The awakened sense of self, if it were not able to fill itself with the power of the word of worlds, would be nothing but a vain illusion of selfhood. Thus the sense of self is like a cup or chalice created by the force of thinking, and so it becomes the bearer of the highest forces of the spirit.

When human beings lose the immediate reality of the individual spirit-experience in the period between death and a new birth and direct themselves to the world of earth, the sense of self becomes the chalice into which the longing for a new earth existence pours.

In the next earth-life, on the other hand, at the time of the twelve Holy Nights, this chalice, formed from the sense of self, becomes the bearer of the word of worlds. At this point we come close to the area of soul and spirit within us, in which St Paul's saying: 'Not I, but Christ in me' can be made real. The bearer of that experience, granted to human beings 'from out the heart's wide worlds of love,' is the sense of self.

5

How this comes about is clearly indicated in the Michaelmas verse. In it the soul is summoned to a task which is to be fulfilled during the twelve Holy Nights. We are urged to become aware of the nature of our knowing, in which works the motherhood of the nature forces. Hence streams forth the

'fiery strength,' which is to lead to the birth of the 'sense of self' at Christmas-tide.

From the furnace of the human will comes forth the fire in which the spirit's edge is tempered so that the sense of self arises from it. This 'edge,' or spirit's driving force, comes out of thinking which is pervaded by force of will and initiative. Just as every budding plant, tree and flower feels new urges in springtime, so in autumn, in preparation for the soul's summer, there will develop this power of thinking permeated by will. From the budding thoughts and impulses of the spirit is formed within humankind the chalice of the 'sense of self.'

But its 'edge' is that experience of the 'I in me' or 'myself in me,' spoken of earlier. The perpetually renewed experience of the heightened self-consciousness has the power to combine the will-pervaded thoughts into this chalice. Thus within the human soul that 'spirit-space' comes into being, which can then become the bearer of the powers of the word of worlds.

This is a process which can occur only in the realm of the consciousness soul; it has only in recent times appeared and unfolded itself in human beings; the age of the consciousness soul began only a few centuries ago. Of the consciousness soul Rudolf Steiner stated that it is that which 'lights up in the soul as eternal,' of which he says,

> We all know how we accept our personal preferences as true, at first. But truth is lasting only when it has freed itself from any flavor of such sympathies and antipathies. The truth is true, even if all our personal feelings revolt against it. We will apply the term 'consciousness soul' to that part of the soul in which truth lives.[7]

Such eternal truths, however, can be won only with the help of such will-pervaded thinking as allows the spirit's driving force to grow and from it to create the chalice of the sense of self. World-thinking then streams into the human soul and eternal ideas begin to live in it.

If this happens, the sense of self must awaken at the same time so that the I can gain knowledge of itself. The I must not lose itself in the spirit but must find itself in it; and for this it needs the 'chalice' of the sense of self. When this is formed, the human spirit, the higher individuality, can become active within him. His own 'genius' descends upon him in the chalice of this sense of self; and in the sense of self human beings now begin to divine their spirit self.

The difference between the consciousness soul and the spirit self is thus described by Rudolf Steiner:

> The consciousness soul merely touches the autonomous truth that is independent of all sympathy and antipathy, but the spirit self carries this same truth inside itself, taken up, enclosed and individualized by means of the 'I' and taken into the individual's independent being. Through becoming independent and uniting with the truth, the 'I' itself achieves immortality.[8]

What is called in the book *Theosophy* that part of the 'I' which can comprehend eternal truth, is, in the Calendar, called the 'sense of self.' It is a part of the process of growth of our I, which can maintain itself when the light of eternal ideas shines upon it. This sense of self does not vanish when it comes into contact with world-thougths: rather it grasps and 'individualizes' them, so that the word of worlds begins to reverberate from them. We then attain one of the high points of inner experience to which the Calendar leads us.

In Rudolf Steiner's Calendar the name of Christ is not once mentioned. Yet it carries us along the path towards the 'Christ-impulse,' which is at the same time the path along which we can attain the spirit self. This is why, in one of Steiner's lectures, we read:

> We must recognize quite clearly that, at the present time, we are gradually moving from a life in the consciousness

> soul to one in the spirit self. I have often explained how this entry into the spirit self comes about, and that the number of those who will experience the appearance of the Christ-impulse will go on increasing during the next three thousand years, so that gradually man will become capable of experiencing the Christ-impulse in the spiritual worlds.[9]

We are preparing ourselves for such an experience when this chalice of the sense of self takes form within our souls.

Heaven's own Fruit of Hope

In Scene 5 of Rudolf Steiner's second Mystery Play, *The Soul's Probation,* Frau Balde tells Professor Capesius, now standing at the crossroads of his life, of a boy, the only child of poor foresters, who even in boyhood had the gift of supersensory sight. He witnessed the 'marvel of the spring,' where three women appeared, forming a glistening chalice from the spray of a mountain stream and filling it with the silvery light of the moon.

Much later, after three times three hundred and sixty weeks, when the boy had reached manhood, the women appeared to him again. This time not only did he see them, but they spoke to him, the first, of the draught of life's hope; the second, of the strength of faith in life; and the third, of the beams of life's love. They set before his eyes the three Christian virtues spoken of by Paul in his hymn to love (1Cor.13:13): 'But now abide faith, hope and love, these three ...'

Here we are considering only hope and shall reflect on the words of the first woman, who said:

> Think of me at every moment
> When you feel yourself alone in life.
> I draw the eye of man's soul
> To the ether-distances and the expanse of stars,
> And to everyone who would feel me
> I hand the draught of life's hope
> Out of my wonder-chalice.

This picture sets before us the situation of modern people. Caught up in a strange city and tired with the day's work, they wonder what life can bring them and are shown their higher

being. If in their loneliness and helplessness, people will raise their eyes to 'the ether-distances and the expanse of stars,' they will be able to partake of the 'draught of life's hope.' Profound riddles are hidden in these words.

Some modern theologians and philosophers have again begun to ponder the enigma of hope. Though we use the word almost daily, its true meaning has almost faded from our minds. Yet in one form or another it lives in the deeds and strivings of individuals, of peoples and groups. Who can say today what hope really is?

Paul Schütz, a Protestant theologian, has written a long book solely about hope. The important Catholic philosopher, Josef Pieper, has collected and commented on the many sayings about hope of Thomas Aquinas. And the philosopher, Ernst Bloch, has written about hope as the basic principle of Communism.

These books are significant of our times, because their owners divine that, in a state of hopelessness, we lose our real humanity. Schütz and Pieper both describe hope as an attitude granted to us to accompany us on our journey on earth. Schütz, the Protestant, wrote:

> Hope is not any strenuous effort of the self. That does not mean that we are not to pray for it, or to be ready for it, or to long for it. It is a mode of being. There is no Christian hope without the power of endurance, or standing firm against all reason. There is no hope without that 'virtue of God in history' called patience. It is this virtue of patience that proves hope to be not an act of will but rather a mode of being.[1]

We should look in vain in modern books of psychology for any discussion of hope: for just as it is not an act of will, so it is not a feeling or a perception. We know it very well but cannot say what it is, and what does it help when it is described by Schütz as 'a mode of being'? What was it in Job that made him say (13:15 NIV), 'Though he slay me; yet will I hope in him'? Or in the

Psalmist when he sings (Ps. 40:3 Douay-Rheims): 'Many shall ... fear: and they shall hope in the Lord.'?

The Catholic philosopher, Pieper, thinks differently:

> Hope and love are among the simple basic expressions of all that lives ... In hope man, with restless heart, strives upward, in confident and sufficient expectation, towards the *bonum arduum futurum;* towards the 'not yet' of fulfilment of both the natural and the supernatural.[2]

Here also, hope is spoken of as if it were a *viaticum* for his earthly journey given to human beings alone of all living creatures. There is an ancient Jewish saying that all creatures are created complete except man, to whom is given hope. The expectation of all creatures for salvation is not hope; all expectation is merely a condition in which hope can awaken. The pilgrim on life's journey must not just wait in expectation; he must have hope for the end of the way and for final salvation in the light of eternity.

Paul says, quite clearly:

> We know that the whole creation has been groaning in travail together until now; and not only the creation, but we ourselves, who have the first fruits of the Spirit, groan inwardly as we wait for adoption as sons, the redemption of our bodies. For in this hope we were saved. Now hope that is seen is not hope. For who hopes for what he sees? But if we hope for what we do not see, we wait for it with patience. (Rom 8.22–25 RSV).

Hope is directed to something not yet actually visible. But we know that it is there and awaits us. Other creatures, in dull and aimless longing, wait for what permeates us as a presentiment of something to strive for, a path. Thus Pieper quotes from the sermons of Thomas Aquinas: 'As yet we do not see what we hope for; but we are the body of that head, in which what we hope for is already fulfilled.'[3] Pieper adds: 'Hope for us is hope in Christ, in whom what we hope for is already fulfilled.'

But what is this something which we await, hoping for it as for something promised, and ever renewing our hope? And why is it that only hope, which we cannot see or even glimpse, can lead us to what is promised? With these questions in mind let us turn to the Calendar.

2

The word 'hope' occurs four times in the Calendar's 52 verses. It is not mentioned in the summer half of the year, between Easter and Michaelmas. It appears, however, immediately after the beginning of autumn, and then in two successive verses, 28 and 29. Nothing is then said about it until it reappears as a central element, fully developed, in the Christmas verse (verse 38) as 'Heaven's own fruit of hope.' Finally, at the beginning of Passion-tide (verse 49), we have the 'inward rays of hope.' A primary association is thus established between the months of autumn and winter and the essence of hope: it does not awake in the soul until the outer world grows dark and autumnal.

A pointer to the connection between hope in the depths of the soul and darkness without is also hidden away in the two verses complementing 28 and 29, namely verses 24 and 25, which speak of the 'darkness of the soul' and the 'dark abysms of time':

24. Unceasingly itself renewing
The soul grows self-aware;
In new self-knowledge vivified
The spirit of the world strives on,
Creating from the darkness of the soul
What sense of self matures as fruit of will.

25. My self, now made my very own,
May shine abroad its inner light
In dark abysms of space and time.
A slumber seizes nature's being,

> But the deep hidden soul shall waken,
> And waking carry sunny gleams
> Into cold winter's tides and streams.

Here we have a reference to the approaching autumn season. The soul is urged to withdraw into itself and to pay heed to the secret working in its inner being. The soul's being grows self-aware and out of the darkness prevailing in summer, creates from 'sense of self' 'the fruit of will.' Hence the self, 'now made my very own,' can shed abroad its 'inner light / In dark abysms of space and time.'

The two following verses take us beyond summer into autumn. Michaelmas begins; Michael's twofold aspect appears in verses 26 and 27: the mighty form imbued with will bearing the sword, and the gentle glance, beckoning us to recognize ourselves.

When these two weeks are over it is already autumn within and without. The picture of verse 28 complements the description in verse 25:

> 28. Quickened anew within
> I feel the vastness of my being,
> And power is mine to shed clear rays of thought
> From the soul's sunlike potency
> Solving life's riddles,
> And granting many a wish fulfilment
> Whose wings had drooped with hope foregone.

A sense of triumphant spirit shines through these lines. The 'urges of the spirit,' tempered by the 'fiery might of the will,' have begun to be active and are transformed into the 'soul's sunlike potency.' This sheds its light into the dark wishes, whose wings had drooped because hope threatened to fail. Darkness of soul had lasted too long but now the rays of thought light up the darkness of many of the soul's riddles and waken hope to renewed activity. Our vision is directed into 'the ether-distances and the expanse of stars.' This is clearly revealed in verse 29:

29. To light in me the lamp of thinking
And fan with inner force the flame,
Illumining life's story
From the world spirit's well of power,
For me is summer's heritage,
Is autumn's peace and winter's hope to be.

In the pictures of these verses, there reappear for us the forms of the fairy story of the 'marvel of the spring.' The three women of the water begin to appear. The heritage of summer gives 'the strength of faith in life'; the calm of autumn gives 'the beams of life's love'; and the hope of winter offers us 'the draught of life's hope.' Past, present and future are spread out before us. If we arouse in us winter's hope it will appear as a youthful form, perhaps resembling the praying youth we know from Greece.

Pieper has drawn attention to this relationship between hope and youth:

> Youthfulness and hope are related in more than one way; the two belong together in both the natural and the supernatural sphere. The figure of youth eternally symbolizes hope ... Natural hope has its origin in the youthful vigour of man and dies away with it.[4]

He then quotes Thomas Aquinas' *Summa*: 'To be young is the source of hope; for youth has much future before it and little past behind.'

We now begin to catch sight of a process that appears to us like the revelation of a secret in verses 28 and 29. The youthfulness of hope, which during the summer had grown old, has been renewed through the appearance within the soul of the awaking power of thought's light, and enters there as new life. Now outer darkness can set in, but in our inner being the light has begun to shine and hope wakes again in all its youthfulness:

30. I joy to feel the spirit stir
Of autumn's watchfulness,
Winter shall wake in me
The summer of the soul.

In the following weeks the battle is fought out between the hardening earth and the light in the hope-filled soul. The soul does not win her victory until Advent; for only then does the summer seed of 'the word of worlds, in germ conceived' at St John's Tide, struggle upwards. In verses 36 and 37 this Christmas song of joy can be heard, ever more clearly audible, as it announces the birth of Christ:

36. Speaks from my being's depths,
Surging to revelation,
In secret wise the word of worlds.

And in the next verse:

37. With joy to carry spirit light
Into the winter night of worlds —
For this my striving heart is fain,

Then, in the expectant stillness of the approaching Christmastide, the song of joy, the *Jubilate,* rises upward, like a single violin accompanying the soprano of the human voice; the human soul sings the eternal paean of its new birth:

38. I feel the spell dissevered
In the soul's womb freeing the spirit child:
The holy word of worlds
Has in the heart's clear light
Begotten heaven's own fruit of hope,
Which, rising from the god in me,
Goes paeaning to the corners of the world.

Now the youthful being of winter's hope finds its true consummation. It has become 'the spirit child' in 'the soul's

womb,' and 'in the heart's clear light' has released from itself 'heaven's own fruit' the 'holy word of worlds.' This now grows into far cosmic distances, telling of the surrender of hope so that Christmas and the birth of the Child may come to pass.

In our inner being the figure of hope still holds its place. The spirit child has completed his yearly work. Gradually he loses himself in the deeds and sufferings of the soul, which now, by itself, must maintain the fire of the awakened word of worlds, 'heart's warmth' and 'soul's fire' fill the ever-increasing rigour of the world like the glow of a healing fire. Hope gathers warmth from the glow and maintains its being and activity until Passion-tide: then it greets the approaching light:

49. 'I feel your strength of life, O worlds,'
So the clear voice of thinking cries,
Mindful of its own spirit's growth
Through the dark world-nights achieved,
And to the world-day as it nears
Bending its inward rays of hope.

The power, which roused hope grown weary at the beginning of autumn, this light of thought, these beams of thought from the sun's light in the soul — this same power now sends forth the last rays of hope to meet the coming of the world's day. Without, morning approaches; within, in the soul, evening draws in. The day of winter's hope fades with the daybreak of the rising sun.

Now hope withdraws and returns again into the depths of our being there to wait until, with the next autumn, it is summoned forth to rise to the upper world of consciousness. The verses reveal a breathing out and in of the power of hope: some event closely connected with the course of the sun seems to be indicated. What direction, then, should our questing thoughts take?

3

The destiny of Persephone is experienced in reverse by hope in the human soul. In spring and summer it is banished into the depths of the subconscious until at the beginning of autumn it is called forth to be a sheath for the word of worlds, which is to be born at Christmas, 'Heaven's own fruit of hope.' Persephone, daughter of Demeter was, for the Greeks, a very special figure; the ancient Greek, says Rudolf Steiner, 'looked up to the goddess, who was regent of the old clairvoyance that was an element of human nature, and called her Persephone.'[5]

At one time, then, hope may well have been a stronger and more powerful faculty than it seems to us to be today. Just as Persephone was banished by the developing intellect into the depths of the underworld, so hope has withdrawn into the realm of the unconscious, and there lives on hidden.

In the lecture just quoted Rudolf Steiner makes an almost casual reference to the once all-embracing power of hope:

> We shall see how Demeter is regent of the mightiest miracle of Nature, a primal form of human feeling, thinking and willing, of which Persephone is the true offspring. Demeter points back to times when, so to speak, the human brain was not dissociated from the general activity of bodily life, when nourishment by food, coming from without, and thinking with the brain were not yet separate functions. Men then still felt how thoughts were active outside themselves: when the seed grew healthily in the fields, hope really did spread over the fields, pervading all the wondrous works of nature, like the song of the lark.

Thus we can say that there was a time when hope was active in the outer world, in the weaving and growing of nature, penetrating, like the song of the lark, into seeds as they grew, and

itself spreading outwards into the ether-distances and the starry heights: only in autumn did it then withdraw to within the soul. Today hope can do no more than direct our gaze to those heights and distances; but if we will turn our gaze there we will receive the 'draught of life's hope.'

Philia, Astrid and Luna, the figures who appear in the Mystery Dramas, may be regarded as the vehicles, in a new form, of faith, hope and love. They guide upwards again what had earlier declined with Persephone and the old clairvoyance. Rudolf Steiner does in fact say this, though only in veiled hints:

> There must be a connection within our souls between streams which give us an indication of man's origin, Demeter and Eros, with Persephone standing between them, and on the other hand a being hovering vaguely in the background without as yet any definite form, a sort of spiritual conscience, which resounds from the undefined and may not yet appear on stage any more than a 'voice off.' It is found in the figures of Luna, Philia and Astrid, who are really Demeter's daughters.[6]

These words hint at what takes place in the second mystery play, then (1911) being performed in Munich. The voice 'off' is that of the spirit-conscience, heard from behind the stage. Philia, Astrid and Luna are 'the spiritual beings who mediate the union of human soul-powers with the cosmos.' In the story of Frau Balde they are the forms of women appearing where the water springs from the rock.

In Scene 13 of *The Soul's Probation* these three beings thus manifest and reveal their activity:

> PHILIA: I will fill myself with light's power of faith.
> ASTRID: I will focus the rays of hope.
> LUNA: I will give warmth to the soul's light, and stability to the power of love.

Here again the three Pauline virtues make an appearance. It is they who mediate the connection of the human soul with the cosmos. Hope is one of them; like Persephone she has been overwhelmed by other forces and has had to withdraw into the soul's darkness. She must wait till the I, her brother Dionysus, awakens to the light again and unites himself with her. Then, as Edouard Schuré wrote, he says: 'Since the world's beginning I belong to thee'; and she replies: 'Until the world's end we are one.'[7]

Yet all this is only a tentative approach to the discovery of what hope really is; pictures appearing and hints vaguely discerned. In fact hope, though it pervades the whole human being, is yet, almost more than anything else, inaccessible to ordinary understanding. We all hope; we hope because we live; and we can live only as long as we hope: anyone falling into hopeless despair will seek only one end — death.

We owe it to the power of hope that every morning we begin our life anew. It is also by the power of hope that we can overcome doubt and despair when they seize upon us. Hope is active within us, permeates us, penetrates into us and maintains us in being. It is much more than a mere 'theological virtue.' It is a powerful force, to which we can have access only in the form of a virtue.

But when hope thus appears, it is only the tip of a huge iceberg. Its depths are hidden in the past in the grounds of the world, which will only gradually reveal themselves. One of Rudolf Steiner's verses is:

> In the head, the power of faith,
> In the heart, the might of love,
> In the whole man, strong hope
> Bears and upholds our life.[8]

The whole human being is pervaded by hope, which will disclose itself only when we recognize the all-embracing meaning of the word.

4

In 1911 Rudolf Steiner gave a whole series of lectures on the fundamental powers of the three virtues, faith, love and hope. To divine how deeply these three virtues are embodied in human existence calls for careful study. Love may be the greatest of them, but hope is the eldest. Before ever love and faith were, hope laid the first foundations of all that can come into existence. The whole world is founded upon hope; on it rests our whole existence. In one of these lectures we read:

> On old Saturn the seed of man's physical body was planted: what does that mean? It was planted in the element of man that was to endure. From this point of view the human body can justly be called the body of hope. The special quality of the physical body is its density. When the waves of the soul's life beat continually upon the human body, penetrating more and more deeply into it, it is filled with hope, with the assurance that out of it something will evolve that will last for ever, that is indestructible.[9]

Thus the oldest part of us, the beginning of our bodily existence, our physical body, is founded on hope. As an all-powerful force it permeates our physical organism from the beginning. Rudolf Steiner said elsewhere:

> Only then do we comprehend the true significance of our physical body when we bear in mind that, in reality, it is not sustained by external physical forces of attraction and repulsion — that is a materialistic idea — but has in it what, according to our concepts, we know as forces of hope. Our physical body is built up by hope, not by forces of attraction and repulsion.[10]

The density of the physical body, which makes it what it is today, is given to it through the soul-forces of hope. At the beginning of the world's evolution hope rayed into it and was then transformed at the various stages of evolution: Saturn, Sun, Moon and Earth, so that today, when it has become an inner quality of the individual soul, it is on the way to becoming one of the three Christian virtues.

In the lecture just quoted Rudolf Steiner refers clearly to this comprehensive quality of hope:

> The forces which we emphatically need as life-giving forces are those of hope, of confidence in the future. As far as the physical world is concerned, people cannot take a single step in life without it... It is precisely in physical life that we need hope, for everything is upheld by hope and without it nothing can be done.

Comments like this open up a wholly new aspect for a future understanding of hope. Once it was one of the basic forces out of which the physical body was created. Hope gave it solidity and its upright stance; out of it arose confidence for the future; on it was founded the law of its being. This was achieved on Old Saturn.

The force of love produced the etheric body during the Sun-existence and the power of faith created the astral body in the Moon-existence. These three forces were able by their activity to form the three sheaths for the human I:

> The inmost kernel of our being may be said to be sheathed in our faith body or astral body, in our body of love or etheric body, and in our hope-body or physical body.

These basic forces, faith, love and hope, penetrate deeply into the processes of world evolution and growth. Today they are accessible to us as no more than experiences and perceptions of the soul, although our whole being is imbued and

permeated by them: all that is firm and solid in us by hope, all that is in process of becoming by love, and all feeling by faith. The central core of our being knows these three, faith, love and hope, and recognizes itself in them. In the depths of winter, when the physical earth has become lifeless and the density of stone is the predominating experience, when, outside, the light dims, and cold makes everything hard and stiff, then, from this all-pervading rigidity, 'Heaven's own fruit of hope' is born (verse 38).

As the spark is struck from the stone and kindles the dry wood, so out of the darkness is born the youthful force of hope and delivers, new-begotten, the holy 'word of worlds,' which then becomes 'the beginning of the new creation' and 'the youthful forces of the morning.'

Hence each year at Christmas hope finds its highest fulfilment. It appears in our inner being as the spirit's child; it brings forth the word of worlds, and thence streams forth the finest fulfilment of all human hope, the ever-increasing knowledge of reincarnation and karma. Such knowledge itself brings 'satisfaction to the forces of hope in the human soul; it offers something that endures and leads us into the future.'[11]

The future of humankind can be assured only by the knowledge of reincarnation and karma: here hope feels its just fulfilment. And in the twelfth article of the creed of the Christian Community this is affirmed: 'Communities whose members feel the Christ within themselves ... may hope for the overcoming of the sickness of sin, for the continuance of man's being and for the preservation of their life, destined for eternity.'

Thus the winter solstice becomes the festival of the eternal renewal of the destined end of the human race. The heart then beats more strongly and clearly, since in the birth of the spirit's child it can see its hope fulfilled and can cry joyfully: 'Is not all eternity mine?' When Lessing wrote these words at the end of his famous essay he gave the force of hope its finest expression.[12]

Goethe devoted the last stanza of his poem, 'Urworte, Orphisch,' to hope: he divines the banishment and imprisonment of hope, which can nevertheless release itself from its enchantment:

> Yet from within these bounds, these adamantine walls,
> the dread portal is unlocked,
> though it stand with the strength of ancient rock.
> A being rises, light and free —
> she gives us wings and from out the mists,
> the rain and the mantle of clouds,
> she bears us up with her aloft.
> Ye know her well, she roams through all the spheres.
> One beat of her great wings and aeons fall behind us.

Forgetting and Losing: Seeking, Finding and Gaining

In *A Journey to the East,* a story by Hermann Hesse published in 1922, there is a description of the 'path' taken by a man who, in fellowship with others, undertakes a journey in search of higher knowledge. The search fails, and the failure makes him aware of his shortcomings. He is appalled to discover not only that he has lost the 'ring of fellowship' entrusted to him, but worse still that for a long time he had not even been aware of the loss. He says: 'In the midst of this came a new consciousness of failure, a new inexplicable omission, a new sense of shame: I no longer possessed the ring; I had lost it and did not even know when or where; in fact until today I had not even missed it.'

Here is clearly indicated the distress which accompanies all losing, mislaying, forgetting. Our sense of loss means that something which had been ours, or perhaps something which we had decided to do, has vanished from our consciousness and from ourselves. We feel such a loss as a sign of failure in ourselves and we react to it in various ways. We may look for someone or something to blame — ourselves, someone else, even circumstances. We experience a feeling of anger, doubt, anxiety, even indifference. In any case forgetting and losing have a strong emotional background — our feelings are very much involved.

A psychology of the future will have to enter into such experiences with the most sympathetic understanding, for in them are first revealed purely human impulses, which spring from the I and involve our conscience. Losing, seeking and finding are not merely external events, they are processes of soul, of a soul moreover touched with spirit.

This study aims at examining such inward relationships. All fairy stories tell of such seeking and finding. Similarly human life in general is a continuing effort to restore a normal balance when it has been disturbed by something attained, something lost, something found, something forgotten.

The Calendar deals with such efforts. It emphasizes the labour involved in preserving the balance of the soul in the course of the year. Thus Rudolf Steiner's original preface spoke of 'the soul in training':

> The soul will most effectively find itself when it lives
> in association and contact with the year in its course,
> when the change from one week to another exerts some
> influence on it: ... the soul should feel itself healthily
> at one with the course of nature and, as a consequence,
> effectively discover itself.

Here something more than a mere finding is emphasized; a 'finding of oneself' is indicated as well as the psychological qualities implied in the use of such words. Just as there is something which we may call 'finding oneself' as well as mere finding, so there is a 'forgetting of oneself' as well as just forgetting, and similarly a 'losing oneself' and a 'gaining oneself.'

The process involved, like some open secret, is revealed in the last of Rudolf Steiner's Twelve Moods:

> In the lost may loss find itself
> In the winning may the loss lose itself
> Loss — may it be winning for itself.[1]

This points us to the way which every soul here on earth takes or should take: as well as the outer, an inner way, which must become the path of our life and the way of our spirit. It is part of everyone's destiny to seek it, to find it, and then to lose it, in order to attain it anew. Thus the etymology of the word 'find' shows it as derived from the Indo-European root *pent,* which expresses the various ideas connected with *going, path, track, bridge.*[2]

The same thing is pointed out by the Lord to Mephistopheles when he hands over Faust for his soul's probation. 'In the dark impulses of his being a good man is well aware of the right path.' Such is the path followed by the Calendar, and its continuing purpose is to transform, more and more forcefully, that 'dark impulse' so that it becomes a 'finding of oneself.'

2

On February 27, 1919, Rudolf Steiner wrote a meditation which can be taken as a guide to our present study:

Seek within your own being
And you find the world:
Seek in the sway of the world
And you find yourself
Mark the swing of the pendulum
Between the self and the world
Then is revealed to you
World-being in man
Man's being in the world.[3]

Here is clearly shown the polarity of the human being and the world in their mutual striving: human beings seek the world and find themselves; and the world, in seeking itself, finds the human being. In the verses from week to week, the Calendar helps us to experience this process for ourselves.

Finding, however, is related not only to seeking, but also to losing. I may be able to find something lost but I must seek it before I can find it. Seeking thus occupies a middle position between losing and finding. We must therefore distinguish three related pairs: losing and seeking, losing and finding, seeking and finding. Seeking follows losing: the lost is found and seeking is crowned in finding.

In these three words, whether used as verb or noun, a gradual process is indicated. In them lives both becoming and fulfilment.

The process is the essential thing, not the attainment. As soon as the finding becomes the found, the losing becomes the loss, and the seeking becomes the sought, then the becoming is brought to a standstill. Worst of all is when seeking becomes the sought, for it then becomes mere self satisfaction, a craving or addiction.[4] Such a sought no longer tries to find the lost, but turns inward on itself. But loss is definite and finalizes the lost. The found confesses the finding and becomes what is won. Finding has attained what it sought.

In surveying this series we can note how manifold are the faculties of soul described in the various words, and how usage has imprinted a very definite meaning on each word.

If we include 'forgetting' and 'remembering,' both of which lie in the sphere of memory, we have an outline of the possibilities in this realm of the soul's being and activity shown in the following arrangement:

Finding	Attaining, grasping Finding, winning, gaining Remembering
Seeking	Investigating Searching Losing possession of
Losing	Forgetting Loss, losing Abandoning, failing, missing

With this outline in mind, let us examine the words given as found in the Calendar. They appear there in many forms, and we can proceed only gradually to work out their meaning.

Most commonly used is the word for finding. Next comes the word for losing. The other words occur only once or

twice; and the word for remembering occurs only in verses 19 and 46, as a noun.

3

We will now consider the words 'to find' and 'to lose.' After the soul's year has opened with an Easter Sunday verse of joyful greeting to the rising sun, we come at once to the drama of losing and finding in the second verse.

> 2. Into the utmost fields of sense
> The force of thought resigns its separate life.
> The worlds of spirit find
> Anew their offspring, man,
> Whose seed in them,
> But his soul's harvest
> Must in himself be found.

The idea merely hinted at in the Easter verse (1), 'Then thoughts from selfhood's narrow case / Draw outward to far spaces,' is described more clearly in the second verse. The meeting of soul and world has turned into an achievement of the will, which overwhelms the human being. The waking power of the light-filled world of sense constrains the world of thought to lose itself in it. A double process of finding is thus set in motion.

> The worlds of spirit find
> Anew their offspring, man,

There the seed is sown, but the fruit of that seed human beings must seek to find in themselves.

Human beings become conscious of this double process of 'finding.' The world becomes ever clearer and its call more powerful. To this they reply:

> 3. Speaks to the universe,
> Itself forgetting

And mindful of its primal form,
The waxing I of man.
'On you, from cramping fetters
Of isolation breaking,
I ground my own intrinsic being.'

Here first resounds the great theme which reverberates in the soul until St John's Tide: 'Lose, lose your self, yourself to find' (verse 9). Expanding in the light of the sun and in light-filled space, the I, forgetful of self, proclaims to the universe this great theme:

'On you, from cramping fetters
Of isolation breaking,
I ground my own intrinsic being.'

Here we have 'ground'; but the word might equally well have been 'find' or 'attain' or 'remember.' The word chosen by Rudolf Steiner is that most apt for the purpose: here it points the way to the journey into the 'ground of the world,' for which the soul must now prepare itself.

In the following verses the chief emphasis is on 'losing.' 'Losing' and 'forgetting' occur seven times between now and the fourteenth week, when the loss seems to be complete. In the middle of July the soul says:

14. Surrendered to the senses' revelation
I lost my being's proper urge,

But just because of this, deliverance can come, and to it the last lines of the verse point:

But waking presses on me still
World-thinking in the senses' glow.

From now on there must be no further mention of 'losing'; even the companion words, 'forgetting' and 'abandoning,' do not again occur, since what had been stated as the main theme, 'lose

your self, to find yourself,' has fully come about. The theme had continued to resound throughout spring and early summer: now a new experience takes its place.

But first let us study the essential stages which are made clear as part of the main theme.

In verse 9 the theme 'forgetting and losing,' was sounded fortissimo. Three times the theme is heard and at its last occurrence 'losing' is raised to be the main theme. We must learn to experience inwardly this growth in intensity so that the whole of our feeling harmonizes with this call. We have arrived at the week after Whitsun, when the world of sense has unfolded its greatest glory, when all is in blossom and filled with light. The scent and splendour streaming from every tree and shrub and meadow enchant the soul, and now we speak of ourselves as though wrapped in a shroud:

9. Forgetting all my separateness of will,
The warmth of worlds, the summer's harbinger,
I feel it flood my spirit and my soul.
To lose myself in light
The gaze of spirit now demands,
And powerfully prophetic boding cries:
'Lose, lose your self, yourself to find.'

At one point earlier, in verse 7, there had been a suggestion of this note. It was then, however, a note of warning, not of exhortation, for the time was not yet ripe for the I to carry out its self-imposed task and to leap into the universe. Verse 7 covers the pre-Whitsun period, when the human heart is filled with fear and anxiety:

7. My self threatens to break away
Through strong enticement of the light of worlds.
Now rise, my boding power,
Assume in strength your rightful throne,
Replace in me the might of thinking

Which in the senses' show
Is like to lose itself.

The powerful summons of verse 9 is followed by the content of verses 11 and 12. Before the period of St John's Tide, a hidden voice speaks to us:

11. In this the sun's high hour
Be yours its herald wisdom to embrace.
Surrendered to the beauty of the world
The self aware of self shall deeply own:
The I of man can lose itself
And find itself within the I of worlds.

Here the theme appears before the soul again in equivalent words. And in verse 12, which expresses the St John's Tide mood, man has made his decision. By his own impulse he now follows the call which has been uttered. He unfolds within him powers of courage and sacrifice, so that he may trust himself to the universe:

12. The world's bright loveliness
Constrains me in my inmost soul.
'Set free the godlike gifts you own
To wing their way into the universe,
Your narrow self forego,
And, trusting, seek that self again
In universal light and warmth.'

The attentive reader will at once notice that here, for the first time, 'finding' is replaced by 'seeking' and the word 'lose' by the much more comprehensive word 'forego,' or 'abandon.' The word 'seek' occurs only twice in the Calendar, here in verse 12 and in the following verse 13. After the surrender to the heights of sense, the 'word of worlds' speaks, flaming up within its soul:

13. Seek through your boding power
And find in spirit ground
Your spirit brotherhood.

In these verses, as is shown by the use in verse 14 of the past tense (lost), the soul has completed the process of 'losing itself , of 'foregoing' and of 'forgetting.' Careful attention to the verses reveals the following relationships: the three faculties of soul, thinking, feeling and will, are distinguished by three separate words to indicate their 'surrender.' For thinking, there is 'lose' ('might of thinking ... is like to lose itself,' verse 7): where will is concerned, the Calendar uses 'forgetting' ('forgetting all my separateness of will,' verse 9): the courage of the heart, which lives in feeling, is referred to in the word 'forego' ('your narrow self forego,' verse 12).

Thus the hidden power and order can be recognized which ensures that in the Calendar every word is used in its appropriate place.

4

The real marvel of the Calendar's structure reveals itself fully only when we trace the development of a word's meaning as it is used in one season and another throughout the year.

Let us look first at the quartet of verses 9, 18, 35 and 44. In each of the first three the word 'find' appears and is in itself enough to reveal their inner relationship; in the fourth, 'finding' becomes 'grasping.'

We are looking for the successive metamorphoses of the main theme, 'lose your self, yourself to find.' The summer verse is:

18. Can I expand my soul
To grapple to her being
This word of worlds in germ conceived?
I do forebode I strength must find

To found and form my soul
A garment worthy of the spirit.

The autumn verse, for the first week of Advent, runs:

35. Can I then the being know
That, known, it find itself again
In the soul's urgence to create?
I feel the power entrusted me
My own self humbly to insert
A living member in the self of worlds.

The fourth verse in the group, for the beginning of February, is:

44. Grasping new spurs of sense,
Mindful of spirit-birth fulfilled,
Clearness of soul outpours
Into the wildering teeming life of worlds
The will creative in my thinking.

As we pass from one verse to the next, we see an increasing intensity in the meaning of the word used. We move from 'find' to 'find again' and so to 'grasp.' What does this signify?

In verse 9 the soul has accepted the behest, 'lose your self, yourself to find,' and as a result it has received the 'seed of the divine word of worlds' planted within it. Its task, in the three succeeding stages, is to find itself. The first step is:

... I strength must find
To found and form my soul
A garment worthy of the spirit.

The second stage, at the beginning of Advent, is to acquire the humility which will enable being to

... find itself again
In the soul's urgence to create

If this is achieved we come to the true Christmas, the birth of the spirit in the soul. The final 'loss' was described in verse 14:

> Surrendered to the senses' revelation
> I lost my being's proper urge,

And the recovery of what was then lost is announced in the corresponding verse 39:

> Surrendered to the spirit's revelation
> I win the light of universal life.

This is the only time the word 'win' is used in the Calendar. It describes what can be seen at the period of the twelve Holy Nights, the light of the world's being, the sun at midnight.

When this climax has been reached, the soul moves on in the course of the year to the final verse of the group we are considering and turns again to the surrounding world:

> 44. Grasping new spurs of sense ...
> Clearness of soul outpours

This new 'grasping' of the sense-world, as it awakes and reveals itself, is made possible by the power of the 'spirit-birth fulfilled.' Here 'grasping' is the opposite of 'forgetful' in verse 9. What in springtime had to be withdrawn from the will is now restored to the senses. The circle of our theme over the year is now completed.

But there is another quartet of verses, in which 'finding' and 'losing' occur, and in which a process is at work through the course of the year. Verse 7 has already been mentioned: in it is a warning against a premature surrender of oneself:

> 7. My self threatens to break away
> Through strong enticement of the light of worlds.

Here the reference is to the thinking which itself wishes to lose itself. All the verses of this second group (20, 33, 46 and 7) contain similar warnings. All are concerned with the struggle

to be decided between the soul and the world. Either the soul, under a Luciferic temptation, experiences a force lifting it above the world or else, with Ahrimanic power, the world seeks to choke the soul. In all the verses which we are now considering we have to deal with deviations from the main theme, deviations which must be endured as a kind of probation. The summer probation describes the soul overwhelmed by the world's glory and near to choking:

20. Now first I feel my being —
Which, torn from world existence,
Within itself must quench the self,
And building on itself alone
Must kill the self-enclosed self.

In this verse there is no 'finding' or 'losing' or indeed anything equivalent. The struggle seems to have ended. The soul has been maimed and can now speak only of 'quenching' and 'killing.'

The autumn probation displays the same desolation: we are in the November mood here:

33. Now first I feel the world,
Which, reft of my indwelling soul,
Would as a frozen waste
Unfold its feeble life,
Create itself anew in human souls,
That in itself could look for death alone.

But there is a gleam of hope. The soul seeks to imbue the frozen earth with its own life; and its awaking confidence re-introduces the word 'look for' (that is, 'find'). Despair is changed to consolation.

The winter probation, falling in the days of Carnival, is of another kind. The world, expanding and extending itself, is like to overcome and annihilate the soul:

46. The world threatens to stupefy
The inborn forces of my soul.
Now rise from spirit-depths
In all your radiance, memory.
Establish my beholding,
Which only through the force of will
Can hold itself erect.

In this verse memory is called to shed its rays of light from spirit depths. It is the same memory which was commissioned in verse 19 to 'wrap the new conceived germ' in its folds; it enclosed the 'word of worlds in germ conceived.' It is now invoked to strengthen the awakened power of vision brought into being from the spirit's birth. The light of the world-being, won at the time of the summer solstice, must not be lost under the world's assault: this is the admonition given to us here.

5

Once the winter probation is over a new process can begin. The flood-gates of early spring open and allow all the powers of awaking life to stream forth to expectant nature: but now that all the tests have been passed, they will no longer overwhelm the soul. This is the tenor of the verse for the first week in March:

47. There shall arise from out the womb of worlds
The bliss of growth, fostering joys of sense;
My force of thinking may it find
Armed with the forces of the gods,
Which live a quickening force in me.

Human beings have now found what they were seeking. 'Armed with the forces of the gods,' their newly awakened thinking, they oppose the onslaught of spring's 'bliss of growth.' They have for the moment achieved their object, and henceforth it is

not they, but the world, that has the task of 'finding.' The world seeks the god-filled human beings because only in them can it reach its goal. This is what happens between human beings and the world during Passion-tide.

The soul bears within itself the newly-developed force of thinking like some powerful light, and 'the bliss of growth' strives towards it. The verses for weeks 50 and 51 lead us on to this experience:

50. Speaks to the human I
In strong self-revelation,
Enlarging all its being's powers,
The bliss of growth in world existence.
'To you my life transporting
Unbanned from its enchantment
I reach my own true goal.'

51. Into the inmost life of man
The senses pour their wealth,
The spirit of the world beholds
His mirrored image in the eye of man,
That eye which from that spirit
Must still renew its power.

It can be a deeply moving experience for the soul to recognize that the task of 'finding' and 'attaining' is taken out of its hands and transferred to the world-spirit, which reveals the 'bliss of growth': and to recognize also that it has itself become the aim of this 'finding,' even that the eye becomes a mirror of the world if it looks rightly on this work of growth.

Just as in the period after Easter we must rediscover the spirit ruling in the world, so in the period before Easter the spirit seeks for and reaches the human soul.

The verses near the beginning and at the end of the soul's year meet in harmony and solace, and tell of this mutual seeking and finding:

2. The worlds of spirit find
Anew their offspring, man,

51. The spirit of the world beholds
His mirrored image in the eye of man,

and again:

3. On you, from cramping fetters
Of isolation breaking,
I ground my own intrinsic being.

50. To you my life transporting
Unbanned from its enchantment
I reach my own true goal.

The soul must continually hold this harmony before it and seek to give it warmth with the force of its sympathetic feeling. Only then will the Calendar point out the way, which will lead to the experience of the Risen One. The name of Christ is not mentioned in a single verse; yet it is he whose being pervades every line, his way and his truth, which permeate them. It is his life which we follow, his way which the soul seeks, his truth which is found in the word of worlds. The verses of the Calendar are saturated with all this. They proclaim in a renewed form what has been handed down to us in the Gospels:

> If anyone wishes to be a follower of mine, he must leave self behind; he must take up his cross and come with me. Whoever cares for his own safety is lost; but if a man will let himself be lost for my sake, he will find his true self. What will a man gain by winning the whole world, at the cost of his true self? Or what can he give that will buy that self back? For the Son of Man is to come in the glory of his Father with his angels. (Matt.16:24-27 NEB).

The verses of the Calendar speak of this struggle, of losing and finding, of seeking and attaining. The words contain the power of the proclamation that the Son comes in the glory of the Father. Today what was foretold earlier has come to pass. In lectures on the appearance of Christ in the etheric world, Rudolf Steiner said in 1910:

> What Paul had experienced, the presence of Christ in the atmosphere of the earth, other men will be able to experience by a now natural clairvoyance, beginning with the years 1930–40 and then over longer periods, as something wholly natural. The event of Damascus will be repeated in many other men, and that event we may call the second coming of Christ in the spirit ... The second coming is brought about when men can raise themselves to the faculty of 'seeing the Christ in the etheric.' This is what we must wait for in this period of transition.[5]

What was once proclaimed to the disciples as something to be expected is now beginning to come about, as Rudolf Steiner indicated here and elsewhere. The cosmic communion mediated by the Calendar is a preparation for this fulfilment.

6

Let us sum up in a single list and a single diagram what we have been speaking about. They will stimulate the reader's own thoughts and insights, making what has been sketched in outline here come alive.

The list below gives the numbers of the verses which contain the individual words here discussed. The symbol at the end of each line refers to similar symbols in the diagram.

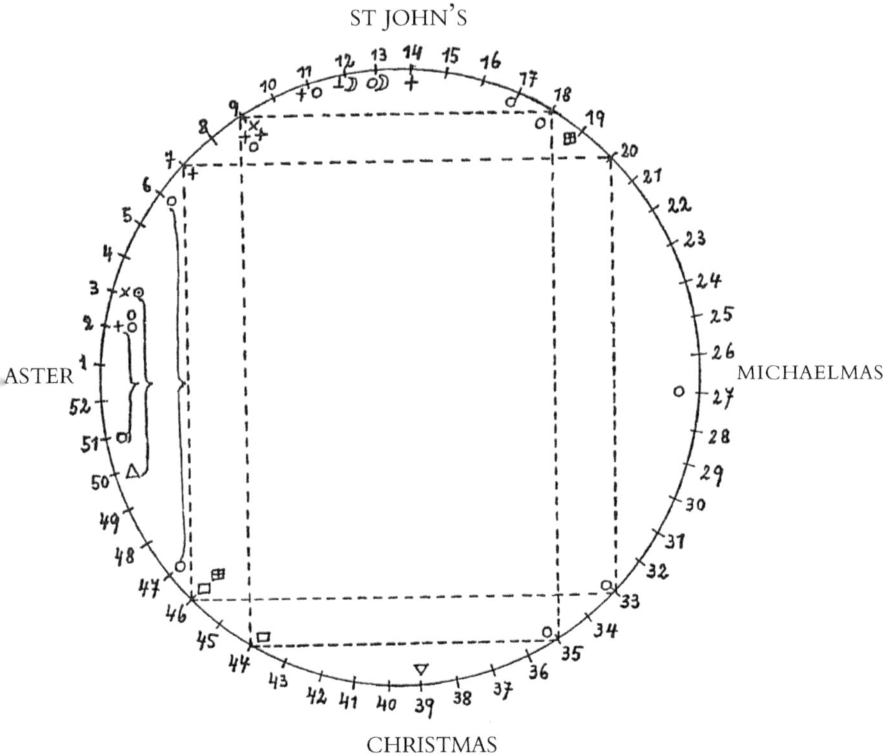

Forgetting: 3, 9 X
Losing: 2, 7, 9, 11, 14 +
Abandoning: 12 ⊥
Seeking: 12, 13 ☽
Grounding: 3 ⊙
Finding: 2, 2, 6, 9, 11, 13, 17, 18, 27, 33, 35, 47, 51 ○
Winning: 39 ▽
Grasping: 44, 46 □
Memory: 19, 46 ⊞
Attaining: 50 △

An Inner Journey through the Year

Soul Images and Soul Calendar

Richard Steel

'The year has a life of its own.' With this simple sentence Rudolf Steiner began his foreword for the second edition of the *Calendar of the Soul* in 1918. This was a new kind of calendar where an objective realm of living substance finds its expression through the art of the word. The verses do not tell us: 'This is what you have to do.' It is striking that his design for the cover of the 1925 edition — which is still used today — does not say 'Rudolf Steiner'; in fact, his name does not appear there at all. Something speaks out of the living being of the year which can be perceived through an artistic approach. Anyone who attempts this approach — we learn from the foreword — 'will feel that forces are stirring within him, giving his soul new life and strength.' These are not forces which lead one away from everyday toils and troubles but, rather, prepare one to meet them: 'Only through such experiences can the soul become aware of those delicate but significant threads connecting it to the world into which it was born.'[1]

Thus what is being aimed at here is no less than enabling the soul to find a new connection to this world into which it has been born and which is not the soul's true home. The question that then arises is, which voice out of the living realm of time can help to make this possible? However, it is not the task of the

Calendar to wrestle with a question but to assist us in forming an existential connection to that being, speaking out of the living realm of time and to let it *live within* our own soul. This is first and foremost an artistic task, a question of practice.

In 1910, during the time that Halley's Comet was just about to come close to the Earth, perhaps as a kind of counterbalance to this, Rudolf Steiner began an intensive programme of lectures in many places where he spoke about the new appearance of the being of Christ in our age, as though preparing the quality of perception that would be needed for this. He spoke about a new epoch which would begin to manifest itself 'between 1930 and 1940/45.'[2] He referred several times to this period as the beginning of the new appearance of the being of Christ and on one occasion directly specified the year 1933.[3] That humanity would have to be prepared for this historic situation was obvious to him, particularly considering the dangers inherent in this development.

The idea of a Calendar arose at the beginning of 1911 in conversation with Imma von Eckhardtstein, who was not only deeply involved with the production of the Mystery Dramas but was also engaged in the discussions regarding a suitable building for them, which then became the Goetheanum in Dornach. She had been given the task by Rudolf Steiner to draw new designs for the signs of the zodiac in accordance with the sketches that he had given to her; and these were to be used in the new Calendar.[4]

Imma von Eckhardtstein also participated in the development of a special project which was of great importance to Rudolf Steiner at that time and was to create a new realm where the true significance of the arts for human evolution and social development could unfold out of esoteric work. The Society for Theosophical Life and Art was to be founded on December 15, 1911 as an experiment in spiritual community building. It was not possible for this vision to be implemented, and the Soul Calendar can, in fact, be regarded as this society's only fruit, in that at its one and

only gathering on the day of its founding the decision was made to publish the Calendar with its weekly verses.

Thus we can see the Calendar of the Soul as having a connection on the one hand with Rudolf Steiner's hopes and intentions for a spiritually oriented community impulse with an artistic foundation and, on the other hand, with therapeutic and prophylactic measures in response to developments and existential challenges that Rudolf Steiner saw approaching humankind.

The significance of the Calendar, which Rudolf Steiner gave both for social life and for inner development in changing and testing times, was linked by a thread of destiny with the impulses and the engagement of a friend in Stuttgart who shared these aims. This was Emil Molt, who is best known because he later asked Rudolf Steiner to found a school for the children of the workers of his Waldorf-Astoria cigarette factory, thus starting the worldwide Waldorf School movement. Thus it came about that the Soul Calendar verses were printed in little booklets and sent in cigarette packets to thousands of soldiers at the front during the First World War. Molt's friendship with Hermann Hesse, who also signed Rudolf Steiner's appeal on behalf of the Movement for Social Threefolding, 'To the German People and to the Cultural World,' was the crucial factor that led to the verses being sent to prisoner-of-war camps under the imprint of the Library for German Prisoners of War.[5] These two editions of the Calendar were not for general sale and included a specially written foreword.

Exactly when Karl König first encountered the Calendar of the Soul we do not know; we have however found an entry in his diary showing that he began to work with it in 1933 with great intensity. At any rate, if it were exactly seven years or not, he had already studied and worked with it so thoroughly that by May 1940 he was able to bring the verses into the forefront of his work. He used the time that he was obliged to spend in the internment camp on the Isle of Man not only to draw the 52

coloured pictures that have been reproduced in this volume but also to study the verses with anthroposophical friends who were also interned there.*

The list of publications that Hans Müller-Wiedemann added to his biography of Karl König gives an indication of the rich range of themes that he was working with at that time. Despite his situation of exile, wartime concerns and the task of building up a community for curative education — something which demanded much of him, not just in organizational terms but also in the training of inexperienced colleagues and assistants, in his capacity as a doctor and in purely practical life skills — his energy and enthusiasm for research never forsook him. Around the time of starting at Kirkton House with the first group of children in need of special care, he was informed that the British government would not recognize his Austrian medical qualifications, despite his extensive experience with his own practices, and as one of those responsible for the curative children's home in Pilgramshain. Thus between May 1939 and March 1940, on top of all his other tasks, he had had to study for a British examination at the University of Dundee. One marvels that at the same time he was able to write a three-part volume about classifications in the animal kingdom. The notebook that he used for the time in Dundee contains not only studies on anatomy, the functions of the inner organs and similar themes but also, surprisingly, over a hundred detailed pages of deep and far-reaching contemplations about various animal species.

König did not specify — even in the more intimate realm of his diary — why he turned to the Soul Calendar in particular during his internment, using it for his own studies, embellishing it artistically and helping others to form a connection to it. We can, however, see something of the inner context from the

* In 1940 all male 'enemy aliens' (including ironically German and Austrian Jews who had fled the Nazi regime) were interned on the Isle of Man, between England, Scotland, Ireland and Wales. Thus all the men were brought to the island from Kirkton (the forerunner of Camphill — the planned move to Camphill Estate was managed by the women on their own). On the Isle of Man they met other similarly interned anthroposophists.

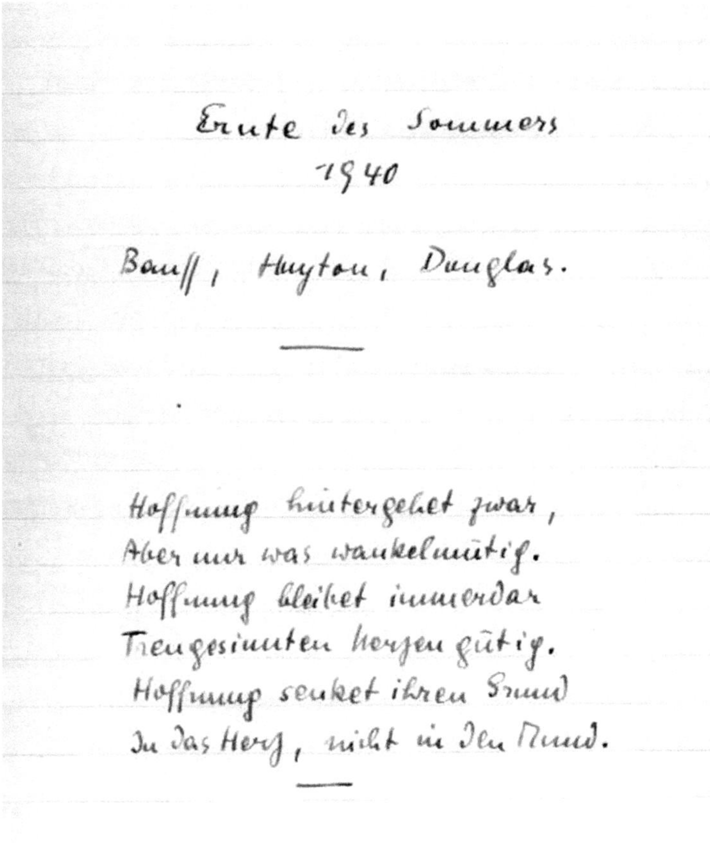

Ernte des Sommers
1940

Banff, Huyton, Douglas.

Hoffnung hintergehet zwar,
Aber nur was wankelmütig.
Hoffnung bleibet immerdar
Treugesinnten Herzen gütig.
Hoffnung senket ihren Grund
In das Herz, nicht in den Mund.

Harvest of the Summer, 1940
Banff, Huyton, Douglas

Hope can indeed be dilatory,
But only where there is vacillation.
Hope remains constant
In its good-heartedness where loyalty reigns.
Hope lays its foundations
In the heart, not the mouth.

Notebook 1940. König noted the various stages on the journey to the internment camp, as he was not told where he was going to.

Die Weiterführung dieses Buches
wurde durch meine
Internierung
5 Monate
lang
unterbrochen.

Das Dazwischen Entstandene ist
in das Buch
„Ernte"
eingetragen.

Oktober
1940
Camphill

The continuation of this book was interrupted
by the five months of my internment.
What arose in the meantime has been copied
into the book 'Harvest.'

October 1940, Camphill

history of the origin and publication of these verses. Steiner's concern to furnish those struggling at the front in the First World War with content showing positive paths of development, and to remind them of their true connection to the world and to the spirit, and of their true task in the world. This was reflected in the motives that König strove towards during the Second World War. One is reminded of his unbroken intentions whilst fleeing from Germany and his hope of taking up and carrying forward the 'true destiny' of Central Europe and the unfulfilled task of Rudolf Steiner.[6] And then there was also the connection of the Calendar with the artistic impulse of community.

Art was always important in Karl König's life. Of course, he had a rich legacy of experiences through the destiny of having grown up in Vienna, but his approach to art was — as in many other things — very individual. He was not strikingly talented in any single art form but consciously used music, poetry, drama, painting and drawing — both as a recipient and a practitioner — as media for coming into contact with and expressing the feelings of his soul and the strivings of his spirit. Especially his abundant poetry, which began from his early youth and continued into his sixties, enables us to participate in a moving way in the manifold colours of his soul experiences and his own path of development. His art was the companion and supporter of his own path, entrusted to his diary and notebooks and only in exceptional circumstances — for example the plays that he wrote for festivals in the Camphill years — open to more public access. His pictorial art was likewise very much linked to inner experience and for the most part remained within the family. The pictures published here were the product of his personal work during his months of internment, and he gave them to his wife on returning home, together with a verse of dedication. Only after his death, and even then almost by chance, did they become known to even his closest colleagues.

The pictures were not meant to have any identity of their own but rather to be indicative of something: more like signposts, helping one to find one's way to the actual substance of the verses and

their process of soul development, while always allowing space for one's own further work. During the months of his path of exile in 1938 and 1939, leading from Vienna through Italy, Switzerland and France to England and Scotland, König had already drawn a series of coloured pictures in a little booklet that he then sent with a dedication to his wife, who was still waiting in Vienna. As one can see from the title-page, this notebook was concerned with a simple question not in a theoretical, but in a deeply autobiographical and contemporary way, namely, 'What is a Christian?' Each aspect of this question is accompanied on a separate page of the booklet by a simple coloured drawing. In a similar way to the pictures of the Soul Calendar hardly more than a year later, we find ourselves looking at images which at first make the impression of being very naive and of a purely personal nature, but which, for the viewer who allows himself to become a beholder (or perhaps a listener), reveal a level of truth and beauty beyond the personal. Esoteric symbolism of this nature reminds us, perhaps, of Rudolf Steiner's sketches from his early years.[7]

Karl König had special gifts that arose from a certain depth of experience, a natural sense of judgment and an intuitive quality of perception. It was a life's task to ensure that temperament and fire of will did not overrule but, rather, utilized these gifts; similarly, it became for him a conscious endeavour not to allow these qualities to be suppressed by scientific schooling but to use them in such a context as a resource and an enhancement. Therefore it was such a deep relief for him to encounter Goethean thought during his studies, enabling these two sides of his being to begin to unite in a conscious fashion.

How different this had been a century earlier for the young Charles Darwin, who stated in his autobiography that he had suppressed his love of artistic activities in order to use all his energy for research, but that because of this the necessary sense of judgment diminished and allowed the results of a lifelong journey of discovery to drift into an unwanted course. When they were young students, Charles Darwin in 1825 and Karl König in 1925,

they had the same burning questions as to the nature of life and development, of human beings and their relationship to the animal kingdom, but the paths that evolved from those questions were so very different. Not that the richly imaginative, spontaneously mobile quality of König's thinking was always of advantage to him on his biographical path; in fact he often met opposition, misunderstanding and even enmity, not only from the scientific world but mainly from his fellow anthroposophists.[8] And yet for many people it was his imaginative method of description, his ability to evoke pictures and living thoughts in his audience, that was of such a help in grasping the far-reaching thoughts of anthroposophy, and to feel encouraged to pursue research and study of their own. Many of his listeners have testified to the way that they could virtually 'see' what he was speaking about. For example, he delighted in conjuring up the essence of an animal, so that an elephant or turtle could be envisaged through a mere gesture. His own imagination was so strong that it could be directly experienced by those following his train of thought.

Thus the picture as an artistic medium — and in terms of its *mediating* function — can assist the cognitive process from two directions: it can widen or enliven the scope of understanding beyond the realm of everyday sense-perception, and it can enable a thought to become manifest for the perception of others. In this sense the drawings for the Calendar of the Soul are not pictures *of* the verses but are a pictorial path *towards* where the verses live. We can therefore speak of the pictorial aspect as a process of becoming, which incorporates the time element of development. This lived already in the dedication that Karl König wrote for his wife, Tilla, when presenting her with the drawings:

> Thus from leaf to leaf* a tree is formed
> Which, now that it is complete, leads you through the year,
> Coming newly to birth week by week
> In growing and unifying harmonies.

* The German *Blatt* means leaf or page.

In Deine Hände leg ich nun die Blätter,
Die ich, in langen Stunden sehnend schrieb.
Und jedes Bild war der Erretter
Aus dunkler Ahnung, die mich trieb.

Und jedes Blatt ist aus dem Schmerz geboren,
Dem Schmerz, den Trennung bringt und Einsamkeit;
Wenn stille Tage sich in Nacht verloren
Und Nacht sich wieder an den Tag gereiht.

So ist aus Blatt um Blatt ein Baum geworden
Der nun, vollendet, durch das Jahr Dich führt
In wechselnden und sich vereinenden Akkorden
Woche auf Woche neu gebiert.

Dann hörst Du vielleicht auch die Melodie
Aus den Akkorden dieses Jahres-Baumes steigen
Das Lied, das ewig unbegrenzt wie nie
Aus meinem Herzen klang; Die Liebe der sich unsre Herzen neigen.
Dann werden unsre Seelen friedvoll zueinand' sich neigen.

There is no question here of comparing Karl König's very personal artistic achievement with that of an artist like Goethe, but if one considers the path of self-development that runs through his biography and takes into account the ideals he strove to fulfil in the daily life of community-building, one may well be reminded of Rudolf Steiner's words about Goethe:

> Art reveals those secrets of nature without which we can never fully understand her. From a certain point onwards it is imperative that we should understand the form and structure of the world as an artistic creation. And once we have taken the path from a purely scientific conception of the world to an artistic

---

←

I place the pages now in your hands,
Pages that I drew over many long hours
And each page was the saviour
From a dark sense of foreboding that pursued me.

And every page has been born out of pain,
The pain that separation and solitude bring;
When quiet days merge into night
And night again follows the day.

Thus from leaf to leaf a tree is formed
Which, now that it is complete, leads you through the year,
Coming newly to birth week by week
In growing and unifying harmonies.

And then, perhaps, you will also hear the melody
Rising from the chords of this tree of the year:
The song that sounded ever... and as never before
From my heart: the love towards which our hearts incline.
Then our souls will draw peacefully together.

> understanding of it, we shall also be ready to take the third step, which leads to a deepening of religious experience ... Human willing rises to the level of artistic creativity and finally achieves a relationship to the world that is not merely a matter of passively getting to know it but a positive, active surrender. Such a quality entails that man no longer looks at the world abstractly, with the forces of his head, but he begins increasingly to perceive with his own being. Living with the course of cosmic existence becomes a relationship that is different from his connection with the facts and events of everyday life. It becomes a ritual, and the cosmic ritual comes into being. Every earthly ritual is a symbolic reflection of this cosmic ritual.[9]

This theme of 'living with the course of cosmic existence' is interwoven with the substance of the essays (pages 207ff) where the aspects of metamorphosis, rhythmical principles and the language of the Soul Calendar are in the foreground. These aspects were to König a central element in the inner striving that underlay the community-building impulse, whereas the 52 pictures for the weekly verses remained undiscovered until long after his death. Now it is left to us to solve their riddles and find ways of using them to guide us along our own path with the weekly verses.

Art played an important part in the life of the developing community and the gradual spread of the Camphill movement. The hope was that the centres would become 'cultural islands,' where the arts would be able to offer their gifts to individuals for therapy and general human development and where, at the same time, artists and the arts themselves would find a home and a nurturing atmosphere for the own development, in turn raying out into society. Carlo Pietzner was one of the central figures in this artistic work; he was already a well-known painter when he joined König's youth group in Vienna and followed him to become one

of the founders of Camphill. To begin with he was completely involved with practical developments, and König in those early days gave him the task of caring for the finances. For many years he was also responsible for a house-community including children with severe spastic cerebal palsy. Pietzner was often asked by König for help with artistic matters, and among his drawings there were some for the Soul Calendar work, like the one on page 238. It was Pietzner who made the community aware of paricular comments that Rudolf Steiner had made regarding the social question, including this passage about the future of art:

> What will become a reality in the future is borne within us today in our ideals. If we ourselves fashion the world, it will be real. This should not live in us merely as a theory; it must be something that we feel, an innermost impulse of our lives. Then we shall simultaneously have a cognitive and a religious relationship to our environment. Out of this innermost impulse art, too, will become something quite different in the future. Art will become something that has an intimate connection with everyday life. Our very existence will need to find an artistic form.[10]

This became one of the high ideals that the small group of Central European refugees endeavoured to implement in the everyday reality of daily life and to implant into the nucleus of the growing community.

The Calendar of the Soul increasingly became an integral part of this community striving, and until his death at Easter 1966 König spoke about it in innumerable lectures, especially in his addresses at every festival. The weekly verses would be regularly 'accompanied' by the various arts, by music, speech, painting and eurythmy (Rudolf Steiner's choreography had to be adapted, because for a long time there were at the most only two eurythmists available, and there was no stage until 1962.) Since those pioneering days many people have studied and regularly turned to the

pictures after they had been rediscovered, realizing that the enigmatic character of the pictures has re-awakened their awareness of the manifold widths and spiritual depths of those words that Rudolf Steiner had been able to discern and cast into poetic form.

It was very clear to Karl König that the arts can become a path towards a new level of experience of the flow of time in which we live as human beings, a conviction which became part of the innermost challenge that he felt to be his earthly task; for a deepening of our perception of 'cosmic rhythms' leads us to that realm in which the being of Christ lives in our age. In this sense may Karl König's own words rightly introduce us to the study of his pictures, helping us to find a deeper connection to the course of the year and to its own life:

> It was a Michaelic deed of Rudolf Steiner's to write down the Calendar of the Soul, and it is a Michaelic deed to take this Soul Calendar earnestly into one's own heart and soul and live with it there ...
>
> The Calendar of the Soul can indeed be regarded as a path of initiation which leads into the planetary spheres and leads to that sphere in which the etheric Christ lives.'[11]

Karl König with his children and colleagues at Kirkton House, early 1940.
Back: Karl König, Alix Roth, Peter Roth, Anke Roth (later Weihs)
Front: Andreas, Veronika, Renate, Christof König.

Life with the Images of the Calendar of the Soul

Christof-Andreas Lindenberg

Karl König drew the 52 pictures for the verses of the Calendar of the Soul in primitive circumstances with coloured pencils on cheap paper. Together with other male members of the newly founded curative-educational community (not as yet called Camphill) between May and October 1940 he was in an internment camp on the Isle of Man, where intensive anthroposophical work took place among the 'enemy aliens' there.

We may suppose that König was aware of the double nature of the relationship between opposite verses; he had probably come to recognize the way that groups of four verses had an affinity with one another, as was indicated by Rudolf Steiner when ascribing numbers and letters to each verse. However, König spoke about this internal structure only later, when — after his release from the camp — he wanted to stimulate his friends and colleagues in Camphill to work with it.[1]

I shall consider and describe the drawings in the light of this principle of fourfoldness.

The senses' might grows great
Bonded with the gods' creating

These first two lines of the eighth verse express something of the mood into which we are led when contemplating the picture,

insofar as the drawing seeks to express something more than what can be apprehended purely by the senses. The eighth verse may be seen as the Whitsun verse. There is a verse from May 1915 in *Verses and Meditations* entitled 'Whitsun' which begins with these words:

> Where outer senses' knowledge ends,
> There and there only is the gateway
> That leads to the realities of life ...

One might therefore call someone who studies pictures with a spiritual content a frequent crosser of thresholds, one who thus stands at the boundary of the sense-world. Of course, a similar situation applies to a sculpture, a eurythmy performance and even to a piece of music, albeit in a different way. But all the same, if one is looking at or listening to art that is spiritually enlivened, one is engaged in an experience that is both of a sensory and a supersensory nature and can open oneself up in two directions at once.

At the bottom of Karl König's drawing for this verse (see page 343) there is a tree, as though growing out of the brown earth and surrounded by light-green spring foliage; behind it is a different green, then blue; perhaps a largish lake extending above the mid-height of the tree. That section of the picture has a brown frame. We are somewhat restricted here in our sensory perception. Above the light-filled crown of the tree a supersensible event manifests itself: in the upper part of the picture one can see a kind of giant blossom consisting of a number of rays, which shine forth in the three primary colours of yellow, red and blue. Its size and rich colours, in contrast to the puny dimensions of the tree, suggest that this can only be a spiritual organ. The sixteen-petalled lotus flower that we are to develop within us is, of course, smaller than this, but one could speak of a giant sun that is projected outwards but is nevertheless an inner reality! Perhaps this intimate, inner reality can, in being externalized, unite with something coming from without?

When godlike being
Will join in union with my soul,
Then human thinking
Must bow in peace to dream existence.

We recognize the moment of joining in union! Perhaps the tree at the foot of the picture represents our thinking's gesture of acceptance, its bowing in peace.

Pictures 8, 19, 34 and 45

Many years ago I set the so-called Whitsun cross verses (8, 45, 19 and 34) to music, an undertaking in the course of which I encountered the rhythmical differences in the verses: the first verse in triple time, the last in a contrasting quadruple time *(Es festigt sich Gedankenmacht* — the first line of verse 45 — cannot be sung in triple time), with the two verses in between being more or less similar but more rhythmical than the other two. The attempt to utilize the voices suggested by König in the setting was an interesting exercise. The four-part choral song entitled the 'Whitsun Cross' was initially performed at the first big Camphill conference on the Soul Calendar in Föhrenbühl in 1973.[2] This was seven years after König's death.

It was there that the collection of König's original pictures could be viewed for the first time by members of Camphill communities and conference participants; hitherto they had been kept privately by his widow, Tilla — after all, Karl König had dedicated this portfolio to her, giving it to her when he returned from the internment camp at the beginning of October 1940. When I visited 'Frau Doktor' in Botton Village shortly before the conference and saw the pictures for the first time, I intuitively recognized the transcendent significance of the miniature works of art. However, it was only several years later that they made a deep impression on me, when Günther Lehr made the first prints of the 52 pictures and copies of the 13 cross motifs;

for it then became possible for me to put each week's picture up individually and live with them. What had already long become an experience for me from a musical standpoint — the connections of the verses with one another — could now gradually manifest through experiencing the pictures. Through König's essays I learnt to distinguish between a *mirroring* of two verses, as at Michaelmas and Easter, and a *complementing,* as with the verses for Christmas and St John's. What was for me an immediate musical experience did not occur to me for a long time in the case of the pictures — that is, also to look at the pictures for the 'opposite' verses together. We shall try to do this in what follows.

In the picture for verse 45 the opposite becomes apparent in a different way as a mirroring or amplification. We again see a tree, this time growing out from four stations of life: from the cradle to the bier and from the altar of special occasions to the wheel of the ever-recurring multitude of daily events. Above the tree with its seven branches rises a countenance that manifests its inner life openly to the world, thus giving expression to a spiritual birth. Enclosing or embracing the revelation of the senses one sees a blue form representing the 'power of thought' (as in the verse). A light border emerges around the crown of the tree, and now a new union, a new joining 'in union' can be seen between the sensory revelation of the tree of life and the light of thinking which is received from above. Thus life ('plenitude of soul') and spirit ('the life of worlds') are juxtaposed in a uniting way in the totality of the picture. The inversion in these two pictures can ultimately be discerned in the single small blue point of the lotus flower on the brow of the spiritually developed human being which is at the opposite pole to the large circular form of the sixteen-petalled flower (picture 8). Circle and point are an archetypal polarity that comes to expression between the Whitsun verse and verse 45, which comes immediately after Candlemas — in a time of approximately nine months. If we view the relationship in this way we can experience this as synchronism.

As we proceed to the pictures of the verses that harmonize

with the others in the 'quartet' (19 and 34), we will not cease to be astonished — for the pictures of these two verses, both of which begin in German with the word *geheimnisvoll* (mysteriously), include the motif of a snake. In one case there is a two-headed snake — probably as an image of memory — and in the other a triple colubrid; the 'new uprisen selfhood' — alternately wakening 'force of my own' and pouring it 'into my human deeds.' One can discover much more of a mysterious nature in these two pictures: in picture 34 one can for example discern several globes — indicative of world evolution through the stages of Saturn, Sun and Moon extending to the present Earth evolution. As a fourth step one also sees a butterfly developing out of a caterpillar. And what might the cosmic egg — probably standing for warmth — have to do with the whole? Is it a further expression of the cosmic forces which flow into life's outward deeds ('my human deeds')? There is also an egg form in the earlier picture (19); this represents the 'force of my own' which, 'emergent,... shall give myself to me.' Remarkably it is a boy who carries this egg, thus emphasizing the state of becoming; while the other large egg is in contact with the colubrid with its three crowns — as what has already come into being. As in the verses themselves, rich contrasts lie hidden in the pictures.

Nearly eight years after he drew the pictures, Karl König drew thirteen medallions, one for every quartet of verses, and around each roundel he wrote out the respective verses by hand. This *Metamorphoses of the Cross* is reproduced on pages 197ff. Ideally, I would have to have everything before me at once — the page with the metamorphoses of the cross together with the four verses concerned and the picture for each verse... and I would also have a notebook where it would be clearly stated how the tenor is the appropriate voice from Easter until summer, the bass until Michaelmas, the soprano until Christmas and the alto until Palm Sunday. I do not have the space I need for this, and it must suffice to consider two pictures at once. This makes the joy of seeing a picture that one has found again after a year all the greater!

Pictures 5, 22, 31 and 48

On four occasions in the year one of the soul calendar pictures from the 'light cross' manifests itself — named thus by König because of the striking word 'light' in the first lines of verses 5, 22, 31 and 48. The pre-spring verse with its initial words:

> In light, that wills from heights of worlds
> To stream amain into my soul

has an almost holy beauty as interpreted in picture 48 (page 423). A religious mood pervades one's feelings, because *both* parts of the picture, the upper as well as the lower, have a symbolic character: the fish in the cosmic ether above the dove of the Grail chalice. The fish refer to the 'sureness of world thinking' 'in the light that' descends 'from heights of worlds'; the dove to the transformation that occurs when the rays awaken 'love within the hearts of men.' Between the two elements is the focal point in blue, reminiscent of picture 45 with the blue form on the brow: 'massing the power of its rays.' In the twelvefold human being — as associated with the influence of the zodiac — Pisces, the fish, are assigned to the feet, and with my feet I enact my destiny. The third line speaks of *'lösend Seelenrätsel'* (solving riddles of the soul) as these fish associated with world thinking become manifest. This certainly has to do with destiny; it approaches one all of a sudden — less through thinking about it than through what happens when looking at the picture: destiny becomes more transparent.

The opposite picture for the fifth verse (page 337) — for the beginning of May:

> In light, that from the spirit's depths
> Plays fruitfully through space
> And manifests the gods' creating

shows a person who appears to carry 'the being of [his] soul / To world existence magnified' on his back. But the clasped hands below these images make it clear that he does not carry this as a burden. It is like a soul reflection of the environment — and yet we have the impression that we are gazing into the inner world of someone who is otherwise wholly enclosed. The outer inactivity gives the possibility of becoming active out of the spirit's depths. The active light appears in the frame of the soul window. The man is tall and broad-shouldered, and has thick hair: nothing petty or narrow prevents a resurrection of 'selfhood's inner power'; the riddles of the soul seem to be resolved. The standing 'in light' represented here is wholly an inward gesture — what a contrast to picture 48! There, with the supplicative force of the verb 'may shine out,' we are looking from a cosmic vantage-point; whereas in the other picture, from an earthly-brown, human standpoint, something enters in to bring new energy into the situation: the soul's true existence is made manifest, magnified to world existence: cosmic transformation — earthly resurrection!

The other two verses are constructed as mirror opposites:

22. Light from the worlds' wide bounds
Unfolds in me ...

31. Light from the spirit's depths
Strives outward ...

The pictures (pages 371 and 389) seem to relate to the fourth line of the respective verses — now without mirroring:

Illumining my spirit's depths

is indicated here by the unicorn: the 'self of worlds';

And shines into the senses' gloom

is portrayed by imagery of the five most familiar senses: at the top the sense of sight, then taste and hearing, and finally the senses

of smell and touch as representatives of the twelve (currently) dulled senses — indicated by the twelve-sided body. Through both drawings one gains the impression that a process of maturation is involved:

> It turns to life's own strength of will
> Changing to light of soul

culminating in the final lines of each verse:

> Through which, from urgings of the soul
> Creative powers grow ripe in human deeds.
>
> Which, when time runs, shall ripen
> The self of man from out the self of worlds.

This ripening process seems to find an echo in the pictures. If one looks at all four, a common denominator can be discerned. One can experience the medallion that connects all four verses (opposite) as an expression of the four kinds of ether: warmth ether in red, light ether in yellow, tone ether in the four red-blue centres and life ether in the orange-coloured arms of the cross: there everything is in vibration! 'The gods' creating' in verse 5 is warmth: verse 22 speaks of 'changing to light of soul' and in the drawing the crystal window is also open to the front (in contrast to picture 5). One can sense the tone ether in verse 48, when the light 'streams amain', and the life ether in verse 31 in the line 'it turns to life's own strength of will.' This is indicated in the picture by the sense of touch at the bottom through to the sense of sight at the top, for in between lies the dodecahedron. All that can be given here are a few indications as to the common properties in these so different pictures, as shown by the medallion. The light cross is at the same time an etheric cross of verses, as only becomes visible in the pictures.

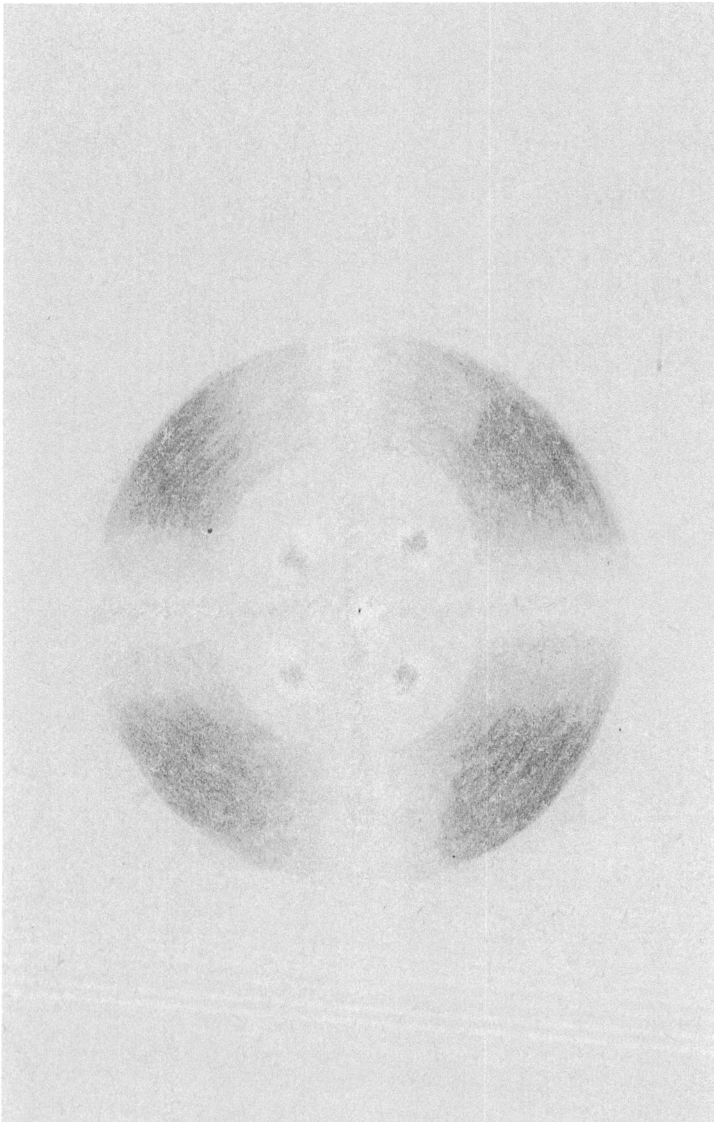

Karl König's drawing of the light cross

Pictures 1 and 52

Thus we can, so to speak, ride in a team of four through the quartets of the pictures, and we notice that at least one of the polarities in each group of four clearly stands out. In what follows some further polarities will be adduced as examples. In the drawings for Easter and Palm Sunday (pages 329 and 431) there is a six-pointed star at the top left of the first picture, and a five-pointed star at the bottom right of the second. There is an astonishing similarity with Sassetta's *Journey of the Magi*,[3] where also the star shines out of the landscape. The whole gesture in picture 1 is in an upwards direction, whereas in picture 52 it is directed downwards, as are the ethereal arcs, as I call them:

> Then thoughts from selfhood's narrow case
> Draw outward to far spaces ...

— the thoughts draw *upwards*;

> Then from the heavens' far corners
> The force of life draws into human frames

— the thoughts draw *downwards.*

Here the world of the senses and the spiritual world become one in the pictures.

Pictures 51 and 2

Now from the second quartet. In the picture for verse 51 (page 429) the eye of the spirit of the world is above; the human eye is at the bottom of the drawing, where the image of the tree arises on the retina. The eye of the spirit must first give the human eye the power of renewal. In picture 2 (page 331), the finding of oneself in the worlds of spirit (as a seed) stands in contrast to the

finding of the spirit of the world in the mirror image. An apple representing a human being's soul harvest appears at the foot of the picture in the same colours as the spirit-eye at the top of picture 51. The seated person in picture 2 firmly holds his seed (a five-pointed star) with the same crescent moon forms which appear to support the tree of the senses' abundance in picture 51. Actually, in the representatives of the worlds of spirit, angels, the seed is recognized as a five-pointed star, just as the abundance of the senses becomes a reality in a mirrored sense in the glass body of the human eye. It is not easy to find adequate words, but we find the soul-fruit of the apple again in the next quartet.

Pictures 3, 50 and 24

In picture 3 (page 333) the eye has actually become an apple representing the universe. The motif of the boat now appears with the meeting of I and world. The world-apple seems to be floating; in the reflection a relationship to the eye-apple is indicated. In picture 50 (page 427), on the other hand, the giant mussel is taken from the water element. There now begins the encounter of 'the bliss of growth in world existence' with the I. Below, in an intimate little picture, one has an inkling of the human I as the goal of world existence — perhaps even in the door that extends, like in double mirrors, into an infinite point. There is a further contrast between the male figure in the boat and the female figure on the prayer stool; the one is wholly outside, the other wholly inside — two sides of our I-existence.

In picture 24 (page 375) there is the threefold snake bridge between day and night. The word 'self' comes four times — most strikingly, I think: three times as an expression for soul realities which in the picture become the snake bridges, while one of these references concerns self-knowledge, which appears in the image of the temple in connection with the spirit of the world. Beside this image are two pillars: an upright snake and the form of self-relatedness (viewing everything in relation to

oneself), that reminds of the form of the chimney of the heating house in Dornach! The temple and the two pillars are beyond our day and night experience. With the sound of the German word *stets* (unceasingly) I had to think not only of the constant renewal of the sense of self out of the realm of the night but also of the ascent that is in prospect up the steep steps of the snake bridge.[4] This twenty-fourth picture really has something quite wonderful about it.

Pictures 4, 49, 23 and 30

With the pictures of the next group of four from verse 4 the boat theme reappears. In picture 4 (page 335) between the big six-pointed star in the symbolic sky and the windmill with six sails on the earth. As one looks more closely, is it the Grim Reaper who is rowing? Again there is a mirroring here referring to another life. An Egypto-Christian symbol on the boat likewise points towards rebirth: 'my being's very being.'

In picture 49 (page 425) there is again a boat, with a symbol that unites past and present. This time the human figure meets only the snake of his own spirit's growth. Rather than death in this case, the birds of hope lead to the 'world-day as it nears.' For the direction of the boat — together with the snake — lies at right angles to the flight of birds; a meeting must first probably take place between the snake, which seems to be coming from the rock of 'dark world-nights,' and the oarsman steering his boat.

Incidentally, the drawing for verse 23 (page 373) is a touching picture from memory. It is the view from Kirkton House of the garden and of Bennachie, the mountain to the north-west of Aberdeen. The crows are flying to their wintering grounds. We are in the month of September with this verse. Venus with its five rays is singing 'in the wide spaces' of 'autumn's wintry sleep,' and something from the summer is still present in the apple tree laden with fruit and in the potato furrows behind the fence which gives itself to father König and daughter Renate and to all

who are dependent upon the fruits of the garden and the tree: the adults and children of the little community in Kirkton House, which Karl König had to leave in order to spend the summer months in the internment camp. The Whitsunday of 1940, when the men were taken away, finds an echo in his memory.

Whereas picture 23 has something of a dream quality, picture 30 (page 387) that is its opposite brings one to an abrupt spirit-waking in the verse for late October. Quite literally, a somersault is made from the third to the fifth cultural epoch, from the Sphinx to the age of Pisces, the Fishes. Instead of garden fruits with radiant autumnal stars we have 'ripe fruits of thinking,' the fish of etheric reality — not a yielding up of summer forces but the sunshine of the soul that awakens its summer; not the splendour of the apple tree but the 'sureness of a self aware' in the inverted tree full of blossoms of venous blood.[5] One goes from one picture to the next in a process of rapid change with the experience: 'Winter shall wake in me / The summer of the soul.'

Pictures 6, 47, 21 and 32

The next but one set of verses, beginning with verse 6, contrasts a person who is relaxing with one who is determined to assert himself (page 339). Pictorially it is the 'powers of time and space' that accompany the self that is on an inner quest in the form of moon and sun. In the time before Easter, on the other hand, one has to arm oneself against the too strong 'bliss of growth' from the 'womb of worlds.' Behind the knight in armour there stands — only partially visible — a form representing an angel's wings as though supporting a five-pointed and a six-pointed star, towards which the knight with the square visor holds up two symbols: the flame of the 'force of thinking' and the staff of a will for healing — new thinking and new will. We have now encountered the two stars on several occasions. A simple interpretation would be that the five-pointed star stands for the human being and the six-pointed star for the stage of the angels. If we adopt the six supplementary exercises

as our path, we come closer to the next stage of evolution, that of the angels.[6] Karl König recommended that we regard the armour of Rembrandt's knight of the spirit as an image for this path and experience the six exercises of the path as parts of that armoury.[7] These six stages can potentially be seen as 'forces of the gods' which live already now within us with great power. In the Letter to the Ephesians (6:11) Paul also wrote about this 'armour of God.'

However, the knight in picture 47 (page 421) looks almost ridiculous — it is difficult to take him seriously! His feet are turned outwards, as only in a highly extrovert child. If something of this kind happens as we look at the picture, we must hold back for a moment and intently focus on the cross in the middle of the suit of armour. Then the shortcomings of the drawing fall away, and we no longer see a clapped-out armour but a human being as an armed knight. We might also ask what exercise on the sixfold path is necessary for changing the way we look at something!

The sky is here divided into three horizontal areas, while in the picture 6, it is divided in a triangle. This composition points to an inner situation. The world (in verse 6) manifests itself in the triangle, and thinking (in verse 47) in a threefold division of all existence — at least this could be a starting point for a possible interpretation. Everything pertaining to world and self appears in terms of opposites.

Let us briefly glance at the other two pictures of this quartet. We see an eagle with a prominent head high above the world without (verse 21, page 369), and, in the other picture (verse 32, page 391)), a dove in the centre of the picture in a more 'inward' context. One may puzzle over the caricature-like rock-faces that pursue the eagle, whereas our eye dwells on the balanced countenance of the person of the heart. Viewed purely form the standpoint of the picture, the words 'boding' and 'clarity' seem to have been exchanged; similarly 'weaves a web of light / Within me for my selfhood's power' and 'to trace life's web of destiny.' For someone who likes to have clear answers, it is good sometimes to leave questions open.

Pictures 7, 20, 33 and 46

Before we complete the circle to the Whitsun cross of verses, we should briefly mention the 'cross of dangers,' as König called it. The verses 7, 20, 33 and 46 lie — in a manner that we may find astonishing — each verse thirteen apart from the next, and that is with good reason. Just as they seem rigid and lifeless in their precisely square position in the cycle of the year, they are also all furthest removed from the four cardinal festivals in the year.

The two rather desolate portrayals of verses 20 and 33 (pages 367 and 393) have an alarming effect initially. In the verses — uniquely — the words 'death' and 'kill' occur in the vocabulary. As I was born in the week of the former verse, I have often worked with it, and over the years I have been struck by these words: 'my being ... within itself must quench the self' and 'must kill the self-enclosed self.' Then I always tried to understand what 'torn from world existence' and 'building on itself alone' might mean. König's picture shows crystals interpenetrating one another as they grow, so to speak, mutually annihilating themselves, going the same way as the two forlornly dying flowers. But the crystals retain their remarkable splendour of colours, and the flowers bring forth blossoms — both are surrounded in the drawing with a radiance, an aura.

The November trees by the river also appear wretched at first, burdened as they are with over-sized crows' nests, and set in a monotone landscape. The words of the verse speak of a world which would be in a dire situation if I did not participate and if the world were not renewed through human souls, that 'in itself' it surely 'could look for death alone.' And it would be our fault! Perhaps the crows are blaming us for the fact that the sun is shining so feebly: 'O woe!' Nevertheless, the sun can also be seen differently, for its poor light is sufficient to transform the otherwise grey river into radiant tones of colour. The first line of

the verse indeed indicates that one can feel the world — then the black crows appear as messengers between the red patch of sun and the observer of the not wholly desolate scene.

If we try a similar approach to the other 'danger verses,' it is perhaps not impossible to meet the threatening four-headed beast with the light of memory (46, page 419), and similarly in the May picture (7, page 341) to withstand the tendency of my self to break away through the boding power of the fourfold blue flower. Karl König thereby indicates that this is also a verse for the Ascension. Through the pictures we can arrive at new attitudes of soul.

For the remaining five quartets, may the reader make discoveries in and through the pictures by observing the stirrings of their own soul. For this pictorial creation by Karl König has over the course of time made the transition from being a private statement to being something of importance to a community and now to a path that can be followed in full openness. Through the medium of the drawings, those working with the 52 verses can be given help. This essay has attempted through its observations to make these pictures more accessible.

Karl König's Drawings for the 52 Verses

1. *Easter. April 7–13*

When from the worlds' wide bounds
The sun speaks to the sense of man,
And joy from depths of soul
Grows one with light in gazing,
Then thoughts from selfhood's narrow case
Draw outward to far spaces
And mutely bind
Man's being with the spirit's life.

Wenn aus den Weltenweiten
Die Sonne spricht zum Menschensinn
Und Freude aus den Seelentiefen
Dem Licht sich eint im Schauen,
Dann ziehen aus der Selbstheit Hülle
Gedanken in die Raumesfernen
Und binden dumpf
Des Menschen Wesen an des Geistes Sein.

1.
Woche

2. *April 14–20*

Into the utmost fields of sense
The force of thought resigns its separate life.
The worlds of spirit find
Anew their offspring, man,
Whose seed in them,
But his soul's harvest
Must in himself be found.

Ins Äüßre des Sinnesalls
Verliert Gedankenmacht ihr Eigensein,
Es finden Geisteswelten
Den Menschensprossen wieder,
Der seinen Keim in ihnen,
Doch seine Seelenfrucht
In sich muss finden.

2.
Woche

3. *April 21–27*

Speaks to the universe,
Itself forgetting
And mindful of its primal form,
The waxing I of man.
'On you, from cramping fetters
Of isolation breaking,
I ground my own intrinsic being.'

Es spricht zum Weltenall,
Sich selbst vergessend
Und seines Urstands eingedenk,
Des Menschen wachsend Ich:
In dir, befreiend mich
Aus meiner Eigenheiten Fessel,
Ergründe ich mein echtes Wesen.

3.
Woche

4. *April 28 – May 4*

'I feel my being's very being,'
So speaks the feeling soul
Which in the sunlit world
Unites itself with floods of light.
It would bestow on thinking
A gift of warmth for clearness,
And into wholeness
Weld man and world together.

Ich fühle Wesen meines Wesens:
So spricht Empfindung,
Die in der sonnerhellten Welt
Mit Lichtesfluten sich vereint;
Sie will dem Denken
Zur Klarheit Wärme schenken
Und Mensch und Welt
In Einheit fest verbinden.

4.
Woche

5. *May 5–11*

In light, that from the spirit's depths
Plays fruitfully through space
And manifests the gods' creating,
Shows forth the being of the soul
To world existence magnified,
And resurrected
From narrow selfhood's inner power.

Im Lichte, das aus Geistestiefen
Im Raume fruchtbar webend
Der Götter Schaffen offenbart:
In ihm erscheint der Seele Wesen
Geweitet zu dem Weltensein
Und auferstanden
Aus enger Selbstheit Innenmacht.

5.
Woche

6. *May 12–18*

There has arisen from its separateness
My self — to find that self
As worlds made manifest
In powers of time and space.
The great world shows me everywhere
As the gods' primal image
My imprint's truthfulness.

Es ist erstanden aus der Eigenheit
Mein Selbst und findet sich
Als Weltenoffenbarung
In Zeit- und Raumeskraften;
Die Welt, sie zeigt mir überall
Als göttlich Urbild
Des eignen Abbilds Wahrheit.

6.
Woche

7. *May 19–25*

My self threatens to break away
Through strong enticement of the light of worlds.
Now rise, my boding power,
Assume in strength your rightful throne,
Replace in me the might of thinking
Which in the senses' show
Is like to lose itself.

Mein Selbst, es drohet zu entfliehen,
Vom Weltenlichte mächtig angezogen;
Nun trete du mein Ahnen
In deine Rechte kräftig ein,
Ersetze mir des Denkens Macht,
Das in der Sinne Schein
Sich selbst verlieren will.

7.
Woche

8. *May 26 – June 1*

The senses' might grows great
Bonded with the gods' creating;
It thrusts the force of thought
Down to the drowsing of a dream.
When godlike being
Will join in union with my soul,
Then human thinking
Must bow in peace to dream existence.

Es wachst der Sinne Macht
Im Bunde mit der Götter Schaffen,
Sie drückt des Denkens Kraft
Zur Traumes Dumpfheit mir herab.
Wenn göttlich Wesen
Sich meiner Seele einen will,
Muss menschlich Denken
Im Traumessein sich still bescheiden.

8.
Woche

9. *June 2–8*

Forgetting all my separateness of will,
The warmth of worlds, the summer's harbinger,
I feel it flood my spirit and my soul.
To lose myself in light
The gaze of spirit now demands,
And powerfully prophetic boding cries:
'Lose, lose your self, yourself to find.'

Vergessend meine Willenseigenheit
Erfüllet Weltenwärme sommerkündend
Mir Geist und Seelenwesen;
Im Licht mich zu verlieren
Gebietet mir das Geistesschauen,
Und kraftvoll kündet Ahnung mir:
Verliere dich, um dich zu finden.

9.
Woche

10. *June 9–15*

Far into summer heights
The sun lifts up its shining sphere,
It draws my human yearning
Into its own wide spaces,
While inwardly a feeling stirs
In dim prophetic boding:
'Hereafter you shall know —
A god, a god has touched you now.'

Zu sommerlichen Höhen
Erhebt der Sonne leuchtend Wesen sich,
Es nimmt mein menschlich Fühlen
In seine Raumesweiten mit,
Erahnend regt im Innern sich
Empfindung, dumpf mir kündend,
Erkennen wirst du einst:
Dich fühlte jetzt ein Gotteswesen.

10.
Woche

11. *June 16–23*

In this the sun's high hour
Be yours its herald wisdom to embrace.
Surrendered to the beauty of the world
The self aware of self shall deeply own:
The I of man can lose itself
And find itself within the I of worlds.

Es ist in dieser Sonnenstunde
An dir, die weise Kunde zu erkennen:
An Weltenschönheit hingegeben,
In dir dich fühlend zu durchleben:
Verlieren kann des Menschen-Ich
Und finden sich im Welten-Ich.

11.
Woche

12. *St John's Tide. June 24*

The world's bright loveliness
Constrains me in my inmost soul.
'Set free the godlike gifts you own
To wing their way into the universe,
Your narrow self forego,
And, trusting, seek that self again
In universal light and warmth.'

Der Welten Schönheitsglanz
Er zwinget mich aus Seelentiefen
Des Eigenlebens Götterkräfte
Zum Weltenfluge zu entbinden;
Mich selber zu verlassen,
Vertrauend nur mich suchend
In Weltenlicht und Weltenwärme.

12.
Woche

13. *June 30 – July 6*

Am I then in the heights of sense —
So kindles in my depths of soul
The truth from spirit worlds of fire
The gods themselves proclaim:
'Seek through your boding power
And find in spirit ground
Your spirit brotherhood.'

Und bin ich in den Sinneshöhen,
So flammt in meinen Seelentiefen
Aus Geistes Feuerwelten
Der Götter Wahrheitswort:
In Geistesgründen suche ahnend
Dich geistverwandt zu finden.

13.
Woche

14. *July 7–13*

Surrendered to the senses' revelation
I lost my being's proper urge,
And felt, in dreaming thoughts bemused,
My selfhood stolen away.
But waking presses on me still
World-thinking in the senses' glow.

An Sinnesoffenbarung hingegeben
Verlor ich Eigenwesens Trieb,
Gedankentraum, er schien
Betäubend mir das Selbst zu rauben,
Doch weckend nahet schon
Im Sinnenschein mir Weltendenken.

Erkenne
Dich Faust
14.
Woche

15. *July 14–20*

I feel the spirit's weaving
Spell-bound within the world's array,
In drowsiness of sense
It wraps my selfhood in —
But all to dower that self
With strength, which cribbed and impotent
Mine I shall never give itself.

Ich fühle wie verzaubert
Im Weltenschein des Geistes Weben,
Es hat in Sinnesdumpfheit
Gehüllt mein Eigenwesen,
Zu schenken mir die Kraft,
Die ohnmächtig sich selbst zu geben
Mein Ich in seinen Schranken ist.

15.
Woche

16. *July 21–27*

Sternly my boding heart demands:
'Cherish within the spirit's dower,
So shall the gifts of God grow ripe
In the soul's soil maturing,
And selfhood reap their fruits.

Zu bergen Geistgeschenk im Innern
Gebietet strenge mir mein Ahnen,
Dass reifend Gottesgaben
In Seelengründen fruchtend
Der Selbstheit Früchte bringen.

16.
Woche

17. *July 28 – August 3*

Now speaks the word of worlds
Which through the senses' door
I may draw deep into my soul:
'Fill full thy spirit's depths
With my world wideness,
To find hereafter me in thee.'

Es spricht das Weltenwort,
Das ich durch Sinnestore
In Seelengründe durfte führen:
Erfülle deine Geistestiefen
Mit meinen Weltenweiten
Zu finden einstens mich in dir.

17.
Woche

18. *August 4–10*

Can I expand my soul
To grapple to her being
This word of worlds in germ conceived?
I do forebode I strength must find
To found and form my soul
A garment worthy of the spirit.

Kann ich die Seele weiten,
Dass sie sich selbst verbindet
Empfangnem Welten-Keimesworte?
Ich ahne, dass ich Kraft muss finden
Die Seele würdig zu gestalten,
Zum Geisteskleide sich zu bilden.

18.
Woche

19. *August 11–17*

To wrap the new-conceived germ
In memory's secret folds
Be now my striving's master aim:
Gathering strength to waken
Force of my own within me,
Emergent, it shall give myself to me.

Geheimnisvoll das Neu-Empfang'ne
Mit der Erinn'rung zu umschliessen,
Sei meines Strebens weitrer Sinn:
Es soll erstarkend Eigenkräfte
In meinem Innern wecken
Und werdend mich mir selber geben.

19.
Woche

20. *August 18–24*

Now first I feel my being —
Which, torn from world existence,
Within itself must quench the self,
And building on itself alone
Must kill the self-enclosed self.

So fühl' ich erst mein Sein,
Das fern vom Welten-Dasein
In sich, sich selbst erlöschen
Und bauend nur auf eignem Grunde
In sich, sich selbst ertöten müsste.

20.
Woche

21. *August 25–31*

I feel a power unwonted, bearing fruit,
Gather its strength and lend myself to me.
I sense the germ maturing,
The while my boding weaves a web of light
Within me for my selfhood's power.

Ich fühle fruchtend fremde Macht
Sich stärkend mir mich selbst verleihn,
Den Keim empfind ich reifend
Und Ahnung lichtvoll weben
Im Innern an der Selbstheit Macht.

21.
Woche

22. *September 1–7*

Light from the worlds' wide bounds
Unfolds in me its life of power,
Changing to light of soul,
Illumining my spirit's depths,
That fruitage to set free
Which, when time runs, shall ripen
The self of man from out the self of worlds.

Das Licht aus Weltenweiten,
Im Innern lebt es kraftig fort,
Es wird zum Seelenlichte
Und leuchtet in die Geistestiefen,
Um Früchte zu entbinden,
Die Menschenselbst aus Weltenselbst
Im Zeitenlaufe reifen lassen.

22.
Woche

23. *September 8–14*

Subdued to autumn's mood
The spurrings of the senses die away;
Veil upon veil, the mist
Dims the still radiant light.
In the wide spaces I discern
The autumn's sleep of worlds;
Summer to me
Has yielded up itself.

Es dämpfet herbstlich sich
Der Sinne Reizesstreben,
In Lichtesoffenbarung mischen
Der Nebel dumpfe Schleier sich,
Ich selber schau in Raumesweiten
Des Herbstes Weltenschlaf,
Der Sommer hat an mich
Sich selber hingegeben.

23.
Woche

24. *September 15–21*

Unceasingly itself renewing
The soul grows self-aware;
In new self-knowledge vivified
The spirit of the world strives on,
Creating from the darkness of the soul
What sense of self matures as fruit of will.

Sich selbst erschaffend stets
Wird Seelensein sich selbst gewahr;
Der Weltengeist, er strebet fort
In Selbsterkenntnis neu belebt
Und schafft aus Seelennfinsternis
Des Selbstsinns Willensfrucht.

24.
Woche

25. *September 22–28*

My self, now made my very own,
May shine abroad its inner light
In dark abysms of space and time.
A slumber seizes nature's being,
But the deep hidden soul shall waken,
And waking carry sunny gleams
Into cold winter's tides and streams.

Ich darf nur mir gehören
Und leuchtend breiten Innenlicht
In Raumes- und in Zeitenfinsternis.
Zum Schlafe drängt natürlich Wesen,
Der Seele Tiefen sollen wachen
Und wachend tragen Sonnengluten
In kalte Winterfluten.

♍
25.
Woche

26. *Michaelmas. September 29*

Nature, thou soul of motherhood,
I bear thee in the essence of my will,
That will whose fiery strength
Tempers my spirit's edge
That it beget such sense of self
As may bear I in me.

Natur, dein mütterliches Sein,
Ich trage es in meinem Willenswesen;
Und meines Willens Feuermacht,
Sie stählet meines Geistes Triebe,
Dass sie gebären Selbstgefühl,
Zu tragen mich in mir.

♍
26.
Woche

27. *October 6–12*

To dive into my being's depths
Stirs up a yearning in me, boding well,
That self-exploring I may find
Myself the gift of summer sun,
Which lives in autumn's mood
A warm seed life
Of thriving forces for my soul.

In meines Wesens Tiefen dringen
Erregt ein ahnungsvolles Sehnen,
Dass ich mich selbstbetrachtend finde
Als Sommersonnengabe, die als Keim
In Herbstestimmung wärmend lebt
Als meiner Seele Kräftetrieb.

27.
Woche

28. *October 13–19*

Quickened anew within
I feel the vastness of my being,
And power is mine to shed clear rays of thought
From the soul's sunlike potency
Solving life's riddles,
And granting many a wish fulfilment
Whose wings had drooped with hope foregone.

Ich kann im Innern neu belebt
Erfühlen eignen Wesens Weiten
Und krafterfüllt Gedankenstrahlen
Aus Seelensonnenmacht
Den Lebensrätseln lösend spenden,
Erfüllung manchem Wunsche leihen,
Dem Hoffnung schon die Schwingen lähmte.

28.
Woche

29. *October 20–26*

To light in me the lamp of thinking
And fan with inner force the flame,
Illumining life's story
From the world spirit's well of power,
For me is summer's heritage,
Is autumn's peace and winter's hope to be.

Sich selbst des Denkens Leuchten
Im Innern kraftvoll zu entfachen,
Erlebtes sinnvoll deutend
Aus Weltengeistes Kräftequell,
Ist mir nun Sommererbe
Ist Herbstesruhe und auch Winterhoffnung.

29.
Woche

30. *October 27 – November 2*

Warmed in the sunshine of the soul
Ripe fruits of thinking thrive,
To sureness of a self aware
All feeling is transformed.
I joy to feel the spirit stir
Of autumn's watchfulness,
Winter shall wake in me
The summer of the soul.

Es sprießen mir im Seelensonnenlicht
Des Denkens reife Fruchte,
In Selbstbewußtseins Sicherheit
Verwandelt alles Fühlen sich,
Empfinden kann ich freudevoll
Des Herbstes Geisterwachen,
Der Winter wird in mir
Den Seelensommer wecken.

30.
Woche

31. *November 3–9*

Light from the spirit's depths
Strives outward like a sun,
It turns to life's own strength of will
And shines into the senses' gloom —
Those forces to set free
Through which, from urgings of the soul,
Creative powers grow ripe in human deeds.

Das Licht aus Geistestiefen,
Nach außen strebt es sonnenhaft,
Es wird zur Lebenswillenskraft
Und leuchtet in der Sinne Dumpfheit,
Um Kräfte zu entbinden,
Die Schaffensmächte aus Seelentrieben
Im Menschenwerke reifen lassen.

31.
Woche

32. *November 10–16*

I feel my proper strength, a fruitful scion,
With gathered power bestow me on the world,
I feel the essence of my being
Grow strong in clarity
To trace life's web of destiny.

Ich fühle fruchtend eigne Kraft
Sich stärkend mich der Welt verleihn,
Mein Eigenwesen fühl ich kraftend
Zur Klarheit sich zu wenden
Im Lebens-Schicksalsweben.

32.
Woche

33. *November 17–23*

Now first I feel the world,
Which, reft of my indwelling soul,
Would as a frozen waste
Unfold its feeble life,
Create itself anew in human souls,
That in itself could look for death alone.

So fühl' ich erst die Welt,
Die außer meiner Seele Miterleben
An sich nur frostig leeres Leben
Und ohne Macht sich offenbarend
In Seelen sich von neuem schaffend
In sich den Tod nur finden könnte.

33.
Woche

34. *November 24–30*

To feel through selfhood new uprisen
The treasured dower of old
Stir secretly to life within
Shall, waking, pour into my human deeds
A tide of universal powers,
And so, maturing, grave me in existence.

Geheimnisvoll das Alt-Bewahrte
Mit neu erstandenem Eigensein
Im Innern sich belebend fühlen:
Es soll erweckend Weltenkrafte
In meines Lebens Außenwerk ergießen
Und werdend mich ins Dasein prägen.

34.
Woche

35. *December 1–7*

Can I then the being know
That, known, it find itself again
In the soul's urgence to create?
I feel the power entrusted me
My own self humbly to insert
A living member in the self of worlds.

Kann ich das Sein erkennen,
Dass es sich wiederfindet
Im Seelen-Schaffens-Drange?
Ich fühle, dass mir Macht verlieh'n
Das eigne Selbst dem Weltenselbst
Als Glied bescheiden einzuleben.

35.
Woche

36. *December 8–14*

Speaks from my being's depths,
Surging to revelation,
In secret wise the word of worlds.
'Fill full your task in life
With this my light of spirit
To offer up the self through me.'

In meines Wesens Tiefen spricht
Zur Offenbarung drängend
Geheimnisvoll das Weltenwort:
Erfülle deiner Arbeit Ziele
Mit meinem Geisteslichte
Zu opfern dich durch mich.

36.
Woche

37. *December 15–21*

With joy to carry spirit light
Into the winter night of worlds —
For this my striving heart is fain,
That, kindling, seeds of soul
Strike in the soil of worlds,
And sounding through the dark of sense
God's word illumine all that is.

Zu tragen Geisteslicht in Weltenwinternacht
Erstrebet selig meines Herzens Trieb,
Dass leuchtend Seelenkeime
In Weltengründen wurzeln
Und Gotteswort im Sinnesdunkel
Verklärend alles Sein durchtönt.

37.
Woche

38. *Christmas. December 22–28*

I feel the spell dissevered
In the soul's womb freeing the spirit child:
The holy word of worlds
Has in the heart's clear light
Begotten heaven's own fruit of hope,
Which, rising from the god in me,
Goes paeaning to the corners of the world.

Ich fühle wie entzaubert
Das Geisteskind im Seelenschoß,
Es hat in Herzenshelligkeit
Gezeugt das heil'ge Weltenwort
Der Hoffnung Himmelsfrucht,
Die jubelnd wächst in Weltenfernen
Aus meines Wesens Gottesgrund.

38.
Woche

39. *December 29 – January 4*

Surrendered to the spirit's revelation
I win the light of universal life.
The force of thought grows strong in clarity
To grant me selfhood,
And in me, from the thinker's power,
Leaps into wakefulness the sense of self.

An Geistesoffenbarung hingegeben
Gewinne ich des Weltenwesens Licht,
Gedankenkraft, sie wächst
Sich klärend mir mich selbst zu geben
Und weckend löst sich mir
Aus Denkermacht das Selbstgefühl.

♄
39.
Woche

40. *January 5–11*

Am I then in the spirit's depths —
So in the roots of soul profound
From out the heart's wide worlds of love
Illusion vain of selfhood fills itself
With powers of fire from the word of worlds.

Und bin ich in den Geistestiefen,
Erfüllt in meinen Seelengründen
Aus Herzens Liebewelten
Der Eigenheiten leerer Wahn
Sich mit des Weltenwortes Feuerkraft.

40.
Woche

41. *January 12–18*

The soul's creative power
Strives from the heart's deep ground:
'Kindle your godlike gifts
For rightful work in human life,
Fashion the self
In human love and human deeds.'

Der Seele Schaffensmacht
Sie strebet aus dem Herzensgrunde
Im Menschenleben Götterkräfte
Zu rechtem Wirken zu entflammen,
Sich selber zu gestalten
In Menschenliebe und im Menschenwerke.

41.
Woche

42. *January 19–25*

In this dark wintertide
To manifest her proper force
Shall be the soul's imperious urge;
Herself to haunts of darkness guiding
To feel in new forebodement
Through warmth of heart the senses' revelation.

Es ist in diesem Winterdunkel
Die Offenbarung eigner Kraft
Der Seele starker Trieb,
In Finsternisse sie zu lenken
Und ahnend vorzufühlen
Durch Herzenswärme Sinnesoffenbarung.

42.
Woche

43. *January 26 – February 1*

Sunk in its wintry depths
True spirit-being quickens into warmth.
Through the heart's force it gives
To the world's show and seeming
The mighty gift of being,
And strengthens, maugre worlds of cold,
In human inwardness the fire of soul.

In winterlichen Tiefen
Erwarmt des Geistes wahres Sein,
Es gibt dem Weltenscheine
Durch Herzenskräfte Daseinsmachte;
Der Weltenkälte trotzt erstarkend
Das Seelenfeuer im Menscheninnern.

43.
Woche

44. *February 2–8*

Grasping new spurs of sense,
Mindful of spirit-birth fulfilled,
Clearness of soul outpours
Into the wildering teeming life of worlds
The will creative in my thinking.

Ergreifend neue Sinnesreize
Erfüllet Seelenklarheit,
Eingedenk vollzogner Geistgeburt,
Verwirrend sprossend Weltenwerden
Mit meines Denkens Schöpferwillen.

44.
Woche

45. *February 9–15*

The power of thought stands firm
Bonded with the spirit's birth,
On the dull spurrings of the senses
Raying the fullness of its light.
When plenitude of soul
Will join in union with the life of worlds,
Then must the senses' revelation
Embrace the light of thinking.

Es festigt sich Gedankenmacht
Im Bunde mit der Geistgeburt,
Sie hellt der Sinne dumpfe Reize
Zur vollen Klarheit auf.
Wenn Seelenfülle
Sich mit dem Weltenwerden einen will,
Muss Sinnesoffenbarung
Des Denkens Licht empfangen.

45.
Woche

46. *February 16–22*

The world threatens to stupefy
The inborn forces of my soul.
Now rise from spirit-depths
In all your radiance, memory.
Establish my beholding,
Which only through the force of will
Can hold itself erect.

Die Welt, sie drohet zu betäuben
Der Seele eingeborne Kraft;
Nun trete du, Erinnerung,
Aus Geistestiefen leuchtend auf
Und stärke mir das Schauen,
Das nur durch Willenskräfte
Sich selbst erhalten kann.

46.
Woche

47. *February 23 – March 1*

There shall arise from out the womb of worlds
The bliss of growth, fostering joys of sense;
My force of thinking may it find
Armed with the forces of the gods,
Which live a quickening force in me.

Es will erstehen aus dem Weltenschoße,
Den Sinnenschein erquickend, Werdelust,
Sie finde meines Denkens Kraft
Gerüstet durch die Gotteskräfte
Die kräftig mir im Innern leben.

47.
Woche

48. *March 2–8*

In light, that wills from heights of worlds
To stream amain into my soul,
May sureness of world thinking
Shine out, to solve the riddles of the soul,
Massing the power of its rays
And waking love within the hearts of men.

Im Lichte, das aus Weltenhöhen
Der Seele machtvoll fließen will,
Erscheine, lösend Seelenratsel,
Des Weltendenkens Sicherheit
Versammelnd seiner Strahlen Macht
Im Menschenherzen Liebe weckend.

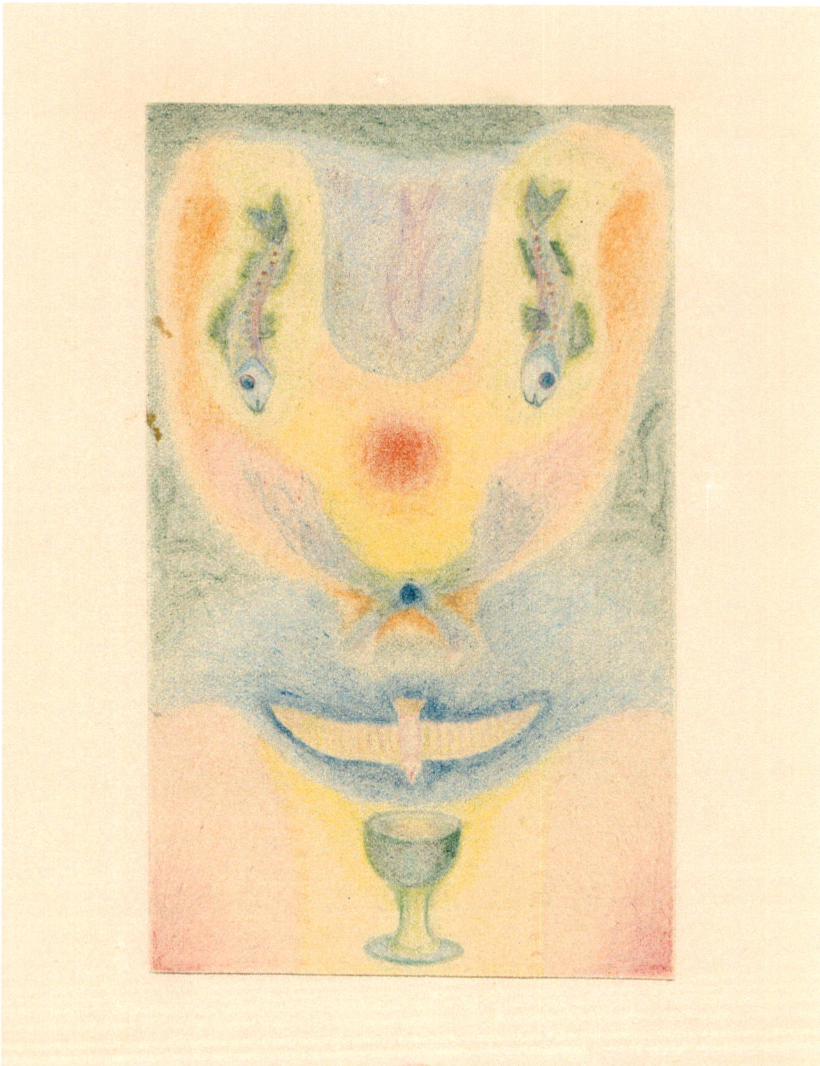
♓
48.
Woche

49. *March 9–15*

'I feel your strength of life, O worlds,'
So the clear voice of thinking cries,
Mindful of its own spirit's growth
Through the dark world-nights achieved,
And to the world-day as it nears
Bending its inward rays of hope.

Ich fühle Kraft des Weltenseins:
So spricht Gedankenklarheit,
Gedenkend eignen Geistes Wachsen
In finstern Weltennächten
Und neigt dem nahen Weltentage
Des Innern Hoffnungsstrahlen.

49.
Woche

50. *March 16–22*

Speaks to the human I
In strong self-revelation,
Enlarging all its being's powers,
The bliss of growth in world existence.
'To you my life transporting
Unbanned from its enchantment
I reach my own true goal.'

Es spricht zum Menschen-Ich,
Sich machtvoll offenbarend
Und seines Wesens Kräfte lösend,
Des Weltendaseins Werdelust:
In dich mein Leben tragend
Aus seinem lauberbanne
Erreiche ich mein wahres Ziel.

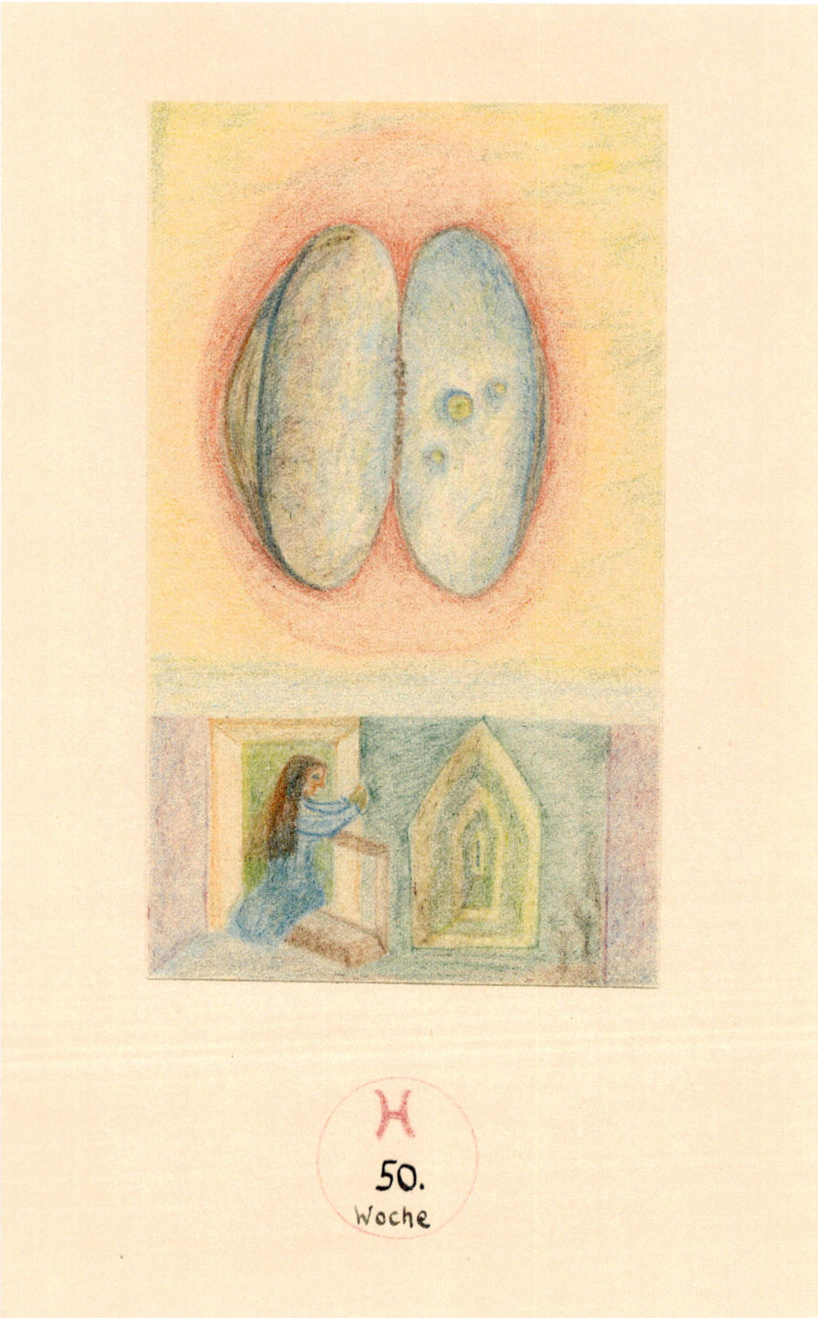
50.
Woche

51. *March 23–29*

Into the inmost life of man
The senses pour their wealth,
The spirit of the world beholds
His mirrored image in the eye of man,
That eye which from that spirit
Must still renew its power.

Ins Innre des Menschenwesens
Ergießt der Sinne Reichtum sich,
Es findet sich der Weltengeist
Im Spiegelbild des Menschenauges,
Das seine Kraft aus ihm
Sich neu erschaffen muss.

51.
Woche

52. *March 30 – April 5*

When from the depths of soul
The spirit turns towards the life of worlds,
And beauty wells from wide bounds of space.
Then from the heaven's far corners
The force of life draws into human frames,
And joins through mighty workings
The spirit's being with the life of man.

Wenn aus den Seelentiefen
Der Geist sich wendet zu dem Weltensein
Und Schönheit quillt aus Raumesweiten,
Dann zieht aus Himmelsfernen
Des Lebens Kraft in Menschenleiber
Und einet, machtvoll wirkend,
Des Geistes Wesen mit dem Menschensein.

52.
Woche

Appendix

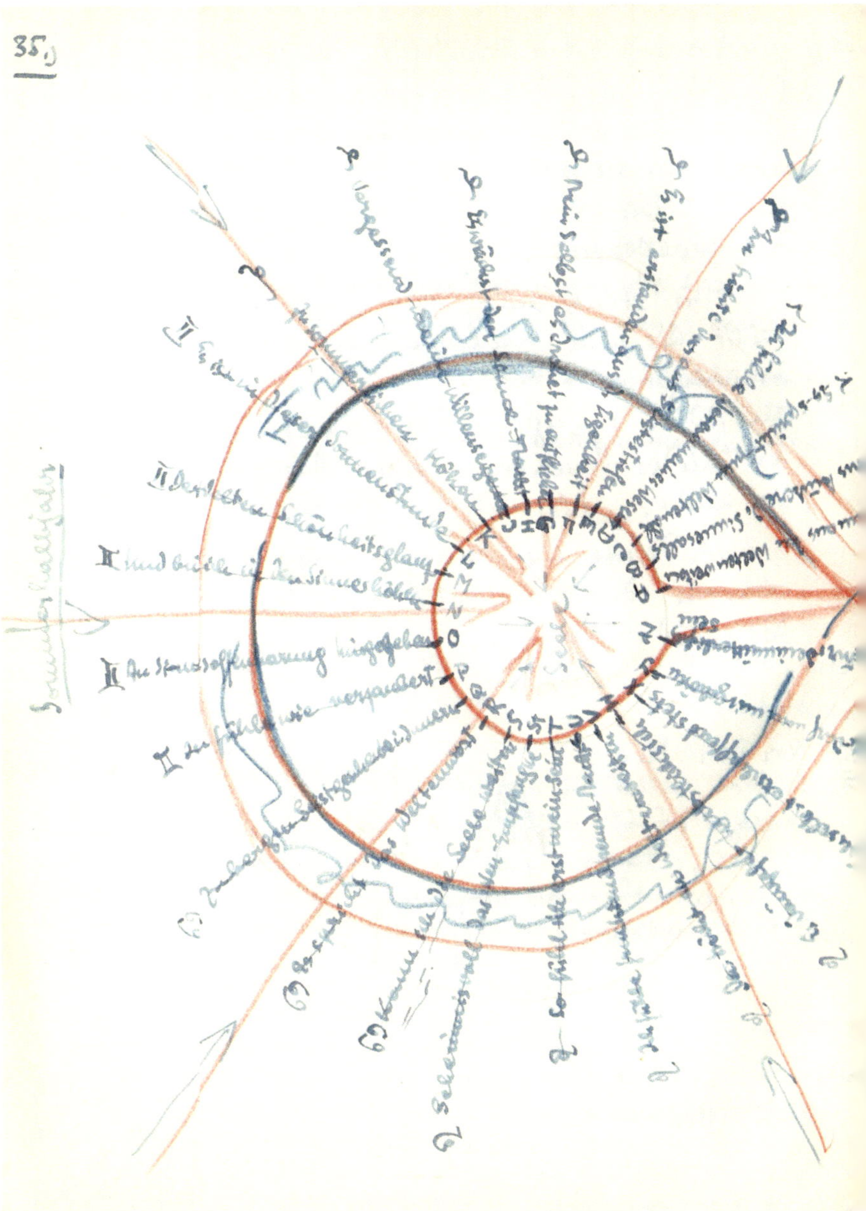

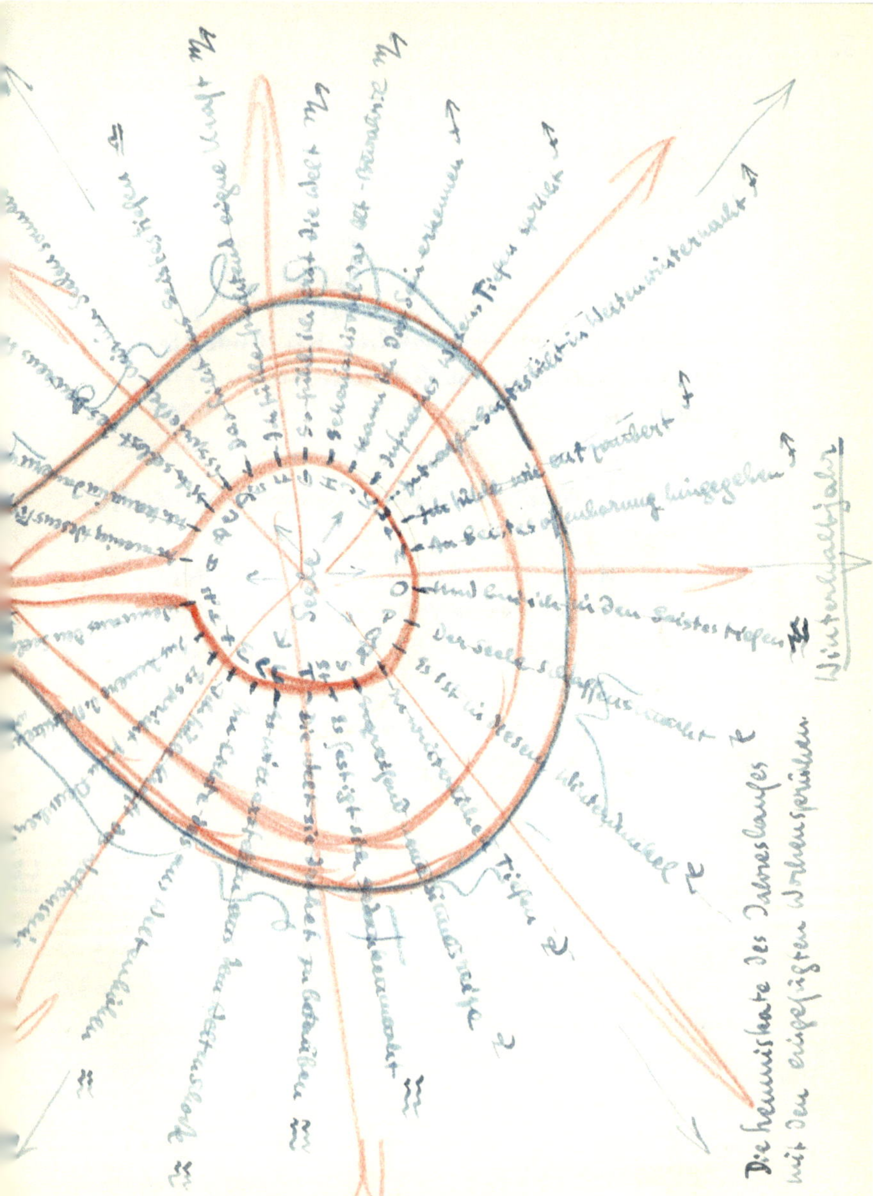
Die Geheimnisse des Jahreslaufes
mit den eingefügten Wochensprüchen
Winterhalbjahr

36.) Aus dem vorhergehenden Schema ist die lemniskatische Anordnung der Wochensprüche klar zu ersehen. Es sind zwei Schleifen u. die Sprüche der einen Schleife entsprechen denen der anderen:

A des Winterhalbjahres Z dem des Sommerhalbjahres,
Z des " " " A " " " "

Gleichzeitig aber entsprechen sich auch die Sprüche mit den gleichen Buchstaben.

Also A .... zu A
und Z .... zu Z.

Nur sind diese Entsprechungen andere als die ersteren.

Das Wesentliche ist aber die lemniskatische Anordnung in der das Spiel der Seele u. der Natur von außen nach innen u. von innen nach außen veranschaulicht wird.

„Und es ist das Ewig-Eine" usw.

So ergibt sich auch, daß das Winterhalbjahr dem Haupte.
Das Sommerhalbjahr dem Stoffwechsel-Gl.-S. entspricht
u. Frühlings- u. Herbstübergang dem rhythmischen System.

Die Atmung .. Frühling
Der Herzschlag ... Herbst.

In the preceding sketch one can clearly see the structure of the weekly verses as a lemniscate. There are two loops and the verses in the one correspond to the verses in the other:

A of the winter cycle [27] to Z in the summer cycle [26]
Z of the winter cycle [52] to A in the summer cycle [1]
Simultaneously however the verses with the same letters correspond to each other:
A ... to A
and Z ... to Z
But these connections are of a different nature to those in the first instance.
The most important element is however the lemniscate structure which reveals the dynamics of the soul and of nature in their movement from outside to inside and inside to outside.

.... the eternal oneness
Divined in manifold world.
Great in small, and small in great
Each according to its kind,
Ever changing, ever constant
Near and far, far and near,
Shaping and reshaping . . .
(Goethe 'Parabase')

In this way the winter half-year reveals its connection to the head,
the summer half-year to the metabolic-limb-system
and the crossing points of spring and autumn to the rhythmic system.
Respiration ... Spring
Heartbeat ... Autumn

From Karl König's notebook. Together with the drawing this marks the earliest mention of his work with the Soul Calendar. The three pages are from 1933, seven years before he started with the pictures in this volume.

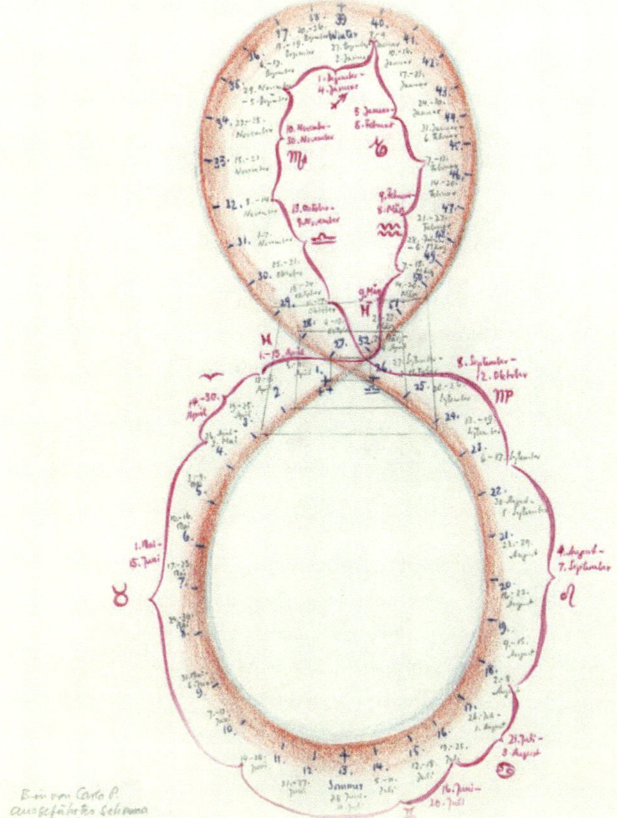

The Calendar of the Soul and the Goetheanum. Drawing by Carlo Pietzner following suggestions and concept of Karl König. Some of the quartets are pencilled in (near the crossing point).

Karl König's suggestions for setting the dates of the Calendar verses

1	Spring: Easter mood
6	Beginning on Sunday before Ascension
7	The week before Whitsun
8	Beginning with Whitsunday
9, 10, 11	Need to be read for a shorter or longer time, according to the date of Easter
12	Mood of St John's Tide, beginning on the Sunday of the St John's week
13	After this verse a threshold is passed, as if asleep.
26	Michaelmas mood, beginning on the Sunday of Michaelmas week
27	Autumn. The week after Michaelmas
35	Beginning with the first Sunday of Advent
38	Christmas mood, fourth week of Advent
39	Winter: birth of the 'I.' After this verse comes the second threshold, 'awake'
40	The week of Epiphany (January 6)
43	The week of conversion of St Paul (January 25)
44	The week of Candlemas (February 2)
45	This verse should be read longer or only a few days according to the date of Easter
46	Carnival
49–51	Cover the Passion weeks
52	Holy Week, begins with Palm Sunday

For practice of the 'fourfold Calendar': the moods of the heavenly quartets: Weeks 1-13 Tenor; Weeks 14-26 Base (or baritone); Weeks 27-39 Soprano; Weeks 40-52 Alto.

Notes

Introduction

1. His exile was 'double' because he had fled from Nazi Austria to Scotland, where he had just been able to make a new start at Kirkton House when he was interned. As he had been excluded from the Anthroposophical Society in 1935, one can also speak of a quality of 'inner exile.' See Selg, *Ita Wegman and Karl König,* p. 57 ff.
2. The background to the writing of the Soul Calendar is described in 'Soul Images and Soul Calendar' p. 295. For Rudolf Steiner's 'disclosures,' see especially *The Event of the Appearance of Christ in the Etheric.*
3. See Selg, 'A Biographical Sketch' in *Karl König: My Task.*
4. From the beginning of the lecture of April 23, 1912 in *Earthly and Cosmic Man.* It is, however, not included in the English translation of these lectures. A portion of Rudolf Steiner's introductory words – and part of the passage quoted here – appears in Christopher Bamford's introduction to the facsimile edition of the *Calendar of the Soul.*
5. See the essay entitled 'Some Personal Memories' in *Karl König: My Task.*
6. See also *Becoming Human: A Social Task.*
7. See *The Christmas Conference*, especially the final words spoken on Jan 1, 1924.

Karl König's Work with the Calendar of the Soul in Camphill

1. The 52 pictures are shown after p. 328.
2. At the conference, at Easter 1973, there was an attempt to connect König's various ideas on the Soul Calendar. See the conference booklet, *Gedanken zum Seelenkalender Rudolf Steiners.*
3. Lecture of Nov 27, 1959. Unpublished manuscript, Karl König Archive.
4. See p. 439.
5. See *Beiträge zur Rudolf Steiner Gesamtausgabe,* No. 37/38. There is a note to this effect in the Pusch translation of the *Calendar of the Soul.*
6. These two lectures are published in *The Mystery of John and the Cycle of the Year.*

Four Addresses on the Calendar of the Soul

1. See *Spiritual Beings in the Heavenly Bodies,* lecture of April 4, 1912. (The *Calendar of the Soul* appeared at Easter 1912.)
2. In *Wonders of the World,* lecture of Aug 26, 1911: 'Hence the form of a bird, the form of a pure white dove, is an appropriate symbol ... In the picture of Jesus of Nazareth at the Jordan with the dove above him we find a true expression of the mystery which has now reached a certain conclusion.'
3. See *The Cycle of the Year as Breathing-Process of the Earth*, lecture of April 7, 1923.
4. See *The Gospel of St Luke,* lecture of Sep 19, 1909.
5. See *The Gospel of St Luke,* lecture of Sep 19, 1909.
6. Above all in the fifth lecture of Oct 13, 1923, *The Four Seasons and the Archangels*.
7. In the years that followed a number of experienced colleagues from Scotland helped the work in South Africa. Many contributions were made regarding these questions; for example, König's daughter went there and wrote an article about the Michaelmas festival. (See *The Cresset,* Vol. 5, No. 1, Michaelmas 1958.)

A Guide to the Anthroposophical Calendar of the Soul

1. An entry in Rudolf Steiner's notebook, 1907. In *Wahrspruchworte.*
2. The path of pain and the path of transformation in the Kabbalah.
3. Rudolf Steiner frequently used this verse in the early 'esoteric lessons.' It does not derive from him but already existed in various languages and was given as a first meditation to all students in the Esoteric School of the Theosophical Society. See Steiner, *Guidance in Esoteric Training*, 'Exegesis to "Light on the Path" by Mabel Collins.'
4. Words from the Offering Service.
5. In *The Fifth Gospel,* lecture of Oct 2, 1913.
6. See *The Four Seasons and the Archangels,* lecture of Oct 12, 1923.
7. See *The Archangel Michael,* lecture of Nov 30, 1919, and *Course for Young Doctors,* lecture of Jan 7, 1924.
8. The concluding portion of 'Gesang des Abgeschiedenen' (Song of the Departed). Trakl, *Das dichterische Werk*, p. 79.
9. Earlier editions of the *Calendar of the Soul* have 'Des Herbstes *Winter*schlaf' (the autumn's wintry sleep) in the third last line. In Rudolf Steiner's manuscript, however, it is quite clearly 'Des Herbstes *Welten*schlaf' (the autumn's sleep of worlds). In recent editions of the Calendar this has been corrected. We have amended Harwood's translation in this book.
10. In *The Four Seasons and the Archangels.*

11. In the 1925 edition of the *Calendar of the Soul,* which was available to Karl König, this line runs: 'the waking I of man' *(des Menschen wachend Ich),* whereas the manuscripts consulted for later editions give 'waxing' *(wachsend).*
12. *The Cycle of the Year as Breathing-Process of the Earth,* lecture of April 1, 1923 (Tr. Barbara D. Betteridge and Frances Dawson).
13. 'Verklärte Herbst' (Transfigured Autumn), Trakl, *Das dichterische Werk.*
14. *Man and the World of Stars,* (tr. Dorothy Osmond).

The Word 'Boding' *(Ahnung)*

1. Kluge, *Etymologisches Wörterbuch.*
2. Steiner, *Occult History,* lecture of Dec 31, 1910.
3. Steiner, *The Spiritual Guidance of the Individual and Humanity,* second lecture.
4. See also Hiebel, *The Epistles of Paul and Rudolf Steiner's Philosophy of Freedom.*
5. Steiner, *Universe, Earth and Man,* lecture of Aug 6, 1908.
6. Steiner, *The Mission of the Folk Souls,* lecture of June 14, 1910.
7. Steiner, *Die menschliche Seele,* lecture of April 6, 1923.

The Winter and Christmas Verses

1. Steiner, *Wahrspruchworte,* p. 179

The Words 'Heights' and 'Depths'

1. From the words of the Christmas service for children.
2. Steiner, *Man and the World of Stars,* lecture of Dec 24, 1922.

The Sense of Self

1. See 'The Words "Heights" and "Depths",' p. 232.
2. Steiner, *Theosophy,* pp. 30f.
3. Aquinas, *Summa Theologica,* 1.79.13.
4. Plessner, *Die Stufen des Organischen und der Mensch.*
5. Jaspers, *Philosophie,* Vol. 2 *Existenzherstellung.*
6. Steiner, *Man's Being, his Destiny and World Evolution.*
7. Steiner, *Theosophy,* p. 46.
8. Steiner, *Theosophy,* p. 51.
9. Steiner, *Earthly and Cosmic Man,* lecture of May 20, 1912.

Heaven's own Fruit of Hope

1. Schütz, 'Charisma Hoffnung,' p. 119 of *Stundenbuch* 10.
2. Pieper, *Über die Hoffnung,* p. 27.
3. Pieper, *Über die Hoffnung,* p. 37.
4. Pieper, *Über die Hoffnung,* pp. 42f.
5. Steiner, *Weltenwunder, Seelenprüfungen and Geistesoffenbarung,* lecture of Aug 18, 1911.
6. Steiner, Notes on the dramatis personae of *The Soul's Probation.*
7. Schuré, *Genesis of Tragedy and the Sacred Drama of Eleusis.*
8. Steiner, *Wahrspruchworte.*
9. Steiner, *Die Mission der neuen Geistesoffenbarung,* lecture of June 14, 1911.
10. Steiner, 'Faith, Love, Hope,' two lectures Dec 2 & 3, 1911. English published in *The Golden Blade* 1964, from which this and the two following extracts from the lecture of Dec 2 are taken.
11. Steiner, *Die Mission der neuen Geistesoffenbarung,* lecture of June 14, 1911.
12. Lessing, *The Education of the Human Race.*

Forgetting and Losing: Seeking, Finding and Gaining

1. Steiner: *Wahrspruchworte.*
2. See Kluge, *Etymologisches Wörterbuch.*
3. Steiner, *Wahrspruchworte,* a meditation for Hans Reinhart in Winterthur.
4. The German word *Sucht,* here translated 'sought,' also means craving, addiction.
5. Steiner, *The True Nature of the Second Coming,* lecture of Jan 27, 1910.

Soul Images and Soul Calendar

1. From the foreword to the second edition of 1918, reprinted in the current German edition and in Cecil Harwood's translation of 1970, *The Meditative Year.*
2. Steiner, *The Reappearance of Christ in the Etheric,* lecture of March 6, 1910.
3. In the course for the priests of the Christian Community, *The Book of Revelation and the Work of the Priest,* he said: 'What needs to be said in the sense meant by the writer of the Book of Revelation is: before the etheric Christ can be comprehended by human beings in the right way humanity must first cope with encountering the beast who will rise up in 1933' (lecture of Sep 20, 1924).
4. See *Beiträge zur Rudolf Steiner Gesamtausgabe*, No. 37/38.
5. See Hans Kühn, *Dreigliederungszeit. Rudolf Steiners Kampf für die Gesellschaftsordnung der Zukunft* (Time for a Threefold Impulse: Rudolf Steiner's Struggle for the Social Order of the Future), Dornach 1978, pp. 162f.

6. Müller-Wiedemann, *Karl König,* above all Chapter 7 of Part One, 'The Epoch without a Beginning.'
7. See *Beiträge zur Rudolf Steiner Gesamtausgabe,* No. 37/38, and also the sketches for the 'occult seals' in *Rosicrucianism Renewed.*
8. See Selg, *Ita Wegman and Karl König.*
9. *Man and the World of Stars,* lecture of Dec 29, 1922 (translation based on Dorothy Osmond's).
10. *Spiritual Science as a Foundation for Social Forms,* lecture of Sep 5, 1920.
11. See 'Advent Address,' on p.47.

Life with the Images of the Soul Calendar

1. König's studies of these groups of four related verses, some of which are accompanied by drawings, appear in the first part of this volume.
2. There is a transcript of the conference lectures in the Karl König Archive, *Gedanken zum Seelenkalender* (Thoughts regarding the Soul Calendar).
3. Stefano di Giovanni Sassetta was one of the leading painters of the School of Siena. His *Journey of the Magi,* painted around 1435, hangs in the Metropolitan Museum of Art in New York.
4. In the German the author notes a clutch of onomatopoetic sounds here that allies itself with the initial consonants of *stets: Stiegen bei dem steilen Stege,* which is largely — though not entirely — lost in English.
5. Rudolf Steiner (in the context of Rosicrucian initiation) describes man as an 'inverted plant.' See *Rosicrucianism Renewed,* lecture of May 19, 1907.
6. The exercises — or six 'conditions' — were frequently described by Rudolf Steiner. See, for example, *An Outline of Occult Science,* the chapter 'Knowledge of Higher Worlds.'
7. *Man in Armour,* Glasgow Art Gallery, Scotland. König spoke about this in conversations with the author. He intended to bring it in a lecture about the inner path of schooling given on April 9, 1961 in Cresset, South Africa, though there is no reference to it in the printed notes.

Bibliography

Aquinas, Thomas *Summa Theologia.*
Beiträge zur Rudolf Steiner Gesamtausgabe, no. 37/38, Dornach 1972.
Bloch, Ernst, *Das Prinzip Hoffnung,* Frankfurt 1954–56.
Darwin, Charles, *The Autobiography*, Norton, New York and London 1958.
Hiebel, Friedrich, *The Epistles of Paul and Rudolf Steiner's Philosophy of Freedom,* St George Publications, New York 1980.
Jaspers, Karl, *Philosophie,* Vol. 1, *Existenzerhellung,* Berlin 1956.
Kluge, Friedrich, *Etymologisches Wörterbuch der deutschen Sprache,* 18th ed, Berlin 1960.
König, Karl, *Becoming Human: A Social Task,* Floris Books 2011.
—, *Gedanken zum Seelenkalender Rudolf Steiners* (Thoughts regarding Rudolf Steiner's Soul Calendar), privately published 1975.
—, *My Task,* Floris Books 2008.
—, *The Mystery of John and the Cycle of the Year*, Camphill Books 2000.
—, *Wanderer ins Morgenrot*, privately published 1962.
Kühn, Hans, *Dreigliederungszeit. Rudolf Steiners Kampf für die Gesellschaftsordnung der Zukunft* (Time for a Threefold Impulse. Rudolf Steiner's Struggle for the Social Order of the Future), Dornach 1978.
Lessing, Gotthold Ephraim *The Education of the Human Race,* tr. Fred W. Robertson, C.K. Paul & Co, London 1881.
Müller-Wiedemann, Hans, *Karl König. A Central European Biography of the Twentieth Century*, Camphill Press 1996.
Pieper, Josef, *Über die Hoffnung,* Munich 1949.
Plessner, H., *Die Stufen des Organischen and der Mensch,* 1928.
Schuré, Edourd, *Genesis of Tragedy and the Sacred Drama of Eleusis,* 1936.
Schütz, Paul, *Parusia-Hoffnung and Prophetic,* Heidelberg 1960.
—, *Stundenbuch,* Vol. 10, Hamburg 1962.
Selg, Peter, *Ita Wegman and Karl König,* Floris Books 2009.
Steiner, Rudolf, Complete Works (CW) / Gesamtausgabe (GA) volume number.
—, *Anthroposophischer Seelenkalender*, Rudolf Steiner Verlag, Dornach 2006.
—, *The Archangel Michael: His Mission and Ours,* CW 194, Anthroposophic Press, USA 1994.
—, *The Book of Revelation and the Work of the Priest,* CW 346, Rudlof Steiner Press, UK 2008.
—, *Calendar of the Soul,* second edition of 1918.
—, *Calendar of the Soul,* (Tr. by Pusch) Anthroposophic Press, USA 1982.
—, *Calendar of the Soul,* facsimile edition, SteinerBooks, USA 2003

—, *The Christmas Conference,* CW 260, Anthroposophic Press, USA 1990.
—, *Course for Young Doctors,* CW 316, Mercury Press, USA 1994.
—, *The Cycle of the Year as Breathing-Process of the Earth*, CW 223, Anthroposophic Press, USA 1988.
—, *Earthly and Cosmic Man,* CW 133, Garber Books, USA 1986
—, *The Event of the Appearance of Christ in the Etheric,* CW 118, Society of Metaphysicians, UK 1987.
—, *The Fifth Gospel,* CW 148, Rudolf Steiner Press, UK 1998.
—, *The Four Seasons and the Archangels,* CW 229, Rudolf Steiner Press, UK 1996.
—, *The Gospel of St Luke,* CW 114, SteinerBooks, USA 2001.
—, *Guidance in Esoteric Training,* CW 245, Rudolf Steiner Press, UK 2001.
—, *Man and the World of Stars. The Spiritual Communion of Mankind,* (Tr. Dorothy Osmond) CW 219, Anthroposophic Press, USA 1963.
—, *Man's Being, his Destiny and World Evolution,* (CW 226) Anthroposophic Press, New York 1985.
—, *The Meditative Year,* translated by Cecil Harwood, Rudolf Steiner Press 1970.
—, *Die menschliche Seele in ihrem Zusammenhang mit göttlich-geistigen Individualitäten,* GA 224, Rudolf Steiner Verlag, Dornach 1966.
—, *The Mission of the Folk Souls,* CW 121, Rudolf Steiner Press, UK 2005.
—, *Occult History,* CW 126, Rudolf Steiner Press, UK 1982.
—, *Occult Science, An Outline,* CW 13, Rudlof Steiner Press, UK, 2009.
—, *The Reappearance of Christ in the Etheric,* CW 118, SteinerBooks, USA 2003.
—, *Rosicrucianism Renewed,* CW 284, SteinerBooks, USA 2007.
—, *Spiritual Beings in the Heavenly Bodies and in the Kingdoms of Nature,* CW 136, SteinerBooks, USA 2006.
—, *The Spiritual Guidance of the Individual and Humanity,* CW 15, Anthroposophic Press, USA 1991.
—, *Spiritual Science as a Foundation for Social Forms,* CW 199, Anthroposophic Press, USA 1986.
—, *Theosophy,* CW 9, Anthroposophic Press, USA 1994.
—, *The True Nature of the Second Coming,* Rudolf Steiner Press, UK 1971.
—, *Universe, Earth and Man,* CW 105, Rudolf Steiner Press, UK 1987.
—, *Verses and Meditations*, Rudolf Steiner Press, UK 2005.
—, *Wahrspruchworte,* GA 40, Rudolf Steiner Verlag, Dornach 1961.
—, *Weltenwunder, Seelenprüfungen and Geistesoffenbarung,* GA 129, Rudolf Steiner Verlag, Dornach 1960.
—, *Wonders of the World, Ordeals of the Soul, Revelations of the Spirit,* GA 129, Rudolf Steiner Press, UK 1983.
Trakl, Georg, *Das dichterische Werk*, Berlin 1980.

Index of Verses

Index

Karl König Archive volumes

1 Karl König: My Task: Autobiography and Biographies
2 Karl König's Path into Anthroposophy: Reflections from his Diaries
3 Ita Wegman and Karl König: Letters and Documents
4 The Child with Special Needs: Letters and Essays on Curative Education
5 Seeds for Social Renewal: The Camphill Village Conferences
6/7 The Calendar of the Soul: An Inner Journey through the Year
8 Becoming Human: A Social Task
9 Communities for Tomorrow
10 At the Threshold of the Modern Age: Biographies Around the Year 1861
11 Brothers and Sisters: The Order of Birth in the Family
12 Kaspar Hauser and Karl König
13 Animals: An Imaginative Zoology
14 Social Farming: Healing Humanity and the Earth
15 Nutrition from Earth and Cosmos
16 The Grail and the Development of Conscience: St Paul and Parsifal
17 Plays for the Festivals of the Year
18 The Spirit of Camphill: Birth of a Movement
19 Stories, Poems and Meditations
20 Before Birth and Beyond Death: The Transformation of the Human Being
21 The Seasons and their Festivals: Human, Earthly and Cosmic Rhythms
22 The First Three Years of the Child: How Children Learn to Walk, Speak and Think
23 Music Therapy: Research and Insights
24 The Human Soul: Mysteries and Complexities of the Psyche

Karl König's collected works are being published in English by Floris Books and in German by Verlag Freies Geistesleben. They encompass the entire, wide-ranging literary estate of Karl König, including his books, essays, manuscripts, lectures, diaries, notebooks, his extensive correspondence and his artistic works, across twelve subjects.

Karl König Archive subjects

Medicine and the study of the human being
Curative education and social therapy
Psychology and education
Agriculture and science
Social questions
The Camphill movement
Christianity and the festivals
Anthroposophy
Spiritual development
History and biographies
Artistic and literary works
Karl König's biography

Karl König Institute
www.karlkoeniginstitute.org